THE MIGHTY EQUALIZER

HOW GOD INTERVENE TO CHANGE EVENTS OF LIFE

Charles E. Kpodzo

Copyright © 2025 Charles E. Kpodzo Maryland, USA

ISBN: 979-8-89324-729-9

United States Library of Congress Catalog in Publication Data – Charles Kpodzo, The Mighty Equalizer – How God changes the balance

The opinions expressed by the Author are not necessarily those held by the Publishers.

The information contained within this book is strictly for informational purposes. The material may include information, products, or services by third parties. As such, the Author and Publisher do not assume responsibility or liability for any third-party material or opinions. The publisher is not responsible for websites (or their content) that are not owned by the publisher. Readers are advised to do their own due diligence when it comes to making decisions.

Published by Franklin Publishers

Printed in the United States of America

For permissions, inquiries, or additional copies, contact:

Franklin Publishers

www.franklinpublishers.com

CHARLES KPODZO

ACKNOWLEDGMENT

In the creation of *"The Mighty Equalizer,"* I have been profoundly guided by the sovereign hand of God, whose presence has been a constant source of strength and inspiration throughout this journey. The sacred truths of Scripture have provided an unshakable foundation for my faith, and it is with deep humility that I extend my heartfelt gratitude to those who have supported and encouraged me along the way. Their contributions to spiritual, intellectual, and practical involvement have been invaluable, and I am deeply moved by their unwavering commitment to this work.

First and foremost, I give thanks to divine providence for directing my path and for entrusting me with the responsibility of edifying the Church through the eternal truths of Scripture. Remaining faithful to the divine commission has been both a solemn duty and a sacred privilege, as I have sought to present the Word of God with clarity and integrity, untainted by personal bias, to lead others toward the redemptive embrace of Salvation.

My pursuit of the knowledge of God has been a central theme in my life and in this work. The Gospel of Christ, with its power to convict and redeem, has been a beacon of truth that has illuminated my path. The insights gleaned from life's experiences and the wisdom shared by fellow believers and seekers have enriched my understanding and strengthened my resolve to share these truths through this book.

To the countless unnamed individuals whose lives and reflections have touched mine, your questions, actions, and shared journeys have been the spark that ignited this endeavor. To the congregations and faith leaders who challenged and inspired me, your examples have been instrumental in shaping this work. To my brethren in faith, your fellowship and dialogue have provided a wellspring of inspiration.

To you, the reader, my appreciation is boundless. Your engagement with this text affirms its purpose and importance. With you in mind, I acknowledge the following guiding principles:

- The call for the Word of God to serve as a transformative force is rightly interpreted and shared.

- The necessity of upholding doctrines that advocate justice, equity, and truth.

- The obligation to convey the Word with integrity, addressing the plight of the oppressed.

- The critical role of Scripture in sustaining the spirit and offering hope to the disheartened.

- The urgency of correcting theological inaccuracies that perpetuate injustice within the Church.

- The responsibility to disseminate God's Word as a means of addressing societal and spiritual disparities.

- The pledge to empower the disempowered through careful and faithful instruction in the Word.

- The commitment to strengthen the Church's mission as an agent of divine justice and redemption.

- The desire to share the knowledge of God as a source of hope and strength for all, particularly the marginalized.

- My gratitude for your dedication to the Word, which validates your inherent worth as a cherished creation of God.

This book was largely completed in the United States, and I am especially grateful to Rev. Dr. Peter Pryce for his biblically rooted guidance. My family has been the bedrock of my strength, and I owe particular thanks to my wife, Rose Ashton Kpodzo, and my son, Sedem Kwami Kpodzo. Sedem, your insightful critique and thoughtful feedback have been instrumental in refining this manuscript.

I also wish to express my deep gratitude to Rev. Christian Fhole and Rev. Theodore Ani, whose spiritual counsel has been pivotal in ensuring the scriptural fidelity and tone of this message. Alongside them, Sedem Kpodzo has provided invaluable support, helping me remain grounded in the truth that the Gospel stands as a cornerstone for the faithful and a challenge for those unanchored in the Word of God.

To all who have contributed to this journey, I extend my heartfelt thanks. May the truths within this book honor God, strengthen His Church, and inspire all who seek His guidance.

DEDICATION

I dedicate this book to my beloved parents, Mr. Emmanuel Yao Kpodzo and Mrs. Emily Yobla Kpodzo, nee Woyome, both of cherished memory. To my dear Rose and to my children, I express my heartfelt gratitude for your unwavering support and encouragement throughout this remarkable journey.

The contributions of my family members, both those present and those who have departed from this world, hold a special place in my heart. I recognize that the foundation laid by those who have gone before us has been instrumental in shaping who I am today. I offer profound thanks to the Almighty God for guiding each of these individuals to make their unique and meaningful contributions to my life.

Reflecting on this dedication, I am reminded of the beginnings of my spiritual journey. My mother, in particular, played a significant role in nurturing my early interest in the Scriptures through her regular reading of the Holy Bible to me. This early exposure sparked my lifelong fascination with the Word of God, a practice inspired by verses such as:

1. **2 Timothy 1:1(KJV)** "Paul, an apostle of Jesus Christ by the will of God, according to the promise of life which is in Christ Jesus,

2. **2 Timothy 1:2(KJV)** To Timothy, my dearly beloved son: Grace, mercy, and peace, from God the Father and Christ Jesus our Lord.

3. **2 Timothy 1:3(KJV)** I thank God, whom I serve from my forefathers with pure conscience, that without ceasing I have remembrance of thee in my prayers night and day;

4. **2 Timothy 1:4(KJV)** Greatly desiring to see thee, being mindful of thy tears, that I may be filled with joy;

5. **2 Timothy 1:5(KJV)** When I call to remembrance the unfeigned faith that is in thee, which dwelt first in thy grandmother Lois, and thy mother Eunice; and I am persuaded that in thee also.

6. **2 Timothy 1:6 (KJV)** Wherefore I put thee in remembrance that thou stir up the gift of God, which is in thee by the putting on of my hands.

7. **2 Timothy 1:7(KJV)** For God hath not given us the spirit of fear; but of power, and of love, and of a sound mind.

8. **2 Timothy 1:8(KJV)** Be not thou therefore ashamed of the testimony of our Lord, nor of me his prisoner: but be thou partaker of the afflictions of the gospel according to the power of God;

Paul, an apostle of Jesus Christ by the will of God, according to the promise of life which is in Christ Jesus... Greatly desiring to see thee, being mindful of thy tears... For God hath not given us the spirit of fear; but of power, and of love, and of a sound mind... Be not thou therefore ashamed of the testimony of our Lord...

The influence of my mother, who diligently passed on the spirit and light of the testimony of our Lord and Savior Jesus Christ, akin to the legacy of Grandmother Lois and Mother Eunice, is something for which I remain eternally grateful. Their unwavering commitment to teaching the Word of God to their children embodies the scriptural ideals as conveyed in

i. **Proverbs 31:1 (KJV)** The words of king Lemuel, the prophecy that his mother taught him.

ii. **Proverbs 31:2 (KJV)** What, my son? and what, the son of my womb? and what, the son of my vows?

iii. **Proverbs 31:3 (KJV)** Give not thy strength unto women, nor thy ways to that which destroyeth kings

The words of king Lemuel, the prophecy that his mother taught him... Give not thy strength unto women, nor thy ways to that which destroyeth kings...

I fondly recall how my mother encouraged me to join my older siblings in attending youth group meetings despite initial resistance from my brothers, who considered it unusual for me to be part of their gatherings at that age. My parents, both church Elders, and my father, a Preacher, imparted invaluable wisdom through their actions and devotion to the Word of God. My mother, in particular, served as a shining example of daily Christian living through her unwavering commitment to reading the Scriptures.

I firmly believe that the influence of my parents in molding my faith and character was not a coincidence but a divine plan ordained from above, aligning with verses such as:

i. **Ephesians 1:3 (KJV)** Blessed be the God and Father of our Lord Jesus Christ, who hath blessed us with all spiritual blessings in heavenly places in Christ:

ii. **Ephesians 1:4 (KJV)** According as he hath chosen us in him before the foundation of the world, that we should be holy and without blame before him in love:

iii. **Ephesians 1:5 (KJV)** Having predestinated us unto the adoption of children by Jesus Christ to himself, according to the good pleasure of his will,

iv. **Ephesians 1:6 (KJV)** To the praise of the glory of his grace, wherein he hath made us accepted in the beloved

Blessed be the God and Father of our Lord Jesus Christ, who hath blessed us with all spiritual blessings... According as he hath chosen us in him before the foundation of the world... Having predestinated us unto the adoption of children by Jesus Christ to himself...

This book stands as a living testament to the lasting impact of my parents, Mr. Emmanuel Yao Kpodzo and Mrs. Emily Yobla Kpodzo, nee Woyome, whose memory I hold dear and whose guidance continues to inspire my journey.

In humble reverence to their legacy, I offer this book as a tribute to their unwavering influence and devotion to the Word of God.

ABOUT THE AUTHOR

Charles Kpodzo,

BA Sociology and Religion,

M.Ed. Instructional Technology

Charles Kpodzo is a distinguished figure whose multifaceted contributions span the fields of technology, education, and spirituality. With a career marked by visionary leadership and scholarly achievements, he has profoundly impacted each of these domains, earning recognition for his innovative approach and unwavering commitment to equity and excellence.

With over 19 years of dedicated service in the driver education industry and its related sectors, Mr. Kpodzo has tackled instructional challenges with unparalleled expertise, becoming a trailblazer in instructional technology and equitable education. His academic foundation is deeply rooted in Sociology and Religion, disciplines that inform his work and enable him to bridge the gap between technology and human-centered learning. This foundation is further enhanced by a Master's degree in Education (M.Ed.) with a specialization in Instructional Technology from Strayer University, Washington, DC.

An accomplished author, Charles Kpodzo has made significant contributions to academic and spiritual literature. His works include a comprehensive handbook on religious and moral education and the critically acclaimed *Christianity Lost in Translation*, which explores the intricate challenges of preserving the essence of Christian doctrine across cultural and linguistic divides. These writings demonstrate his dedication to fostering a deeper understanding of faith and education while championing the importance of spiritual equity.

In the business realm, Mr. Kpodzo has served as the President and CEO of the Starlinx Group of Companies since 2007, showcasing his leadership and commitment to safety and educational excellence. His strategic partnership with Tajintech in 2010 highlights his forward-thinking approach, focusing on innovation in instructional management and driving consultancy services. His work has

FOREWORD

BY DR. EKWOW SPIO-GARBAH

*I*t has been my absolute privilege to know Charles Kpodzo for over a decade. Throughout this time, I have not only witnessed firsthand the depth of his commitment and the breadth of his knowledge across various sectors, but I have also had the distinct pleasure of crossing paths with him in the realms of politics and civic engagement. Charles is not merely a visionary leader; he is a profound scholar, a compassionate advocate for equity, justice, and spiritual enlightenment, and a dedicated participant in our political and civic discourse.

His academic background in Sociology and Religion, paired with a Master of Education in Instructional Technology and Information Systems, lays a solid foundation for his extensive contributions. Charles has masterfully intertwined these disciplines to address complex issues in education, spirituality, technology, and beyond, making significant strides toward enhancing understanding and accessibility in these fields. Our collaboration and discussions in political and civic arenas have further illuminated his dedication to using his vast knowledge and leadership skills for the greater good, advocating for policies and initiatives that foster community development and social justice.

In the realm of business and education, Charles has demonstrated exceptional leadership as the President and CEO of the Starlinx Group of Companies. His strategic alliances and innovative approaches have not only advanced the company's mission but also set new standards in driver education and instructional technology. His ability to forge meaningful partnerships reflects his dedication to creating opportunities for learning and growth, a principle that he carries into his civic and political endeavors, always aiming to bridge gaps and build stronger, more informed communities.

Furthermore, Charles' scholarly work, including his critical examination of Christian doctrine and his comprehensive handbook on religious and moral education, showcases his commitment to fostering dialogue and understanding across cultural and linguistic divides. His publications are a testament to his scholarly depth and his relentless pursuit of knowledge, enriching our political and civic discussions with insights that draw from a deep well of interdisciplinary expertise.

Beyond his professional achievements, Charles's spiritual advocacy and outreach are truly inspiring. Through his podcast, "Christian Sunday Live," and his publications like "The Mighty Equalizer," he has touched the lives of many, offering guidance, hope, and a sense of community to those in need. His spiritual leadership extends into his political and civic engagement, where he embodies the principles of compassion, equity, and justice in every action.

In conclusion, Charles Kpodzo is a remarkable individual whose contributions to technology, education, faith, and our shared political and civic landscapes have made a lasting impact on countless lives. I am honored to have known him for over a decade and to have stood alongside him in efforts to effect positive change in our community and beyond. I am confident that his work will continue to inspire, educate, and empower individuals around the world. Charles is not just a leader; he is a beacon of hope and a catalyst for positive change in every arena he touches.

BY DR. EKWOW SPIO-GARBAH

PREFACE

My Christian journey began in early childhood, deeply influenced by my devout parents, Mr. and Mrs. E. Y. Kpodzo, who served as respected Church Elders (Presbyters) within our faith community. Their unwavering dedication to their faith provided me with a firm foundation in Christianity, and I was baptized and confirmed as a member of the Evangelical Presbyterian Church.

As a young believer, I actively participated in church programs and youth initiatives, such as the Christian Youth Builders (C.Y.B). These experiences shaped my spiritual growth and connection to the teachings of the faith, as I represented my peers in Bible studies and competitions. However, as I entered early adulthood, my spiritual fervor waned, and my commitment to faith gave way to sporadic church attendance, reading or studying of the Word, and a diminishing relationship with the principles I once cherished.

Through life's trials and tribulations, however, I was preserved by an unshakable grace, kindness, and mercy that guided me back to the path of faith. A pivotal moment came during an unimaginable period of loss in 2010, when I experienced the passing of three siblings, Marlon, William, and Daniel, within a span of three months. This devastating time served as a profound awakening, reigniting my faith and compelling me to reexamine my purpose.

Even before these heartbreaking losses, I had endured the premature passing of my immediate brother, Robert, in 1990, which took a heavy toll on my mother's health and eventually led to her death in 1995, and our oldest sister in 2006. These cumulative losses deeply impacted my family, leaving me as the sole surviving son, a position that seemed divinely preserved for a greater purpose. This realization became a turning point in my understanding of my journey and my faith.

Looking back, I can see the divine hand guiding me, shielding me from spiritual calamity, and preserving me for a mission yet to unfold. My relocation to the United States marked another pivotal chapter, offering not just refuge but a platform for growth, reflection, and the pursuit of the purpose for which I was spared.

This book is both a testimony to that preservation and a call to others to rediscover the transformative power of faith. It is written as a guide to those seeking to reconnect with the core truths of Christianity, emphasizing a return to foundational principles and the pursuit of truth in the face of a world often clouded by misleading interpretations.

Through my journey, I have come to understand that salvation is not found in mere rituals or appearances but in the transformative power of genuine faith and a deep connection to divine teachings. It is my prayer that this book serves as a tool to inspire others to seek truth, reclaim the core tenets of their faith, and build a stronger foundation for their spiritual lives.

In the midst of personal adversity, I found strength, peace, and deliverance not in external validations but in the enduring truths of faith. My hope is that this work illuminates a path for those who may have strayed, providing clarity, encouragement, and a renewed trust in the principles that hold the power to transform lives. May this book serve as a beacon for those searching for purpose, guiding them to a deeper connection with the enduring truths of faith and the grace that sustains us all.

Also, by the Same Author:

- *A Handbook on Religious and Moral Education*
- *Christianity Lost in Translation*

May this journey through "The Mighty Equalizer" be a source of spiritual enlightenment, strengthening the faith of those who have strayed and leading them back to the path of Christ.

INTRODUCTION

HOW TO UNDERSTAND THE TITLE OF THE BOOK

THE MIGHTY EQUALIZER

Divine Intervention: How God Shapes the Course of Our Lives"

====================

FIAYI - Ewe symbol of authority

====================

*I*n ***The Mighty Equalizer***: *Unveiling the Power of Justice and Mercy*, the message here reveals a profound understanding of the divine as the ultimate force of balance in human existence. This concept transcends time, culture, and creed, urging us to reflect on the nature of divine intervention in addressing the imbalances of life, restoring fairness, and offering hope to the oppressed.

At its core, this work explores the idea of God as the Mighty Equalizer, whose nature embodies both unwavering justice and boundless mercy. It highlights the intricate balance between holding wrongdoers accountable and extending forgiveness to those who seek redemption. This duality offers a timeless message for humanity, reminding us of the possibility of transformation and renewal when true repentance meets divine grace.

The enduring relevance of this perspective is not limited to spiritual understanding but extends into societal structures and interpersonal relationships. It challenges us to consider how divine principles of fairness and compassion can shape our responses to the injustices of the world. By intervening to right wrongs, lift the oppressed, and bring accountability to those who resist change, the Mighty Equalizer sets an example of how fairness and kindness can coexist without compromising integrity.

This book also delves deeply into the transformative power of genuine repentance and redemption. By examining how divine justice is satisfied while mercy prevails, we see a universal truth of fairness and love can operate in harmony, offering the possibility of restoration while addressing the consequences of wrongdoing.

To further illuminate this idea, *The Mighty Equalizer* draws on additional insights that underscore divine impartiality and care for humanity. We reflect on how this principle applies to real-world situations where fairness is restored, where the downtrodden are lifted, and where oppressive systems are dismantled. These themes resonate across all facets of human life, showing the profound and practical implications of divine balance in action.

Ultimately, *The Mighty Equalizer* is a call to reflect on justice and mercy, to understand the intricate balance that shapes human existence, and to embrace the transformative power of grace. It offers hope for a world that yearns for fairness and compassion, reminding us that true equilibrium is found when accountability meets love and when justice and mercy coexist as guiding principles for all. **Colossians 3:25 (KJV)** "But he that doeth wrong shall receive for the wrong which he hath done: and there is no respect of persons."

> **Romans 2:11(KJV)** "For there is no respect of persons with God."
>
> **Psalm 9:7 (KJV)** "But the LORD shall endure for ever: he hath prepared his throne for judgment."
>
> **Psalm 9:8 (KJV)** "And he shall judge the world in righteousness, he shall minister judgment to the people in uprightness."
>
> **Psalm 146:7 (KJV)** "Which executeth judgment for the oppressed: which giveth food to the hungry. The LORD looseth the prisoners:"
>
> **Psalm 146:8 (KJV)** "The LORD openeth the eyes of the blind: The LORD raiseth them that are bowed down: The LORD loveth the righteous:"
>
> **Psalm 146:9 (KJV)** "The LORD preserveth the strangers; he relieveth the fatherless and widow: but the way of the wicked he turneth upside down."

Understanding *"The Mighty Equalize"* begins with the fundamental principle that every action, whether righteous or unjust, carries its consequences. This book takes readers on a journey through divine justice, exploring how the balance of fairness and accountability plays out in our world. Drawing from timeless wisdom, historical lessons, and contemporary challenges, it illuminates how the unseen hand of justice shapes destinies, addresses societal wrongs, and restores hope to the oppressed.

Through a rich tapestry of reflections, the book portrays God as the ultimate **"Equalizer,"** a force that governs the universe with compassion and integrity. It invites readers to consider how divine justice influences individual lives, family dynamics, and the larger social order. By examining the interplay of justice and mercy, the book unveils how the equilibrium of life is maintained and how ultimate accountability is inescapable for those who does not repent and seek salvation through our Lord and Savior and Jesus Christ.

Real-world examples bring these truths to life, illustrating the consequences of unrighteous actions by those in positions of power. Whether in unethical business dealings, corrupt leadership, or neglect of the vulnerable, the book explores how divine justice prevails despite human inequity. It challenges those in authority to reflect on their responsibilities, emphasizing the moral imperative to act with integrity, fairness, and compassion.

At its heart, *The Mighty Equalizer* reveals a profound truth about God, The Lord God. While justice is inevitable, mercy is accessible. The book emphasizes that sincere repentance, coupled with genuine efforts to make amends, opens the door to forgiveness and restoration.

In a world marked by imbalance and strife, *The Mighty Equalizer* offers a message of hope, urging readers to align their lives with principles of justice and mercy. It underscores the transformative power of redemption and the enduring relevance of living with purpose, integrity, and compassion. This exploration of divine justice serves as a guide for those seeking to understand their place in the grand design of fairness, accountability, and grace.

CHAPTER 1

THE SPIRITUAL BEFORE THE PHYSICAL: UNDERSTANDING THE DIVINE ORDER OF EXISTENCE

======================

FAWOHODIE

"Independence"

Asante philosophical symbol of Independence, Freedom, Emancipation,

Self-Governance

======================

In the vast tapestry of existence, two distinct dimensions emerge: the spiritual realm and the physical realm. The spiritual realm, eternal and transcendent, holds primacy over the physical, influencing and shaping it in ways that transcend human understanding.

These dimensions are imbued with profound significance, offering timeless insights that illuminate the nature of existence. Together, they reveal a broader perspective on life, guiding us toward a deeper understanding of our purpose and connection to the divine. This exploration seeks to unravel the relationship between these realms, delving into their intricacies and uncovering the transformative messages they convey.

In Matthew 6:10, we are guided to pray, "Thy kingdom come. Thy will be done on earth, as it is in heaven." This prayer serves as a reminder of the spiritual influence on the physical world.

This verse points to the connection between the heavenly or spiritual realm and the earthly or physical realm, suggesting that the spiritual realm precedes, influences, and surpasses the physical world we inhabit

> **1 Corinthians 15:44 (KJV)** "It is sown a natural body; it is raised a spiritual body. There is a natural body, and there is a spiritual body."

> **1 Corinthians 15:46 (KJV)** "Howbeit that was not first which is spiritual, but that which is natural; and afterward that which is spiritual."

> **Ephesians 1:4 (KJV)** "According as he hath chosen us in him before the foundation of the world, that we should be holy and without blame before him in love."

> **Ephesians 1-5 (KJV)** "Having predestinated us unto the adoption of children by Jesus Christ to himself, according to the good pleasure of his will."

This is yet another scripture that emphasize the existence of both physical and spiritual aspects of our being. These verses invite us to contemplate the transition between our physical and spiritual existence and the profound implications of this transformation.

The precedence of the natural world before the spiritual. This insight encourages us to appreciate the intricate balance between the two realms and the divine order in which they operate.

The eternal nature of our connection to the spiritual realm and God's divine purpose in our lives and highlights the concept of God's divine plan.

> **1 Timothy 3:16 (KJV)** "God was manifest in the flesh, justified in the Spirit, seen of angels, preached unto the Gentiles, believed on in the world, received up into glory."

> **1 Peter 1:20 (KJV)** "Who verily was foreordained before the foundation of the world, but was manifest in these last times for you."

Dear reader, the idea of divine adoption and God's sovereignty offers a glimpse into the divine plan that predates our earthly existence, highlighting our predestination as children of God if only you believe in the scripture. As we delve into the realm of the spiritual, we encounter parables and teachings that reveal the profound divide between the children of God and the children of darkness.

Within these two realms, there are individuals who align with the controllers of each realm: Today, the devices you hold in your hands, filled with videos and statements widely shared on social media, have the power to blur the line between truth and deception. In a world where information can be manipulated to mislead, it's easy to lose sight of what is real. But let me assure you, Scripture

remains the ultimate guide, unshaken by trends and untouched by the distortions of the digital age. It offers clarity and truth far beyond the screens you scroll, protecting us from the enemy's attempts to deceive God's true children. Turn to the Word of God, it is more reliable than any video or post you might encounter.

Matthew 13:38 (KJV) "The field is the world; the good seed are the children of the kingdom; but the tares are the children of the wicked one."

Luke 16:8 (KJV) "And the lord commended the unjust steward, because he had done wisely: for the children of this world are in their generation wiser than the children of light."

John 8:44 (KJV) "Ye are of your father the devil, and the lusts of your father ye will do. He was a murderer from the beginning, and abode not in the truth, because there is no truth in him. When he speaketh a lie, he speaketh of his own: for he is a liar, and the father of it."

Ephesians 5:8 (KJV) "For ye were sometimes darkness, but now are ye light in the Lord: walk as children of light."

1 Thessalonians 5:5 (KJV) "Ye are all the children of light, and the children of the day: we are not of the night, nor of darkness."

The interplay of righteousness and darkness within both the physical and spiritual realms compels us to reflect on our true identities and the allegiances we form in life. These realms shape the essence of who we are as in person, whether we align ourselves with divine light or remain enveloped in darkness. Yet, within this duality lies the profound possibility of transformation, a call to embrace a higher purpose and step into the illumination of truth and grace.

Humanity's shared essence transcends physical appearances and cultural differences, reminding us of the unity that binds all people. Beneath the surface, our biological makeup, there is more in common that points to our shared composition, interconnectedness, and common origins, which affirms the intrinsic oneness of the human race. This universal connection underscores the shared journey of humanity, urging us toward mutual respect, compassion, and an acknowledgment of the deeper spiritual truths that unite us all.

Acts 17:26 (KJV) "And hath made of one blood all nations of men for to dwell on all the face of the earth, and hath determined the times before appointed, and the bounds of their habitation."

However, the unity of the physical realm stands in contrast to the spiritual realm, where humanity is categorized as children of God or children of the Darkness based on their faith, beliefs,

and alignment with divine truth. As such, it is vital to understand that in the spiritual realm, we speak the language of our spiritual lineage and act according to the principles of our spiritual Father.

Moreover, this teaching underscores the truth revealed in the Word of God, that we are all one in Christ and must endeavor to treat one another as children of the same Father, united in Christ Jesus. This chapter explores the profound distinctions between the spiritual and physical realms as revealed in the Bible. It highlights God's divine plan, established before our earthly existence, the coexistence of light and darkness, but light overcomes darkness and the possibilities for transformation and redemption. While all humans share a common physical nature, they are spiritually categorized into two groups: those who align with God's principles and those who follow the ways of darkness. The difference lies in their understanding and commitment to the Word of God. Recognizing this spiritual division is essential, enabling us to engage in meaningful conversations with those open to the Word, while wisely refraining from contentious debates with those who reject it. Understanding these realms and their roles is vital for a deeper connection with our spiritual journey and the divine purpose guiding our lives.

(Genesis 25:23-25) reveals a profound message about God's sovereignty and purpose in creation, particularly in the diversity of humanity:

> **Genesis 25:23 (KJV)** "And the LORD said unto her, Two nations are in thy womb, and two manner of people shall be separated from thy bowels; and the one people shall be stronger than the other people; and the elder shall serve the younger.
>
> **Genesis 25:24 (KJV)** "And when her days to be delivered were fulfilled, behold, there were twins in her womb."
>
> **Genesis 25: 25 (KJV.** "And the first came out red, all over like an hairy garment; and they called his name Esau."

In this passage, God reveals to Rebekah a profound truth about the twins in her womb, Jacob and Esau. He foretells that they will become two distinct nations and "two manner of people," highlighting their unique destinies and characteristics. While Esau's physical appearance is vividly described as "red, all over like a hairy garment," there is no description of Jacob's outward features. This omission speaks volumes, drawing attention away from physical traits and toward the deeper significance of purpose and character in God's plan.

This account invites us to look beyond superficial distinctions and recognize the inherent worth of every individual. Jacob and Esau, though physically different, were both created with divine intention, reflecting the diversity and richness of God's creation. Their destinies were not determined by their appearances but by the unique purposes, God had designed for each of them.

The emphasis on Esau's appearance, juxtaposed with the lack of detail about Jacob, teaches an important lesson: God's focus is not on external attributes but on the roles and purposes He assigns to each life. It is a reminder that judging others based on outward differences, such as skin color or physical traits, diminishes our ability to see the divine image in which every person is made. Such judgments not only disregard the uniqueness of God's creation but also challenge His sovereignty in determining the value and purpose of each life.

This is a call for humility and respect, urging us to embrace the diversity of humanity as an expression of God's creative will. By focusing on the heart and the purpose of each individual, we align ourselves with a higher understanding of worth, one that sees beyond the surface and celebrates the divine plan for every life.

> **Amos 9:7 (KJV)** "Are ye not as children of the Ethiopians unto me,
> O children of Israel? saith the LORD. Have not I brought up Israel
> out of the land of Egypt? and the Philistines from Caphtor, and the
> Syrians from Kir?

Almighty God does not care about the color. As we have read above, God, speaking through the prophet Amos, emphasizes that all nations are significant to Him and under His control. By comparing Israel to the Ethiopians and mentioning other nations He has guided and liberated, God is reminding Israel that His love, authority, and care extend beyond one specific group. This particular scripture verse conveys the idea that all people are part of God's creation, and their value is not tied to ethnicity, color, or national identity (boundaries) but rather to their relationship with Him.

The focus on Esau's distinct appearance, contrasted with the lack of a description for Jacob, invites a deeper reflection on the essence of identity and purpose. This omission shifts attention away from external characteristics, emphasizing that true significance lies not in physical traits but in the unique roles and purposes assigned to each individual. The portrayal of Jacob and Esau as "two manners of people" suggests that their differences extend beyond what is visible, highlighting their destinies and the distinct paths shaped by a higher design.

By omitting Jacob's physical features, the narrative challenges us to look beyond outward distinctions when understanding identity. It calls us to consider character, purpose, and the divine plan rather than surface-level differences such as color or appearance. This perspective serves as a reminder that worth is determined not by external attributes but by the values and purposes woven into each person's life.

The message is clear: to judge or discriminate based on physical traits is to ignore the deeper essence of humanity. Differences in appearance or origin are secondary to the larger purpose and connection that each individual holds within the grand design of creation. The absence of Jacob's

description may be a deliberate reminder to adopt this broader, more meaningful view of others, focusing on their inner qualities and divine potential.

In this way, the scripture encourages us to align our perspective with a higher understanding of value and purpose. It challenges us to reject superficial judgments and instead embrace the uniqueness of each individual, recognizing that true significance comes not from outward differences but from living in alignment with the purpose and virtues that transcend the physical.

> **Galatians 3:28**: **(KJV)** "There is neither Jew nor Greek, there is neither bond nor free, there is neither male nor female: for ye are all one in Christ Jesus."

In conclusion, this message serves as a poignant reminder that in the presence of divine love and purpose, distinctions rooted in outward appearances fade into insignificance. The diversity of our gifts, traits, and cultures is not a basis for division but a testament to the beauty of our differences, designed to complement and enrich one another in meaningful ways. This harmonious interplay reflects the profound wisdom and sovereignty behind creation.

The true measure of value lies not in external attributes but in the essence and purpose embedded within each individual. This story compels us to honor that truth by embracing both the unity that connects us and the diversity that enhances us. Together, we embody the divine nature and a shared purpose that transcends all superficial distinctions, uniting us in a greater, collective harmony

Who is Abraham According to the Bible?

According to the Bible, Abraham, originally named Abram, is a central figure in the book of Genesis and is known as the "father of faith." Abraham, originally Abram, is a pivotal biblical figure and patriarch revered in Judaism, Christianity, and Islam. His journey, detailed in the Book of Genesis, marks the beginning of a profound legacy. Born into a society steeped in idol worship, including his own family in Ur of the Chaldees, Abram was raised in a culture where polytheism and the worship of other gods were commonplace

> **Joshua 24:2 (KJV)** "And Joshua said unto all the people, Thus saith the LORD God of Israel, Your fathers dwelt on the other side of the flood in old time, even Terah, the father of Abraham, and the father of Nachor: and they served other gods."

> **Joshua 24:3 (KJV)** "And I took your father Abraham from the other side of the flood, and led him throughout all the land of Canaan, and multiplied his seed, and gave him Isaac."

> **Genesis 12:1 (KJV)** "Now the LORD had said unto Abram, Get thee out of thy country, and from thy kindred, and from thy father's house, unto a land that I will shew thee."

> **Isaiah 51:2 (KJV)** "Look unto Abraham your father, and unto Sarah that bare you: for I called him alone, and blessed him, and increased him."

Abraham, a man of extraordinary faith, stands as a timeless symbol of trust and obedience to divine will. Responding to God's call, he left his homeland of Ur of the Chaldees to journey to Canaan, embodying the unwavering belief in God's plan for his life. As the progenitor of the Israelites through Isaac and the Ishmaelites through Ishmael, his lineage also extends to the Edomites and Midianites, establishing him as a central figure in history and faith. Through God's covenant, Abraham was promised countless descendants and the blessing that all nations would be touched by his faith in our creator, which has become a cornerstone of the Abrahamic religions.

One of the most profound moments in Abraham's life is his willingness to sacrifice his son, Isaac, an act halted by divine intervention. This story highlights his remarkable trust and loyalty, serving as a testament to faith under trial. Known for his great hospitality and moments of vulnerability, Abraham's life portrays a relatable blend of faithfulness and humanity. He remains a spiritual patriarch in Christianity and a symbol of enduring faith and obedience in Judaism, leaving an indelible mark on the Abrahamic faiths.

The story of Abraham's journey intertwines deeply with geographical and cultural history. Along with his wife and nephew Lot, Abraham departed from Egypt, a region integral to his story. Notably, he amassed significant wealth, with cattle, silver, and gold, emphasizing his affluence in both Egypt and Canaan. This connection to Africa enriches the biblical narrative, fostering an appreciation for the diverse landscapes and cultures that shaped this spiritual heritage.

As believers, our spiritual relationships transcend bloodlines and physical ancestry, connecting us to a shared heritage that is rooted in divine purpose rather than biological ties. Abraham's spiritual legacy reminds us that our identity as children of God is not confined by geography, culture, or lineage but is anchored in a relationship with the divine. This universal connection emphasizes that spiritual lineage is defined by faith and the divine calling, rather than the circumstances of birth.

A recurring question often arises among certain individuals, particularly within non-Christian circles, and it is sometimes amplified on social media: "Why should I pray through someone else's ancestor, like Abraham, instead of ancestral figures from my own heritage?" This line of reasoning is often used to sow confusion among those who are not firmly grounded in the faith.

The answer lies in recognizing that God, in His sovereignty, chooses whom He wills as vessels for His divine purpose. Abraham is not merely an "ancestor" in a cultural sense but was divinely appointed as the father of faith, through whom God initiated His covenant of redemption for all humanity. It is not about rejecting one's heritage or cultural identity, but rather about acknowledging and embracing the divine provision for salvation that transcends all earthly genealogies.

To insist on an exclusive focus on personal or cultural ancestors over God's chosen vessels is to misunderstand the universal nature of God's plan. His purpose is not bound by ethnicity or geography but is directed toward the redemption of all nations through faith in Him. Let us, therefore, remain steadfast in the truth of God's Word and avoid being swayed by arguments that aim to undermine the foundation of our faith.

Abraham's story highlights the deeper truths of faith, obedience, trust, and the fulfillment of divine promises. These qualities transcend personal lineage, illustrating that God's plans are not bound by human constructs of ancestry or heritage. His calling and covenant with Abraham established a spiritual lineage open to all who align themselves with God's purpose and promise.

This perspective challenges us to look beyond cultural or physical distinctions and recognize the universal nature of spiritual connection. Abraham's legacy is a call to reflect on the depth of our own spiritual journey, reminding us that the relationship with God is personal, transformative, and transcendent, uniting believers across all divides in the pursuit of divine truth and grace.

> **Romans 11:17 (KJV)** "And if some of the branches be broken off, and thou, being a wild olive tree, wert graffed in among them, and with them partakest of the root and fatness of the olive tree;"

> **Romans 11:18 (KJV)** "Boast not against the branches. But if thou boast, thou bearest not the root, but the root thee."

> **Galatians 3:29 (KJV)** "And if ye be Christ's, then are ye Abraham's seed, and heirs according to the promise."

These New Testament scriptures metaphorically illustrate how those outside the lineage of Israel are spiritually grafted into the same family tree, sharing in the blessings and promises originally made to Abraham and his descendants. They highlight that in God's divine plan, distinctions such as ethnicity, social status, or gender are transcended, uniting all believers as heirs to Abraham's legacy through faith.

Consider this in the context of a town, city, or kingdom where an individual family is chosen or inherits the role of king or chief. Does this mean that because they are not directly of your bloodline, they are not your king or queen? Of course not! Their royal position represents and unites all citizens by virtue of belonging to the same town, city, or kingdom. Similarly, through faith, believers are united as one people under God's covenant, regardless of their origin.

Those who align themselves with God's will and live in obedience, regardless of their earthly ancestry or nationality, are embraced as part of God's spiritual family. This integration underscores that faith and commitment, rather than physical lineage, are the defining factors in inheriting the promises made to Abraham.

The concept of being "grafted" into this spiritual lineage serves as a reminder of the inclusivity of God's covenant, inviting all who follow His commandments and believe in His redemptive plan to share in the blessings of Abraham's heritage. This unity reflects the transformative power of faith, which transcends earthly boundaries to bring all believers into a shared relationship with God.

> **Genesis 24:2 (KJV)** "And Abraham said unto his eldest servant of his house, that ruled over all that he had, Put, I pray thee, thy hand under my thigh."

> **Genesis 24:3 (KJV)** "And I will make thee swear by the LORD, the God of heaven, and the God of the earth, that thou shalt not take a wife unto my son of the daughters of the Canaanites, among whom I dwell."

> **Genesis 24:4 (KJV)** "But thou shalt go unto my country, and to my kindred, and take a wife unto my son Isaac."

The narrative of Abraham seeking a wife for his son Isaac offers a profound reflection on faith, obedience, and divine guidance. Entrusting the mission to his servant, Abraham demonstrates unwavering reliance on a higher plan, trusting that the path forward is guided by divine purpose.

This journey, filled with faith and intention, underscores the belief that life's significant decisions are best made with a focus on spiritual alignment and trust in unseen guidance.

The servant's preparation and journey to a distant land stand as a powerful testament to obedience and unwavering trust in the mission he was given. His actions go beyond mere logistics, carrying with them the profound expectation that divine providence would manifest at the appointed time. This unwavering trust reveals a profound truth: that human effort, when aligned with a higher purpose, becomes an instrument for the fulfillment of God's divine plan.

Brothers and sisters, place your trust in the Lord in whatever task or mission lies before you. Just as the God of Abraham enabled His servant to fulfill a critical part of His divine purpose, so too will He make a way for you where there seems to be none.

This story serves as a timeless lesson, reminding us of the essential role of faith and the importance of seeking guidance that transcends human understanding. It highlights the interconnectedness of our choices, relationships, and spiritual purpose, demonstrating how God's direction can surpass cultural and geographical boundaries to achieve His will.

> **Romans 2:11 (KJV)** "For there is no respect of persons with God."

> **Galatians 3:28 (KJV)** "There is neither Jew nor Greek, there is neither bond nor free, there is neither male nor female: for ye are all one in Christ Jesus."

God's Word makes it clear that He judges with perfect justice, without favoritism or partiality. In His eyes, no race, nation, or social class holds a higher status than another. His judgment is based on the condition of the heart, not outward appearance or human distinctions. Any belief that seeks to elevate one group above another stands in direct opposition to His divine truth.

In Christ, all barriers of division fade away. The foundation of God's kingdom is unity, where love, faith, and obedience define a person's worth, not earthly labels. True identity is found in a relationship with Him, not in race, status, or background.

While the Bible contains historical accounts specific to certain peoples and times, its spiritual truths are timeless and universal. The principles of faith, righteousness, and divine guidance apply to all who seek Him, regardless of their origin. Any attempt to misuse Scripture to justify discrimination or division is a distortion of God's eternal purpose.

As we stand before Him, let us remember that His judgment is not based on color, status, or heritage, but on the condition of our hearts. The call is clear to reject the false pride of human divisions and embrace the unity found only in Christ. For in the end, only those who walk in His righteousness will stand justified before His throne.

CHAPTER 2

RELIGION AND POLITICS –

DID GOD ALMIGHTY PROPHESY ABOUT DEMOCRACY?

======================

EBAN

"Fence"

Asante philosophical symbol of Love, Safety, Security

======================

*I*n the vast design of the Divine, we frequently contemplate if the concept of modern democracy was anticipated. Let's delve into these Bible verses to reflect on this idea:

> **Acts 15:18 (KJV)** "Known unto God are all his works from the beginning of the world."

> **Isaiah 46:10 (KJV)** "Declaring the end from the beginning, and from ancient times the things that are not yet done, saying, My counsel shall stand, and I will do all my pleasure."

Democracy is often defined as governance "of the people, by the people, and for the people." This ideal, however, can encounter challenges in practice, sometimes diverging from its foundational principle.

In democracies like the United States, the process can be complex and layered, influencing how the democratic will of the people is expressed:

The system includes the Electoral College, a body that convenes post-election to cast votes, which can sometimes differ from the popular vote due to certain legal frameworks.

The Electoral College's votes are then certified by the State Secretary, requiring a candidate to secure 270 votes from this body to become President.

This process raises questions about the direct impact of individual votes when a single certification has significant implications.

Following this, the US Congress meets to count and certify these State-certified votes.

The President-Elect's assumption of power is contingent on this physical meeting of Congress, highlighting a crucial step in the process.

The President is officially sworn in by the Chief Justice of the Supreme Court.

In this system, despite the collective power of the Senate, a single Senator can influence decisions, sometimes opposing measures supported by the majority, such as financial aid during crises.

This layered approach can sometimes place the people's voices and votes in the background, emphasizing the role of unelected bodies and officials. It brings to light situations where an individual's decision can impact the collective will, reflecting on the complexities within democratic systems.

Such scenarios prompt reflection on the essence of democracy, especially when minority voices hold significant sway over the majority's preferences.

Turning to biblical perspectives, democracy's emergence can be contemplated through the lens of **1 Samuel 8** in the Old Testament. This chapter discusses Israel's transition from a system of judges to a monarchy, initiated by the people's desire for a king. It illustrates a shift from God's direct rule to a human-led monarchy, prompted by the Israelites' request to the prophet Samuel, offering insights into the evolution of governance systems.

> **1 Samuel 8:1 (KJV)** "And it came to pass, when Samuel was old, that he made his sons judges over Israel."
>
> **1 Samuel 8:2 (KJV)** "Now the name of his firstborn was Joel; and the name of his second, Abiah: *they were* judges in Beer-sheba."
>
> **1 Samuel 8:3 (KJV)** "And his sons walked not in his ways, but turned aside after lucre, and took bribes, and perverted judgment."
>
> **1 Samuel 8:4 (KJV)** "Then all the elders of Israel gathered themselves together, and came to Samuel unto Ramah,"

In these verses, the context is that the prophet Samuel was growing old and had appointed his sons, Joel and Abiah, as judges over Israel. However, the people of Israel were dissatisfied with Samuel's sons as their leaders. They accused his sons of being corrupt and taking bribes, which led them to seek a change in the system of governance

> **1 Samuel 8:5 (KJV)** "And said unto him, Behold, thou art old, and thy sons walk not in thy ways: now make us a king to judge us like all the nations."

> **1 Samuel 8:6 (KJV)** "But the thing displeased Samuel, when they said, Give us a king to judge us. And Samuel prayed unto the LORD."

> **1 Samuel 8:7 (KJV)** "And the LORD said unto Samuel, Hearken unto the voice of the people in all that they say unto thee: for they have not rejected thee, but they have rejected me, that I should not reign over them."

> **1 Samuel 8:8 (KJV)** "According to all the works which they have done since the day that I brought them up out of Egypt even unto this day, wherewith they have forsaken me, and served other gods, so do they also unto thee."

> **1 Samuel 8:9 (KJV)** "Now therefore hearken unto their voice: howbeit yet protest solemnly unto them, and shew them the manner of the king that shall reign over them."

The people approached Samuel with a request for a king to rule over them, desiring a centralized monarchy similar to the systems of neighboring nations. This marked a departure from the decentralized leadership of judges, which had defined their governance up to that point. Their desire to conform to the practices of other nations reflected a shift in priorities, one that troubled Samuel deeply.

Samuel perceived their demand as a rejection of divine leadership, and in his distress, he sought guidance. The response he received was striking: he was instructed to honor the people's request but to also make them fully aware of the consequences of their decision. This moment revealed the tension between human desires for tangible leadership and the spiritual reality of divine authority.

This ancient narrative resonates with modern governance, echoing the complexities of collective decision-making and the challenges of balancing human autonomy with higher principles. It serves as a timeless reminder of the consequences of choices made without fully considering the broader implications, offering insight into the dynamics of leadership and the enduring interplay between human will and divine purpose.

As Christians navigating a world intertwined with secular systems like democracy, it's important to thoughtfully consider how these systems align with our spiritual beliefs, especially regarding the acknowledgment of God's sovereignty over leaders and nations. The complexities and challenges of integrating Christian values into such human-made systems can sometimes lead to a conflict between personal interests and divine principles.

In reflecting on democracy, particularly in contexts like the United States and globally, it's crucial for Christians to discern whether the practices within these systems are in harmony with the teachings of Christ. For instance, the disparity between the compensation for high-profile roles, such as lawyers and retired politicians, and the wages of everyday workers raises questions about justice and fairness from a Christian perspective. This contrast can be seen as a call for Christians to advocate for a more equitable distribution of resources and support for those who labor diligently.

In essence, as Christians engage with democratic systems, it's important to continually seek guidance on how best to reconcile these earthly structures with the heavenly kingdom's values, ensuring that our actions and choices reflect Christ's teachings of justice, fairness, and compassion.

> **1 Samuel 8:16 (KJV)** "And he will take your menservants, and your maidservants, and your goodliest young men, and your asses, and put *them* to his work."
>
> **1 Samuel 8:17 (KJV)** "He will take the tenth of your sheep: and ye shall be his servants."

Many of those elected as legislators and leaders identify with a belief in God or align themselves with one faith or the other. However, this raises critical questions about their true principles and the direction of their moral compass. How do their decisions reflect a genuine commitment to humanity? What will the ultimate judgment of their actions be when held to the highest standard of accountability?

The narrative explored in ***The Mighty Equalizer*** examines the profound responsibility of governance. It reflects on the inherent risks of placing trust in human authority over divine guidance. Leadership, as depicted in the ancient story of Samuel and the people's demand for a king, warns of the potential for leaders to exploit their positions for personal or political gain, often at the expense of the very people they are meant to serve. The imagery of a ruler drafting sons of others into armies, assigning daughters to labor, and exploiting resources underscores the burdens that unchecked authority can impose on society.

This story serves as a timeless cautionary tale, prompting us to reflect on the systems we rely on to govern ourselves. While democracy offers the promise of representation and equality, it is not immune to the pitfalls of corruption and manipulation. Leaders who prioritize personal gain or political power over the collective good betray the trust placed in them and undermine the very principles they were chosen to uphold.

As believers, there is a higher calling to ensure that governance reflects justice, integrity, and care for the vulnerable. Those entrusted with power bear a sacred responsibility to act in the best interests of the people they serve. Their actions are observed, and their motives will ultimately be judged by the Divine Almighty, who holds all authority accountable.

This reflection also warns of the consequences of placing unwavering trust in human systems without seeking divine wisdom. History reveals that leadership driven by ambition rather than service can lead to disillusionment, hardship, and suffering. It challenges us to evaluate the balance between reliance on human governance and adherence to higher, divinely inspired principles.

In the end, the call is clear: leadership must be rooted in justice, humility, and an unwavering commitment to the greater good. The lesson is not just for those in power but for all of u, to seek wisdom, discernment, and accountability in those we choose to lead, ensuring they embody the values we wish to uphold in our communities and nations

> **2 Thessalonians 2:11-12 (KJV)** "And for this cause God shall send them strong delusion, that they should believe a lie:

> **2 Thessalonians 2:12 (KJV)** "That they all might be damned who believed not the truth, but had pleasure in unrighteousness."

Rejecting God's truth and choosing unrighteousness comes at a significant cost. those who find pleasure in ungodliness and turn away from the truth of God risk facing His judgment. As a true child of God, you are called to discern His truth in every decision, whether as a leader or a follower. When guided by God's wisdom, your actions and choices will reflect His righteousness, guarding you from the dangers of deception and leading others in the path of His light.

The biblical account in 1 Samuel subtly critiques human governance by showing how systems like democracy, where people collectively make decisions, can be seen as diverging from God's direct rule. It raises the question: does democracy genuinely empower the people, or does it risk becoming a tool where the will of a few can override the needs and values of the majority?

While democracy aims to reflect the people's voice, it can, in practice, be vulnerable to corruption and manipulation. Self-serving politicians or leaders may exploit this system, undermining the genuine interests of the populace. This potential for misuse highlights the need for godly integrity and accountability within democratic structures.

As a follower of God, you are called to ensure that democracy reflects His will on earth. This means governing with honesty, transparency, and compassion, putting the welfare of the people above personal gain.

> **Micah 6:8 (KJV)** "He hath shewed thee, O man, what is good; and what doth the LORD require of thee, but to do justly, and to love mercy, and to walk humbly with thy God?"

In every decision, whether as a leader or a citizen, remember that God is watching, and He will judge each according to how they serve His people. By upholding justice and mercy and by aligning democratic choices with God's values, we can work toward a society that honors Him and truly benefits all His children.

> **Colossians 3:23 (KJV)** And whatsoever ye do, do it heartily, as to the Lord, and not unto men;

> **Colossians 3:24 (KJV)** Knowing that of the Lord ye shall receive the reward of the inheritance: for ye serve the Lord Christ.

God Almighty prophesied that in your democracies, as in America and around the world, when the Government and the President and his family and friends would be doing all the above evil deeds to you, that is when you would cry to God Almighty for help, and GOD ALMIGHTY WILL SAY, NO!

> **1 Samuel 8:18 (KJV)** "And ye shall cry out in that day because of your king which ye shall have chosen you; and the LORD will not hear you in that day."

Why is democracy really the rule of a few powerful men, but the people are deceived into thinking, saying, and repeating that it is the rule of the people? In all the so-called Presidential and Parliamentary forms of Government, it is the will, the idea, the position, and the desire of the President or the Prime Minister and their unelected cabinet officials that supersedes, overrides, and tramples the will of the people!

Even Jesus Christ, who did not kill a single person and never lied, was not immune from rebuke, insult, and a sham trial before a corrupt legal Roman and Jewish court, and yet, these politicians have immunity from prosecution while in office and after they have left office, thus, giving them a free hand to kill people, arrest people who rebuke them, commit many crimes in office, and then walk away free of charge!

> **1 Samuel 8:19 (KJV)** "Nevertheless the people refused to obey the voice of Samuel; and they said, Nay; but we will have a king over us;"

> **1 Samuel 8:20 (KJV)** "That we also may be like all the nations; and that our king may judge us, and go out before us, and fight our battles."

> **1 Samuel 8:21 (KJV)** "And Samuel heard all the words of the people, and he rehearsed them in the ears of the LORD."

> **1 Samuel 8:22 (KJV)** "And the LORD said to Samuel, Hearken unto their voice, and make them a king. And Samuel said unto the men of Israel, Go ye every man unto his city."

To explore the concept of democracy's prophetic presence in the Bible, we turn to the book of 1 Samuel. In this biblical passage, the people of Israel express a desire for a king to rule over them, rejecting the Lord's direct governance:

> **1 Samuel 8:7 (KJV)** "And the Lord said unto Samuel, Hearken unto the voice of the people in all that they say unto thee: for they have not rejected thee, but they have rejected me, that I should not reign over them."

This verse implies that the people's desire for a human king and this can be seen as a rejection of God's direct rule, suggesting that human-made governance systems like democracy can stand in contrast to the Lord's divine authority, if the leader rule out of their own desire and will.

As the passage unfolds, God, through Samuel, warns the people about the consequences of having a human king. It is prophesied that the king would take their sons and daughters, resources, and labor for his own purposes, revealing the potential for rulers to exploit their power for personal gain:

Furthermore, when we explore democracy in the context of the Bible, it prompts reflection on the potential consequences and challenges of human-made governance systems in comparison to the divine authority of God. It encourages us to consider whether democracy, while purporting to be the rule of the people, can, in practice, result in centralized power and the suppression of the collective voice of the majority.

In today's political climate, there is a troubling irony where some politicians and their supporters seem to pray for their own nation's downfall if it means discrediting their opponents and opposing every good idea in the name of opposition without considering the devastating effects this may have on ordinary citizens. Despite its flaws, democracy remains the best system of government available to humanity, though still far beneath the infinite wisdom and knowledge of God Almighty.

The unfortunate reality is that when one political group wins, the opposing side often wishes for their failure, even if it means the country suffers. This approach undermines the very fabric of love, patriotism, and community. If we truly love our neighbors, our country, and our fellow human beings, why should we harbor ill will or wish for their destruction?

Such negative intentions reflect humanity's shortcomings, revealing our inability to create a perfect system free of victimization, division, and harmful ambitions. But rather than allowing these flaws to define us, we should strive for unity, compassion, and understanding.

Let us set aside divisive politics and join hands in love, care, and mutual respect to build a peaceful and thriving world for all. True progress comes not from tearing each other down but from working together for the greater good.

The LORD Jesus Christ be with your spirit. The LORD Jesus Christ give you understanding.

CHAPTER 3

THE RULE OF GOD (LAW)!

====================

DZINUDZEZI

(SYMBOL OF WOMANHOOD)

Ewe symbol of womanhood

====================

*T*hroughout history, laws have been fundamental in shaping human behavior and societal norms. Laws establish boundaries, determining what is permissible and what is not. But beyond human-made laws lies a higher standard divine law, the Rule of God. Divine law provides not only guidance but a framework for righteousness, helping us to understand concepts like guilt and sin. Without divine law, the lines between right and wrong blur, making it challenging to discern moral truth.

The Rule of God, as laid out in the Holy Scriptures, holds a special place in our lives, serving as the ultimate measure of justice and morality. This divine law illuminates the path of righteousness, helping us differentiate virtuous actions from sinful ones. Human laws, while essential for societal order, often fall short of God's divine standard and may lack moral clarity. When laws contradict the principles established by God, they undermine the natural order and are viewed as abominations.

In today's world, we must examine the fairness and justice of human legal systems. Although these systems strive to maintain order, they frequently overlook or even oppress the marginalized.

Laws that disregard divine principles or deviate from natural order can lead to societal chaos, moral decline, and ultimately, collapse, as witnessed in the Roman Empire, where deviation from God's design led to its downfall.

Divine law serves as the moral compass instilled within each of us. This internal guidance aligns our actions with God's principles, fostering a sense of justice that transcends human limitations. Those who distance themselves from God's guidance risk losing this moral compass, leading to actions that stray from divine values. When society replaces God's law with human interpretation, history shows that it often invites social unrest and moral decay.

The Rule of God reminds us that true justice is not simply about maintaining order but about upholding the dignity and worth of every individual. Human laws, though valuable, often lack a safety net for the vulnerable and may fail to address the needs of the less privileged. Only God's law is truly just and fair, offering a foundation for ethical living that human systems often cannot replicate.

> **Psalm 19:7 (KJV)** "The law of the LORD is perfect, converting the soul: the testimony of the LORD is sure, making wise the simple."

> **Micah 6:8 (KJV)** "He hath shewed thee, O man, what is good; and what doth the LORD require of thee, but to do justly, and to love mercy, and to walk humbly with thy God?"

> **Proverbs 14:34 (KJV)** "Righteousness exalteth a nation: but sin is a reproach to any people."

> **Romans 13:1 (KJV)** "Let every soul be subject unto the higher powers. For there is no power but of God: the powers that be are ordained of God."

> **Romans 13:2 (KJV)** "Whosoever therefore resisteth the power, resisteth the ordinance of God: and they that resist shall receive to themselves damnation."

In conclusion, while human laws serve to maintain societal order, true justice is realized only when these laws reflect the higher principles of divine wisdom. Divine law calls humanity to embody justice, compassion, and humility, fostering ethical living and inspiring leaders and citizens alike to act with integrity. Rooted in universal truths, these laws transcend mere regulation, aiming to transform hearts and minds, strengthen communities, and cultivate nations grounded in righteousness.

Disregarding divine principles leads to moral decay and societal decline, as these laws are not arbitrary but purposeful, offering guidance to protect and uplift. They set clear boundaries to preserve the dignity and well-being of individuals and societies, warning of the inevitable consequences of stepping outside these limits. When human governance aligns with these higher principles, it reflects the legitimacy and authority derived from the ultimate source of truth and justice.

God's laws are given not to constrain but to guide humanity toward lives of meaning and purpose. They serve as safeguards against destructive practices, protecting spiritual and moral integrity. By honoring these principles, we avoid embracing harmful customs or traditions that deviate from the intended path and risk eroding the fabric of our collective well-being.

In embracing divine law, we not only uphold justice but also honor the values that sustain life and harmony. This alignment creates societies built on fairness, compassion, and a shared commitment to higher ideals, ensuring that we live in accordance with a purpose greater than ourselves. It is through this alignment that we find not only order but true fulfillment and enduring peace.

> **Leviticus 18:22 (KJV)** "Thou shalt not lie with mankind, as with womankind: it is abomination."

> **Leviticus 18:23 (KJV)** "Neither shalt thou lie with any beast to defile thyself therewith: neither shall any woman stand before a beast to lie down thereto: it is confusion."

> **Leviticus 18:24 (KJV)** "Defile not ye yourselves in any of these things: for in all these the nations are defiled which I cast out before you."

> **Leviticus 19:26 (KJV)** "Ye shall not eat any thing with the blood: neither shall ye use enchantment, nor observe times."

> **Galatians 4:9 (KJV)** "But now, after that ye have known God, or rather are known of God, how turn ye again to the weak and beggarly elements, whereunto ye desire again to be in bondage?"

> **Galatians 4:10 (KJV)** "Ye observe days, and months, and times, and years."

Many people celebrate holidays like Christmas and Easter, believing them to be purely Christian traditions. However, these observances have roots in pagan customs that were later adapted and incorporated into Christian practices. While the intention behind celebrating these days may focus on honoring Christ, it's essential to understand their origins and consider whether they align with God's original commandments.

Traditions, even those embraced in the name of faith, can sometimes lead us away from the clarity of God's teachings. Over time, customs rooted in human traditions may obscure the true essence of worship, placing greater emphasis on cultural practices rather than spiritual truth. This doesn't mean that participating in such celebrations is inherently wrong; often, the intention behind the celebration can transform its meaning and purpose. However, making informed decisions based on a deeper understanding of these origins allows us to evaluate our actions more thoughtfully.

For those who desire to align their lives more closely with God's instructions, it may be worthwhile to consider how these traditions fit within a life guided by divine principles. Avoiding such celebrations, not out of legalism but from an informed conscience, can be an act of devotion and faithfulness. Ultimately, the focus should always remain on God's commandments as the foundation of worship, ensuring that our practices reflect His truth rather than human tradition.

This perspective encourages readers to seek wisdom and discernment in their choices. By examining the origins and implications of certain customs, believers can make intentional decisions that align with their faith, prioritizing the purity of worship over adherence to traditions that may obscure the divine purpose.

Deuteronomy 12:29 (KJV) "When the LORD thy God shall cut off the nations from before thee, whither thou goest to possess them, and thou succeedest them, and dwellest in their land;"

Deuteronomy 12:30 (KJV) "Take heed to thyself that thou be not snared by following them, after that they be destroyed from before thee; and that thou enquire not after their gods, saying, How did these nations serve their gods? even so will I do likewise."

Deuteronomy 12:31 (KJV) "Thou shalt not do so unto the LORD thy God: for every abomination to the LORD, which he hateth, have they done unto their gods; for even their sons and their daughters they have burnt in the fire to their gods."

Colossians 2:8 (KJV) "Beware lest any man spoil you through philosophy and vain deceit, after the tradition of men, after the rudiments of the world, and not after Christ."

Jeremiah 10:2 (KJV) "Thus saith the LORD, learn not the way of the heathen, and be not dismayed at the signs of heaven; for the heathen are dismayed at them."

Jeremiah 10:3 (KJV) "For the customs of the people are vain: for one cutteth a tree out of the forest, the work of the hands of the workman, with the axe."

Jeremiah 10:4 (KJV) "They deck it with silver and with gold; they fasten it with nails and with hammers, that it move not."

Matthew 7:22 (KJV) "Many will say to me in that day, Lord, Lord, have we not prophesied in thy name? and in thy name have cast out devils? and in thy name done many wonderful works?"

Matthew 7:23 (KJV) "And then will I profess unto them, I never knew you: depart from me, ye that work iniquity."

Mark 7:13 (KJV) "Making the word of God of none effect through your tradition, which ye have delivered: and many such like things do ye."

1 Thessalonians 5:22 (KJV): "Abstain from all appearance of evil."

As Christians, it is important to thoughtfully consider the origins of certain celebrations and traditions that have become widely accepted within our faith. Many of the days we honor, such as Christmas and Easter, as well as practices like decorating trees or engaging in certain rituals, often have roots in pagan customs that were later adopted and adapted by Christians. While these celebrations may now carry new intentions focused on honoring Christ, understanding their origins allows us to make informed choices about how we approach them.

The key question is not merely about participating in these traditions but whether they truly align with our devotion to God and reflect His will. In a world where societal norms often influence even the most devout believers, it is vital to ensure that the practices we adopt do not dilute our worship or compromise the integrity of our faith. While the intention behind celebrating certain days may sanctify them to some degree, we should critically evaluate whether they enhance our connection to God or serve as remnants of worldly customs.

Consider holidays like Halloween, whose origins are deeply tied to pagan rituals and the glorification of themes such as darkness, death, and the occult. These elements starkly contrast the Christian message of life, hope, and the light of Christ. While many participate in Halloween without malicious intent, its historical associations warrant careful reflection for those who seek to live lives that honor God fully.

This discussion is not about condemning those who partake in such celebrations but about encouraging an informed conscience. As followers of Christ, we are called to live with intentionality, ensuring that the traditions we observe align with God's teachings. Abstaining from practices rooted in darkness or that conflict with biblical principles is not about fear or legalism but about demonstrating our commitment to the purity of worship and the truth of the Gospel.

Ultimately, avoiding such celebrations based on informed conviction allows us to focus more fully on living lives that reflect our devotion to God. It also sets an example for others, inspiring deeper discernment and a commitment to honoring God in all aspects of life. While intentions can redeem certain practices, choosing to forgo traditions with origins that conflict with our faith can deepen our spiritual walk and affirm our dedication to the principles that guide us as children of light.

Ephesians 5:11 (KJV) "And have no fellowship with the unfruitful works of darkness, but rather reprove them."

Deuteronomy 18:10 (KJV) "There shall not be found among you any one that maketh his son or his daughter to pass through the fire, or that useth divination, or an observer of times, or an enchanter, or a witch,"

Deuteronomy 18:11 (KJV) "Or a charmer, or a consulter with familiar spirits, or a wizard, or a necromancer."

Deuteronomy 18:12 (KJV) "For all that do these things are an abomination unto the Lord: and because of these abominations the Lord thy God doth drive them out from before thee."

1 Thessalonians 5:22 (KJV) "Abstain from all appearance of evil."

2 Corinthians 6:14 (KJV) "Be ye not unequally yoked together with unbelievers: for what fellowship hath righteousness with unrighteousness? and what communion hath light with darkness?"

Our human limitations and personal efforts often fall short in keeping us consistently on the path of righteousness. As we interact with others, we may be vulnerable to outside influences and subtle pressures that can divert us from our true purpose. The Word of God, however, remains our steadfast guide, giving us the clarity to discern between right and wrong. As followers of Christ, we bear the responsibility to continually examine whether our actions align with the divine will of our Heavenly Father or are shaped by worldly influences.

Aligning our lives with God's will requires cultivating a deep, personal relationship with Him. This alignment is not achieved in a single moment but through a daily commitment to seeking His guidance and living by His love, grace, and truth. Through this dedication, we draw closer to God's heart and learn to walk consistently in the light of His purpose.

The LORD Jesus Christ be with your spirit. The LORD Jesus Christ give you understanding.

CHAPTER 4

THE MIGHTY EQUALIZER: A DIVINE MESSAGE FOR
THE PRESIDENT AND THE FIRST LADY

=====================

LAMB OF GOD

Ewe symbol for Lamb of God

=====================

*I*n the complex fabric of global governance, leaders such as presidents, prime ministers, and those in power often hold influence that extends far beyond ordinary authority. However, the forces at play are not always aligned with righteousness; many leaders operate in concert with dark influences that shape the direction of nations. Governing a nation is not just a human responsibility; it is a profound calling meant to reflect divine purpose and justice. When leaders sever their connection to God, they open the door for malevolent forces to exert control, distorting the true purpose of their power.

The foundation of any nation lies in its alignment with God's will. Without this sacred relationship, leaders may fall prey to influences that lead nations astray, prioritizing worldly agendas over divine guidance. True leadership should seek God's wisdom, ensuring that governance serves to uplift and protect rather than subjugate and mislead. In a world where many rulers have turned from God's path, it is essential to recognize the spiritual battle underlying global affairs and to pray for leaders to seek righteousness in their roles.

Proverbs 21:1 (KJV) "The king's heart is in the hand of the Lord, as the rivers of water: he turneth it whithersoever he will."

For those who rise to positions of leadership, whether as presidents, prime ministers, or local governors, a profound truth stands: true leadership is a calling meant to be anointed by God. It is a divine appointment, one that carries immense responsibility. Leaders are entrusted with the well-being and destiny of the people under their care, who, in a spiritual sense, are God's people.

However, there is an opposing force at work. The enemy, or the devil, also seeks to influence and control the destinies of these people by manipulating leaders and swaying them from God's path. This spiritual battle over leadership is intense, as the enemy knows that influencing those in power can impact entire nations. Leaders who neglect their divine purpose or fall into worldly temptations open the door for dark forces to shape their decisions, ultimately steering people away from God's intended plan.

Therefore, it is essential for leaders to seek God's guidance and to remember their role as stewards, not rulers, of God's people. In a world where spiritual influences are ever-present, a leader's alignment with God's will serves as a safeguard against the enemy's schemes, ensuring that governance uplifts and protects rather than leading people astray.

This responsibility is a unique and profound privilege, one that sets leaders apart. With this privilege comes an equally significant duty. Leaders are entrusted with the welfare of those they serve, including their well-being, and spiritual and physical needs. It is a calling that requires integrity and compassion, recognizing the impact leadership has on the lives of others.

In the forthcoming pages, we shall embark on a journey to unravel the divine responsibilities entrusted to rulers, with a specific focus on Head of States (Presidents/Prime Ministers) and their first ladies. Our exploration delves deep into the significance of this calling, the profound expectations it bears, and the substantial impact it wields upon the lives of those under their governance. Above all, we ponder a question that resounds through the annals of leadership: "What will The Lord, The Lord God, say to you, the President, and the First Lady, when you stand before Him to give an account of your stewardship?" These inquiries are anchored in the wisdom of the Holy Bible, emphasizing that those blessed with great privilege and responsibility are held to a higher standard of accountability and care, especially those who assume positions of leadership.

Our journey is illuminated by the timeless wisdom found in the Bible, which beckons us to consider the profound significance of leadership and the divine expectations that accompany it. The sacred scriptures remind us that leaders are called to serve with righteousness and compassion, guided by the principles laid out in the Word of God.

Psalm 82:3-4 (KJV) "Defend the poor and fatherless: do justice to the afflicted and needy."

Psalm 82:3-4 (KJV) "Deliver the poor and needy: rid them out of the hand of the wicked."

The role of leaders, including presidents and first ladies, is to champion justice and care for the vulnerable.

Furthermore, we are reminded of the weight of leadership responsibilities by the counsel of God.

Proverbs 31:8 (KJV) "Open thy mouth for the dumb in the cause of all such as are appointed to destruction."

Proverbs 31:9 (KJV) "Open thy mouth, judge righteously, and plead the cause of the poor and needy."

Leaders are called to be advocates for those who cannot speak for themselves and to uphold righteousness in their judgments, especially on behalf of the underprivileged.

In our exploration, we'll also draw inspiration from **Matthew 25:40**, where Jesus teaches, "And the King shall answer and say unto them, Verily I say unto you, inasmuch as ye have done it unto one of the least of these my brethren, ye have done it unto me." This verse underscores the profound connection between serving the marginalized and serving the divine purpose. Thus, as we delve into the divine responsibilities of rulers, we do so with a firm understanding of the biblical expectations placed upon leader, who bear the duty of compassionate and just governance, with a watchful eye on the welfare of all.

Luke 12:48 (KJV): "But he that knew not, and did commit things worthy of stripes, shall be beaten with few stripes. For unto whomsoever much is given, of him shall be much required: and to whom men have committed much, of him they will ask the more."

1 Peter 5:2-3 (KJV): "Feed the flock of God which is among you, taking the oversight thereof, not by constraint, but willingly; not for filthy lucre, but of a ready mind; Neither as being lords over God's heritage, but being ensamples to the flock."

There is no kingdom without God, for He is the ultimate sovereign over all creation. A true leader of people must be anointed by God, as leadership is a divine calling and a sacred trust. As a leader, you bear a unique and God-ordained responsibility to care for His people. This responsibility is a privilege granted only to you by God's will.

If you are not leading under the influence of evil but as a servant of God, you must make decisions guided by divine wisdom, ensuring that they positively impact God's children. This sacred duty requires humility, discernment, and a heart aligned with God's purpose.

The scripture also calls on citizens and subjects to submit themselves to the authority of such leader, as long as that authority aligns with God's principles. In doing so, the community thrives under leadership that honors God and nurtures His people.

> **Hebrews 13:17 (KJV)** "Obey them that have the rule over you, and submit yourselves: for they watch for your souls, as they that must give account, that they may do it with joy, and not with grief: for that is unprofitable for you."

> **1 Corinthians 4:2 (KJV)** "Moreover it is required in stewards, that a man be found faithful."

The truth is that all authority is established by God, and those in positions of leadership, rulers and leaders alike, are placed there according to His divine purpose. Their authority is not their own but is granted by the Creator, who guides the hearts of kings and rulers like streams of water, directing them as He wills. God, in His infinite wisdom, sets up leaders and removes them at the appointed time, sometimes using unexpected or even undesirable rulers as instruments of His will.

When God's children become wayward, arrogant, or disobedient, He may allow a leader to rise who challenges their pride and complacency, serving as an instrument to fulfill His divine will. Just as He hardened Pharaoh's heart to bring Israel back to alignment, God can permit a leader to redirect His people toward repentance and restoration. Such leadership, even when it appears harsh or unwelcome, is often a refining fir, designed to compel the disobedient to return to God's path.

However, those chosen for such roles must remember that their position is not an endorsement of their actions but a fulfillment of God's purpose. Just as Judas played his part in the betrayal of Jesus to fulfill the scriptures, leaders who fail to embrace their unique role for good may also find themselves expendable in God's plan. Woe to the one who fulfills God's will through actions of harm or neglect, for they will face divine judgment for their choices. Leadership is a sacred trust, and those who misuse it for selfish gain or divisiveness will bear the consequences before the One who appointed them.

In His sovereignty, God can use the foolish to confound the wise and the weak to reveal His strength, showing that no ruler rises outside His control. Leaders, whether exalted or despised, are tools in His hands, working to accomplish His divine plan and guide His people back to Him. This truth reminds us that God's purpose prevails, even through circumstances that challenge our understanding, as He works all things for the ultimate good of those who love Him.

> **Romans 13:1 (KJV)** "Let every soul be subject unto the higher powers. For there is no power but of God: the powers that be are ordained of God."

> **Proverbs 21:1 (KJV)** "The king's heart is in the hand of the LORD, as the rivers of water: he turneth it whithersoever he will."

Daniel 2:21 (KJV) "And he changeth the times and the seasons: he removeth kings, and setteth up kings: he giveth wisdom unto the wise, and knowledge to them that know understanding:"

1 Samuel 16:13 (KJV) "Then Samuel took the horn of oil, and anointed him in the midst of his brethren: and the Spirit of the LORD came upon David from that day forward. So Samuel rose up, and went to Ramah."

Psalms 75:6 (KJV) "For promotion cometh neither from the east, nor from the west, nor from the south."

Psalms 75:7 (KJV) "But God is the judge: he putteth down one, and setteth up another."

Timothy 2:1 (KJV) "I exhort therefore, that, first of all, supplications, prayers, intercessions, and giving of thanks, be made for all men;"

1 Timothy 2:2 (KJV) "For kings, and for all that are in authority; that we may lead a quiet and peaceable life in all godliness and honesty."

1 Timothy 2:3 (KJV) "For this is good and acceptable in the sight of God our Saviour;"

1 Timothy 2:4 (KJV) "Who will have all men to be saved, and to come unto the knowledge of the truth."

First of all, Mr. President, your foremost duty is to ensure that the divine plan for the well-being of God's people prevails. The President is entrusted with the task of advancing social justice and equality for all citizens, irrespective of their ethnicity, background, religious beliefs, gender, or their past electoral choices. As the leader of the nation, advocating for policies and initiatives aimed at rectifying systemic inequalities and discrimination is imperative. The President or Prime Minister should exemplify a lifelong dedication to serving and caring for their fellow citizens. Protection of the people from harm such as flood, hunger, disease, and natural events or disasters.

Leadership, in its truest sense, transcends party affiliations, ethnic loyalties, or personal grievances. A leader's foremost responsibility is to serve and care for all the people under their charge, irrespective of who supports them or is aligned with their ideology. When leaders allow partisan biases or regional allegiances to dictate their actions, they fail to honor the sacred duty entrusted to them.

Recently, an instance emerged where a leader publicly expressed reluctance to assist communities affected by disaster, suggesting their lack of past support for him or his political organization. Such remarks and the subsequent lack of meaningful action highlight a concerning disregard for the suffering of citizens who depend on leadership for guidance, protection, and hope in times of crisis.

True leadership is measured by the ability to rise above divisions and serve with equity and compassion. It calls for a heart that prioritizes the collective good, fostering unity and trust among the people. When leaders neglect this responsibility, they betray the very essence of governance and fail the people they were chosen to serve.

> **James 2:15 (KJV)** "If a brother or sister be naked, and destitute of daily food,
>
> **James 2:16 (KJV)** And one of you say unto them, Depart in peace, be ye warmed and filled; notwithstanding ye give them not those things which are needful to the body; what doth it profit?"
>
> **Proverbs 31:8 (KJV)** "Open thy mouth for the dumb in the cause of all such as are appointed to destruction.
>
> **Proverbs 31:9 (KJV)** Open thy mouth, judge righteously, and plead the cause of the poor and needy."

So, I politely ask you, Mr. President, again, what will God say to you when you stand before His judgment throne? Refusing to assist certain communities in their time of distress based on political affiliation or voting history is a profound violation of the principle of equal treatment. Leadership demands fairness, compassion, and the commitment to serve all citizens equally, regardless of their political choices or loyalties.

Every citizen deserves equal access to government assistance, especially in moments of crisis. Denying aid or withholding comfort from those in need because of perceived differences is not only troubling but reveals a failure to uphold the sacred trust placed in you as a leader. What account will you give before the Lord, who sees all and holds leaders to the highest standard of justice and mercy? Will you be found faithful, or will your actions testify against you?

> **Proverbs 21:13 (KJV)** "Whoso stoppeth his ears at the cry of the poor, he also shall cry himself, but shall not be heard."
>
> **Matthew 25:40 (KJV)** "And the King shall answer and say unto them, Verily I say unto you, Inasmuch as ye have done it unto one of the least of these my brethren, ye have done it unto me."

You have forsaken the sacred duty entrusted to you by God to care for all the people under your leadership. An elected leader bears the moral responsibility to serve the entire nation, not only those who support them. Neglecting to assist communities in need, particularly during times of crisis, is a breach of this fundamental obligation.

Through such actions and words, Mr. President, you have taken a partisan stance that fosters division rather than unity, undermining the very foundation of your leadership. God, in His infinite justice, will hold you accountable for the stewardship entrusted to you. Such choices risk widening

the divisions within the nation, deepening mistrust among communities, and threatening the unity and cohesion of the country.

The moral authority of a leader is rooted in the trust and confidence of the people. When assistance is withheld based on political considerations, it erodes that trust and damages the credibility of the leader's ability to govern with fairness and impartiality. A true leader unites, serves, and protects all citizens, reflecting the justice and mercy of the One who ordained their authority.

What will The Lord say to you for your neglect of the vulnerable and marginalized communities? Most often, they suffer the most from this kind of discrimination. These communities may already face numerous challenges and hardships, and denying them assistance based on political considerations can have devastating consequences for them.

> **Matthew 25:42(KJV)** "For I was hungred, and ye gave me no meat: I was thirsty, and ye gave me no drink:"

> **Matthew 25:43 (KJV)** "I was a stranger, and ye took me not in: naked, and ye clothed me not: sick, and in prison, and ye visited me not."

> **Matthew 25:44 (KJV)** "Then shall they also answer him, saying, Lord, when saw we thee hungry, or athirst, or a stranger, or naked, or sick, or in prison, and did not minister unto thee?"

> **Matthew 25:45 (KJV)** "Then shall he answer them, saying, Verily I say unto you, inasmuch as ye did it not to one of the least of these, ye did it not to me."

Mr. President, such behavior undermines the principles of fairness and the cornerstone of democratic rule, which demands that leaders serve and represent all citizens, irrespective of their political affiliations or preferences. True leadership is marked by courage, impartiality, and an unwavering commitment to the well-being of all people. Ethical and moral leadership requires the exhibition of empathy, compassion, and dedication to the common good values that transcend political considerations.

Refusing aid or assistance based on political bias violates these principles and diminishes the trust and unity necessary for good governance. It reflects a departure from the high standard of care and fairness expected of those in positions of authority.

You will be held accountable, Mr. President, not only by the people you serve but also by God Almighty, whose commands call for justice, mercy, and humility in leadership. Discriminatory actions raise profound moral questions about the integrity and purpose of leadership. Woe to those who abandon their divine mandate, for they will answer to both conscience and the Creator who entrusted them with such responsibility.

Proverbs 16:5 (KJV) "Every one that is proud in heart is an abomination to the Lord: though hand join in hand, he shall not be unpunished.'

Jeremiah 17:10 (KJV) "I the Lord search the heart, I try the reins, even to give every man according to his ways, and according to the fruit of his doings."

Leaders may make promises, whether good or bad, but their true legacy lies in the policies they implement and the direction they set, which ultimately shape the lives of the people they govern. A single statement, such as your public confession that certain communities do not historically support you due to tribal, religious, or political differences, cannot justify a decision to ignore their suffering or punish them. Such actions, coupled with pride and disregard for moral principles, carry consequences that cannot be ignored or go unpunished.

This serves as a sobering reminder that leaders, like all individuals, are subject to divine judgment for their actions. Scripture teaches us that God examines the hearts and deeds of all, including those in authority, and holds them accountable according to their ways. Leadership is not exempt from this divine scrutiny, and every decision carries spiritual and moral weight.

Mr. President, by your words and refusal to assist certain communities based on their voting history, you risk violating ethical principles, undermining trust, and deepening divisions within the nation. A true leader is called to rise above political biases and prioritize the welfare of all citizens, irrespective of their political choices.

Take this to heart, Mr. President, and recognize the sacred stewardship entrusted to you by God. Your role is not one of favoritism or retribution but of service, justice, and compassion toward all of God's people.

A landslide victory is not a license for wickedness, nor does it grant the authority to overplay your hand by allowing campaign promises of divisiveness or malice to shape your actions as president. Such a victory should instead remind you of the weight of responsibility entrusted to you to govern with fairness, justice, and humility.

Your presidency belongs to the people, if you truly represent them. It is your sacred duty of serving and representing their collective interests, not just those who supported you. The office you hold is not a platform for personal vendettas or political retribution but a calling to unify and uplift the nation.

Let not the rhetoric of the campaign trail cloud the moral clarity required of your leadership. The promises of harm or exclusion made to secure power must not define the legacy of your governance. Leadership rooted in wickedness will ultimately be judged and held accountable by both history and the God who grants authority.

Mr. President, remember that your actions today shape the lives of millions and leave an indelible mark on your stewardship. Lead with integrity, compassion, and the commitment to serve all citizens equally, as the privilege of leadership demands.

> **Proverbs 29:2 (KJV)** "When the righteous are in authority, the people rejoice: but when the wicked beareth rule, the people mourn."

Mr. President, it is essential to trust in the Lord wholeheartedly and lean not on your own understanding, acknowledging Him in every decision you make. By seeking His wisdom and guidance in all matters, you allow Him to direct your path and ensure that the choices you make positively impact the lives of those you serve. True leadership comes from relying on God's divine insight, recognizing that human understanding alone is insufficient for the weight of such responsibility.

> **Proverbs 3:5 (KJV)** "Trust in the Lord with all thine heart; and lean not unto thine own understanding."

> **Proverbs 3:6 (KJV)** "In all thy ways acknowledge him, and he shall direct thy paths."

Mr. President, choose this day whom you will serve with unwavering loyalty to God, your Creator, and to the people He has entrusted to your care. Your devotion should be evident in your actions, demonstrating a steadfast commitment to their well-being and welfare. True leadership calls for a heart fully dedicated to honoring God's purpose while serving His people with integrity and compassion.

> **Joshua 24:15 (KJV)** "And if it seem evil unto you to serve the Lord, choose you this day whom ye will serve...but as for me and my house, we will serve the Lord."

Lead with humility, considering the needs and interests of the people above your own. Let your actions reflect selflessness and a genuine commitment to their well-being, even when it demands personal sacrifice. True leadership is marked by a heart that values others and serves with compassion and dedication, placing the greater good above individual gain.

> **Philippians 2:3 (KJV)** "Let nothing be done through strife or vainglory; but in lowliness of mind let each esteem other better than themselves."

> **Philippians 2:4 (KJV)** "Look not every man on his own things, but every man also on the things of others."

Dear leader of the people, set an example in every aspect of your life, demonstrating integrity, love, faith, and moral character that inspires others to follow. Live in a manner that is worthy of respect and emulation, upholding a high standard of ethical conduct and becoming a beacon of righteousness for those you lead. Let your actions speak louder than your words, showing the way through a life of virtue and purpose.

> **1 Timothy 4:12 (KJV)**— "Let no man despise thy youth, but be thou an example of the believers, in word, in conversation, in charity, in spirit, in faith, in purity."

Lead with a clear and purposeful vision that inspires hope and guides your people toward progress and prosperity. Without direction, communities falter, but a leader who diligently pursues a meaningful plan for the betterment of their nation brings stability and growth. Let your vision illuminate the path forward, providing guidance and purpose for those you serve.

> **Proverbs 29:18 (KJV)** "Where there is no vision, the people perish: but he that keepeth the law, happy is he."

Do not be afraid, for He is with you; do not be dismayed, for He will strengthen and uphold you as you face difficulties. Lead with courage and fairness, ensuring that your actions are rooted in justice and compassion. By standing firm in what is right and seeking divine guidance, you can effectively manage any crisis without succumbing to fear or bias. Let your leadership reflect a steadfast reliance on God's direction, instilling hope and confidence in those you serve.

> **Isaiah 41:10 (KJV)** "Fear thou not; for I am with thee: be not dismayed; for I am thy God: I will strengthen thee; yea, I will help thee; yea, I will uphold thee with the right hand of my righteousness."

Let integrity and uprightness guide you in every action and decision, ensuring that your leadership reflects honesty and moral strength. A leader's true worth is measured by their character, and those who walk in integrity not only earn the trust of the people but also align their path with righteousness.

Maintain a commitment to truth and justice, refusing to compromise your principles for personal gain or fleeting advantages. Let your life serve as a moral compass for your nation, standing as an example of ethical leadership. As you pursue a path of integrity, you safeguard the nation's foundations, fostering trust, stability, and progress among the people you are called to serve.

> **Proverbs 11:3 (KJV)** "The integrity of the upright shall guide them: but the perverseness of transgressors shall destroy them."

> **Psalm 26:11 (KJV)** "But as for me, I will walk in mine integrity: redeem me, and be merciful unto me."

Let your decisions be guided by a deep sense of justice, compassion, and humility, striving always to do what is right in the eyes of God and beneficial for humanity. True leadership calls for moral courage to choose what is good and decent, even when it goes against popular opinion or immediate convenience.

Walk humbly, recognizing that your authority is not for personal gain but a sacred trust to serve others with fairness and integrity. Act justly, ensuring that your decisions uplift the oppressed, honor the truth, and reflect the values of righteousness. Show mercy, extend compassion, to those in need, for a leader's greatness is seen in their kindness and willingness to stand up for what is right, no matter the cost. In doing so, you align your leadership with divine purpose and become a beacon of hope and justice for your people.

> **Micah 6:8 (KJV)**— "He hath shewed thee, O man, what is good; and what doth the Lord require of thee, but to do justly, and to love mercy, and to walk humbly with thy God."

Mr. President, your position comes with profound ethical and moral responsibilities, requiring a commitment to justice, integrity, and the well-being of all citizens. As the leader of the nation, you are called to serve every citizen, not just those who supported you at the ballot box or aligned with your political or ethnic affiliations. Leadership demands a higher purpose, one rooted in fairness, compassion, and the pursuit of what is right in the eyes of both God and humanity.

What will the Lord say to you when you stand before His judgment throne, having neglected the people entrusted to your care? Refusing assistance to those in need based on past political choices violates the principles of good governance and contradicts the essence of democracy. In what just system must everyone vote for you to be counted as citizens? You are not just the leader of your supporters or your kinsmen; you are the President of the entire country, entrusted with the sacred duty to protect and uplift all people under your care.

And to the First Lady, your role is one of extraordinary influence and responsibility. What will God say to you, who holds a position designed to advocate for the voiceless? You are uniquely positioned to champion the cause of the vulnerable the widows, the fatherless, and the destitute echoing the principles of justice and mercy found in God's Word. This is your reasonable service, a divine calling to reflect God's heart for the oppressed and to stand as a beacon of hope for those who cannot fight for themselves.

Both of you, as leaders in your respective roles, are accountable to a higher standard. Your actions must align with the principles of compassion, equity, and divine stewardship. Leadership is not a privilege for self-serving agendas but a sacred responsibility to serve all people with humility and righteousness. May you reflect on these truths and lead in a way that honors the God who has entrusted you with such great authority.

> **Isaiah 1:17 "KJV)** "Learn to do well; seek judgment, relieve the oppressed, judge the fatherless, plead for the widow."
>
> **Psalm 68:5 (KJV)** "A father of the fatherless, and a judge of the widows, is God in his holy habitation."

Today's First Ladies or wives of leaders in our world hold unique positions of influence, not just as partners to prominent figures but as stewards of divine purpose. These roles are not merely ceremonial or self-serving; they are sacred callings that carry immense responsibility. The example of Esther provides a timeless blueprint for how women in such positions can rise to the occasion and fulfill their God-given purpose.

Esther's story is one of courage, selflessness, and divine timing. She found herself in a position of power not for personal gain but to stand in the gap for her people during a time of crisis. She raised awareness of the plight of the Jewish people, risking her own life to intercede before the king. This demonstrates the courage required to confront difficult issues, even when it means challenging authority or risking personal comfort.

In today's world, First Ladies, whether in the church or government, are called to emulate this example. As wives of leaders, they often have unparalleled access to decision-makers, a privilege that comes with the responsibility to advocate for the vulnerable, uplift the marginalized, and bridge divides in society. Like Esther, they must ask themselves whether they have been placed in their roles for "such a time as this," to champion causes that promote justice, equity, and compassion.

Modern challenges demand the courage and focus of women like Esther. Are you using your influence to protect the rights of women and girls, to advocate for those who suffer injustice, and to foster unity and harmony in your community? Are you raising awareness of the struggles faced by the abused, the neglected, and the oppressed? Or are you consumed by materialism, focused on appearances and personal luxury rather than the urgent needs around you?

To those who have embraced worldly titles such as "First Ladies" in churches, you are not exempt from the divine calling that comes with your role. The spiritual leadership of the congregation places upon you the responsibility to embody humility, faith, and action. Your position is not one of mere recognition but one of profound influence and service.

Women and girls in the church look to you for guidance, inspiration, and mentorship. Are you actively investing in their spiritual and personal growth, creating opportunities for them to thrive, and standing boldly against the societal ills that threaten their well-being? Or have you become complacent, content to rest in the shadow of your title, neglecting the deeper purpose for which God has placed you in this position?

Your role calls for far more than appearances or occupying a seat beside your husband in the front row. It demands a wholehearted commitment to being a living reflection of Christ's love, a champion for truth, and a source of hope and inspiration for the next generation. This position is not about titles or recognition but about using your God-given influence to nurture hearts, uplift spirits, and transform lives. Embrace the higher calling to serve with purpose and humility, leaving a legacy that glorifies God and impacts lives for eternity.

The modern Esther has every resource at her disposal to effect changes, as well as a mega social platform, networks of influence, and access to the corridors of power. The question is whether these tools are being used to heal, build, and reconcile or squandered on vanity and complacency. Just as Esther's bravery saved her people, today's women in leadership can be instruments of God's will, provided they prioritize service over self and embrace their roles as advocates for righteousness and justice.

This is your moment to stand in the gap, to lift your voice for the oppressed, and to be the change that reflects God's heart for His people. Anything less is a failure to recognize the divine purpose behind your position. Let the legacy of Esther inspire you to rise above the ordinary and leave an indelible mark on the lives you are called to serve

> **Esther 4:14 (KJV)** "For if thou altogether holdest thy peace at this time, then shall there enlargement and deliverance arise to the Jews from another place; but thou and thy father's house shall be destroyed: and who knoweth whether thou art come to the kingdom for such a time as this?"

First Lady, have you truly reflected on why God has placed you in this position of influence as the spouse of your nation's leader? Your role is far more than ceremonial or symbolic; it is a divine appointment, a calling to intercede for the voiceless and champion transformative social change. You have been entrusted with a sacred opportunity to be a voice for the marginalized, to advocate for justice, and to bring hope to the downtrodden. This is not a position of privilege for personal gain but a responsibility to serve those who cannot fight for themselves.

Your position as the wife of a President, Prime Minister, or King gives you a platform like no other, one from which you can bring attention to the struggles of the widow, the orphan, and the oppressed. It is not a role for passive observation or quiet comfort but one demanding active compassion and bold action. You must speak for those who cannot speak for themselves, defending the cause of the destitute with the courage that only God can provide.

Consider the example of Esther, who did not shy away from the responsibility placed upon her. She recognized that her role as queen was not an accident but a divine placement to bring deliverance to her people. When faced with the potential annihilation of her people, she did not remain silent or passive. Instead, she prepared herself with fasting and prayer, then approached the king, risking her own life to intercede for her people. She chose to act despite the danger, saying, "If I perish, I perish." Her bravery united her people, bridged divisions, and saved lives. Her story demonstrates that true leadership requires sacrifice, faith, and a commitment to the greater good.

In your role, are you raising awareness about the injustices and hardships faced by your people? Are you advocating for the vulnerable, such as women and children, who face abuse and inequality?

Are you using your influence to create opportunities and bring lasting change to your society? Or are you distracted by the trappings of luxury and personal status, neglecting the sacred duty you have been entrusted with?

As the First Lady, you have a unique opportunity to be a voice for women who have been silenced, to uplift the next generation of girls, and to champion fairness and equality. Your proximity to the President gives you influence that can shape policies and priorities for the betterment of your nation. Let your actions mirror the courage and selflessness of Esther, who rose to her divine calling and changed the fate of her people.

True greatness lies not in titles or adornments but in serving others with integrity, humility, and compassion. Use your resources to empower the vulnerable, promote justice, and model a life of faith and purpose. Be a beacon of hope and a role model for the youth, showing them that leadership is about lifting others, not elevating oneself. This is your time, your moment to fulfill the divine purpose for which you have been placed in such a position. Let your legacy be one of courage, compassion, and a life lived for the good of others.

> **Esther 4:16 (KJV)** "Go, gather together all the Jews that are present in Shushan, and fast ye for me, and neither eat nor drink three days, night or day: I also and my maidens will fast likewise; and so will I go in unto the king, which is not according to the law: and if I perish, I perish."

May you, as the First Lady, draw inspiration and strength from these carefully prepared biblical teachings, presented as a story to guide you in understanding and fulfilling your role with wisdom, compassion, and courage. Let these lessons illuminate your path, empowering you to embrace your divine calling with purpose and grace.

The Compassionate Women of Influence (First Ladies): A Divine Calling of Leadership and Responsibility

In every corner of society, from the corridors of government to the boardrooms of corporations, from the pulpits of churches to the palaces of kings, there are women whose roles place them near seats of power. They are wives, partners, and confidants to leaders or CEOs, ministers of God, presidents, prime ministers, and kings. These women, admired for their grace and strength, hold positions of profound influence. Their lives are a testament to the potential of leadership rooted in compassion, faith, and responsibility.

One day, a great calamity struck a disaster that laid bare the vulnerabilities of many. It was a moment that called for decisive action, for voices to rise above the chaos and lend strength to the afflicted. Among those who held the power to make a difference was a woman of influence. She stood not just as a spouse or supporter but as a beacon of hope, her heart stirred by the suffering she saw.

She reflected on her role, understanding that her proximity to power was not incidental but purposeful. She was reminded of a queen from history, a woman placed in a position of influence during a time of great peril. This queen faced a pivotal choice: to remain silent and risk the destruction of her people or to act with courage and intercede for their lives. Her decision to step forward, despite the risks, not only saved her nation but demonstrated the profound truth that leadership is about serving others and fulfilling a divine calling.

Inspired by this example, the woman resolved to use her influence to bring relief to those in need. She understood that her position was not a privilege to be enjoyed but a responsibility to be carried. Seeking wisdom, she reflected on the actions of others who had wielded great power. She thought of those who had honored God through their decisions and those who had faltered, allowing personal desires to cloud their judgment.

She remembered the leader who lost his authority because he prioritized himself over his people. She recalled the judge who, though mighty, was undone by betrayal of his sacred vows. She reflected on the king who, despite his wisdom, allowed his kingdom to fracture because he strayed from the principles of justice and humility.

These lessons strengthened her resolve. She recognized that her role as a wife to a leader, whether in governance, business, or ministry, was a mantle of responsibility. She saw the potential to be an advocate for widows, orphans, and vulnerable women whose voices were often silenced. Her proximity to power gave her the ability to amplify their cries, shine a light on their struggles, and act as a force for justice and compassion.

Determined, she set out to make a difference. She rallied resources, called on allies, and lent her voice to the voiceless. Her actions were not driven by ambition or the allure of recognition but by a deep sense of duty to her people and to God. She understood that leadership was not about titles or appearances but about meaningful action and unwavering service.

Through her efforts, she became an example of what true leadership looks like a commitment to aligning one's actions with divine principles of love, mercy, and fairness. She brought hope to the destitute, inspired unity among the divided, and became a testament to the transformative power of faith and selflessness.

As she reflected on her journey, she hoped that when her time came to stand before the Creator and give an account of her stewardship, she would hear the words, "Well done, my faithful servant."

This story of a woman of influence is a reminder to all wives of leaders whether in government, business, or ministry that their roles are not incidental but divinely appointed. Leadership, at any level, is a sacred trust that requires courage, humility, and an unwavering commitment to the welfare of others. May all women entrusted with such roles embrace their calling with wisdom, compassion, and faith, leaving a legacy that honors God and uplifts His people.

End of story, Women of Influence. May the grace and wisdom of the Lord guide you always, and may your actions fulfill the divine purpose for which you have been placed in your position.

CHAPTER 5

THE MIGHTY EQUALIZER: A DIVINE MESSAGE FOR THE RACIST

====================

====================

*T*he physical world may divide us by appearance, but the spiritual realm exposes a far greater reality. God does not judge by race, nationality, or skin color. Humanity is separated not by earthly distinctions but by the condition of the heart and alignment with His truth. To claim superiority based on physical traits is to rebel against the Creator who formed all people with purpose. The arrogance of racism is not just an offense against fellow humans; it is an affront to God Himself. He sees beyond flesh and weighs the soul, and no veil of prejudice will shield anyone from His righteous judgment. Discrimination is not merely a moral failing, it is a spiritual corruption that invites divine wrath. Those who persist in exalting themselves over others will one day stand before the Almighty, stripped of their illusions, forced to reckon with the reality that in His eyes, the only distinction that matters is between those who walk in righteousness and those who walk in darkness. God's judgment is certain, and no earthly privilege will grant escape.

God's love is immeasurable and boundless, reaching every corner of humanity without prejudice or limitation. It is not confined by race, ethnicity, status, or background but instead embraces the entirety of the human family. This profound truth reminds us that God's love is not reserved for

a select few who deem themselves special or superior. Instead, it is a divine gift extended freely and equally to all, underscoring the universality of His grace. It is a love so deep and so vast that it encompasses every soul, offering hope and salvation to anyone who believes. Such love calls us to reflect on its inclusivity and challenges us to embody the same boundless compassion in our interactions with one another.

The Word of God stands firmly against partiality and favoritism, making it clear that to show bias or hatred toward others is a direct violation of His divine principles. How, then, will you stand before the Creator, you who harbor racism in your heart, who judge and mistreat others solely because of the color of their skin or their heritage? Such actions are not only an affront to those you demean but also to God Himself, who created every person with intention and dignity.

Discrimination based on race is a grievous sin, for it denies the fundamental truth that we are all crafted in the image of God. Each person, regardless of their background or appearance, bears the imprint of His likeness, a testament to their worth and equality in His eyes. To deny this truth through acts of hatred or exclusion is to reject the very essence of God's creation.

The impartiality of God should be a guiding light for us all, calling us to love without condition and to see His reflection in every face we encounter. Racism not only divides humanity but stands in direct opposition to the command to love one another as God loves us. Such behavior invites judgment, for it contradicts the divine purpose of unity and equality. May we, therefore, examine our hearts, repent of any bias, and strive to live in harmony, celebrating the beauty of God's diverse creation.

> **John 3:16 (KJV)** "For God so loved the world, that he gave his only begotten Son, that whosoever believeth in him should not perish, but have everlasting life."
>
> **James 2:9 (KJV)** "But if ye have respect to persons, ye commit sin, and are convinced of the law as transgressors."
>
> **Genesis 1:27 (KJV)** "So God created man in his own image, in the image of God created he him; male and female created he them."

The command to love one's neighbor is a cornerstone of faith, a divine call that transcends all boundaries of race, ethnicity, or likeness. This love is not limited to those who share our culture, appearance, or beliefs but extends even to those we might consider our enemies. The parable of the Good Samaritan profoundly teaches this truth, reminding us that genuine love is active, sacrificial, and indiscriminate. It challenges us to break down the barriers that society or prejudice might erect and see every person as worthy of care and compassion.

The call to reconciliation is a thread woven throughout Scripture, urging us to live in peace, unity, and harmony with one another. Racism, by its nature, stands in stark opposition to this

divine purpose. It fosters division, animosity, and mistrust, tearing apart the fabric of healthy human relationships and denying the inherent dignity God bestows on all His children. If you, as a professed follower of Christ, engage in or tolerate such sin, what will the Lord God say to you? Will He see in your heart the reflection of Christ's love, or the influence of the deceiver, the father of lies, who delights in hatred and division?

Christ came to break down the walls of hostility that divide humanity, calling us to a life of love, peace, and service. To harbor prejudice or discrimination is to reject the work He accomplished and to walk not in His light but in the darkness of falsehood. True worship and devotion to God require that we overcome these sinful attitudes. How can we claim to love God, whom we have not seen, if we hate our brothers and sisters, whom we see daily? Such hypocrisy is a betrayal of the faith we profess.

Racism is not an innate trait but a learned behavior that is a result of upbringing, societal influences, and false ideologies. Yet, as children of God, we are called to renew our minds and reject such teachings. It is our reasonable service to God to dismantle prejudice, overcome hatred, and embrace every person as a neighbor, as Christ commands. Only in this way can we truly honor Him and live in accordance with the principles of His kingdom. Let us examine our hearts, seek forgiveness where we have failed, and commit to walking in love, the ultimate expression of faith.

> **Luke 10:25 (KJV)** "And, behold, a certain lawyer stood up, and tempted him, saying, Master, what shall I do to inherit eternal life?"

> **Luke 10:26 (KJV)** "He said unto him, what is written in the law? how readest thou?"

> **Luke 10:27 (KJV)** "And he answering said, Thou shalt love the Lord thy God with all thy heart, and with all thy soul, and with all thy strength, and with all thy mind; and thy neighbour as thyself."

> **Luke 10:28 (KJV)** "And he said unto him, Thou hast answered right: this do, and thou shalt live."

> **Luke 10:29 (KJV)** But he, willing to justify himself, said unto Jesus, And who is my neighbour?

> **Luke 10:30 (KJV)** And Jesus answering said, A certain man went down from Jerusalem to Jericho, and fell among thieves, which stripped him of his raiment, and wounded him, and departed, leaving him half dead.

> **Luke 10:31 (KJV)** "And by chance there came down a certain priest that way: and when he saw him, he passed by on the other side."

> **Luke 10:32 (KJV)** "And likewise a Levite, when he was at the place, came and looked on him, and passed by on the other side."

Luke 10:33 (KJV) "But a certain Samaritan, as he journeyed, came where he was: and when he saw him, he had compassion on him,"

Luke 10:34 (KJV) "And went to him, and bound up his wounds, pouring in oil and wine, and set him on his own beast, and brought him to an inn, and took care of him."

Luke 10:35 (KJV) "And on the morrow when he departed, he took out two pence, and gave them to the host, and said unto him, Take care of him; and whatsoever thou spendest more, when I come again, I will repay thee."

Luke 10:36 (KJV) "Which now of these three, thinkest thou, was neighbour unto him that fell among the thieves?"

Luke 10:37 (KJV) "And he said, He that shewed mercy on him. Then said Jesus unto him, Go, and do thou likewise."

Ephesians 2:14 (KJV) "For he is our peace, who hath made both one, and hath broken down the middle wall of partition between us;"

1 John 4:20 (KJV) "If a man say, I love God, and hateth his brother, he is a liar: for he that loveth not his brother whom he hath seen, how can he love God whom he hath not seen?"

Racism, in its many forms, often stems from deeply rooted insecurities, jealousy, and envy, manifesting as a destructive force against others' achievements, possessions, and knowledge. In a world marked by disparities, it is not uncommon for some to feel entitled, perceiving themselves as more deserving than others. This entitlement, coupled with hubris and conceit, fuels the toxic belief in superiority based on race, ethnicity, culture, or nationality. Such attitudes perpetuate the mistreatment and marginalization of those deemed "less deserving," creating a cycle of contempt and animosity.

Discrimination often manifests in tangible barriers, especially for racial minority groups. These barriers, whether in employment, education, housing, or career advancement, are deliberately crafted to maintain systems of inequality. The result is a persistent cycle of poverty and limited opportunities for those unfairly marginalized. Racism in these forms is not only a denial of justice but a refusal to recognize the inherent dignity and worth of all peopl, as established by their Creator.

At its core, this issue is often rooted in fear and misunderstanding. What people do not comprehend, they often fear, and what they fear, they may seek to destroy. This fear of diversity, fueled by ignorance, blinds individuals to the beauty and richness of humanity's collective differences. Instead of appreciating diversity as a reflection of God's boundless creativity, some view it as a threat to their comfort, identity, or perceived status. The beauty of creation lies in its diversity, where each part enhances and complements the other. One color standing alone cannot fully display the

brilliance and depth of beauty; it is only when colors blend and contrast that their true magnificence is revealed. In the same way, humanity, with its vast array of colors, cultures, and characteristics, reflects the intentional design of the Creator.

A friend recently sent me a YouTube video with the disturbing caption: **"No Black People Allowed in South Africa's White-Only Land."** The video showcases the Afrikaners of Orania, a self-segregated community of Dutch descendants who arrived at the Cape of Good Hope in 1652. Shockingly, Section 235 of South Africa's constitution permits this form of self-determination, allowing racial exclusivity to persist under the guise of cultural preservation.

This is not just a relic of history; it is a chilling reminder of how deeply ingrained human laws can be in sustaining division and discrimination. But what does God say? **Racism is not just a social injustice, it is a sin.** The very notion of excluding an entire group of people based on race is an affront to the Creator, who made all humans in His image. The Bible is clear: **"There is neither Jew nor Gentile, neither slave nor free, nor is there male and female, for you are all one in Christ Jesus"**. Any system or ideology that seeks to elevate one race over another defies God's design for unity and love among His creation.

Man's rule may justify exclusion, but God's justice will not allow it to stand. History has shown that such walls of separation always crumble under the weight of truth and righteousness. Apartheid fell. Segregation fell. And in time, any human institution built on racial superiority will fall because **God is not mocked.** Let this be a sobering call: we must reject racism not just as a moral failing, but as an outright rebellion against God's divine order.

> **Genesis 1:27(KJV***)* "So God created man in his own image, in the image of God created he him; male and female created he them."
>
> **Galatians 3:28 (KJV***)* "There is neither Jew nor Greek, there is neither bond nor free, there is neither male nor female: for ye are all one in Christ *Jesus."*
>
> **Galatians 6:7 (KJV)** "Be not deceived; God is not mocked: for whatsoever a man soweth, that shall he also reap."

We are one unit, crafted in unique forms, each carrying distinct gifts and attributes. Just as a masterpiece is painted with many hues and textures, so too is humanity a collective work of art, where differences are not flaws but essential elements of the whole. Our variety is not meant to divide but to enrich, as each person brings something irreplaceable to the tapestry of life.

This diversity is evidence of the Creator's boundless creativity and wisdom. It reminds us that no single group or individual can fully encompass the image of God on their own. Together, in our unique forms, we reflect His glory more completely. It is through our unity in diversity that we can truly thrive, supporting, learning from, and celebrating one another as part of one grand design.

Such attitudes are a profound failure to recognize that diversity is not a flaw but a testament to the brilliance of God's design. Humanity's varied cultures, colors, and perspectives are meant to complement and enrich one another, not divide and diminish. By rejecting this truth, we fail to grasp the fullness of what it means to be made in God's image, a tapestry of unity in diversity.

To combat this, we must confront the root causes of racism, pride, envy, and fear. Only by fostering understanding and empathy can we dismantle the systems and mindsets that perpetuate such evil. This requires humility, a willingness to learn from and about others, and a commitment to justice and love in all interactions. The path to healing and unity begins with recognizing that no one is entitled to more dignity or worth than another, for we are all equal in the eyes of our Creator. Only then can we move toward a world that reflects the harmony and equity of God's kingdom.

> **Leviticus 19:18 (KJV)** "Thou shalt not avenge, nor bear any grudge against the children of thy people, but thou shalt love thy neighbour as thyself: I am the LORD"

> **Hebrews 13:2 (KJV)** "Be not forgetful to entertain strangers: for thereby some have entertained angels unawares."

> **Ephesians 2:19 (KJV)** "Now therefore ye are no more strangers and foreigners, but fellowcitizens with the saints, and of the household of God;"

Scripture warns us of the father of lies, Satan, whose ultimate aim is to sow division and disrupt the unity of God's children. Racism is one of the tools he wields to plant seeds of discord, animosity, and violence among humanity, creating barriers where God intended fellowship and love. Through the poison of prejudice, Satan seeks not only to divide but to obscure the truth of God's grace and hinder individuals from fully embracing His transformative love.

Racism serves as a snare, pulling hearts away from the core teachings of faith, love, unity, and justice and replacing them with hatred, arrogance, and enmity. This destructive mindset contradicts the purpose for which we were created: to live in harmony as reflections of God's image. As we seek to confirm our understanding and confront this evil, let us turn to the truth of Scripture, which provides the foundation for our doctrine and calls us to reject the lies of the enemy.

> **John 8:44 (KJV)** "Ye are of your father the devil, and the lusts of your father ye will do. He was a murderer from the beginning, and abode not in the truth, because there is no truth in him. When he speaketh a lie, he speaketh of his own: for he is a liar, and the father of it."

> **Ephesians 2:14 (KJV)** "For he is our peace, who hath made both one, and hath broken down the middle wall of partition between us;"

Ephesians 2:15 (KJV) "Having abolished in his flesh the enmity, even the law of commandments contained in ordinances; for to make in himself of twain one new man, so making peace;"

Ephesians 2:16 (KJV) "And that he might reconcile both unto God in one body by the cross, having slain the enmity thereby:"

Racism, with its roots in prejudice and pride, often leads to oppression and injustice, leaving marginalized and vulnerable individuals to bear the weight of unfair treatment. The exploitation, abuse, and violence that stem from such attitudes are grievous violations of the dignity and worth of every human being, particularly targeting those who are perceived as inferior by the dominant group. Black people, along with other marginalized communities, have often faced systemic injustice and dehumanization as a result of this evil.

These outcomes stand in stark contrast to the biblical mandate for justice, mercy, and humility. God calls His people to defend the oppressed, uphold the rights of the vulnerable, and walk humbly in righteousness. True worship of God is inseparable from active care for those who are marginalized. To ignore their plight or, worse, to perpetuate their sufferin, is to turn away from God's heart and will.

Scripture teaches that God is the defender of the weak and the protector of the marginalized. He lifts up those who are bowed down and thwarts the plans of those who perpetuate injustice. Racism, by its nature, opposes this divine mission, seeking to tear down rather than build up, to exclude rather than embrace. It is a sin that not only wounds its victims but also grieves the heart of God, for it denies His call to love, justice, and equity.

Psalms 146:7 (KJV) "Which executeth judgment for the oppressed: which giveth food to the hungry. The LORD looseth the prisoners:"

Psalms 146:8 (KJV) "The LORD openeth the eyes of the blind: the LORD raiseth them that are bowed down: the LORD loveth the righteous:"

Psalms 146:9 (KJV) "The LORD preserveth the strangers; he relieveth the fatherless and widow: but the way of the wicked he turneth upside down."

Micah 6:8 (KJV) "He hath shewed thee, O man, what is good; and what doth the LORD require of thee, but to do justly, and to love mercy, and to walk humbly with thy God?"

James 1:27 (KJV) "Pure religion and undefiled before God and the Father is this, To visit the fatherless and widows in their affliction, and to keep himself unspotted from the world."

In the eyes of God, all people are created equal, regardless of their ethnicity, social status, or cultural background. Scripture consistently calls us to uphold justice, love, and respect for one another, reminding us that every human being is precious in the sight of the Creator. Discrimination, favoritism, nepotism, and prejudice are not just social ills; they are sins, direct violations of God's command to love one another as He loves us.

God's Word emphasizes the shared humanity of all people, revealing that we are all part of the same divine family, bound together by the love and grace of our Maker. Our differences, be it racial, economic, or cultural, are not meant to divide us but to enrich the tapestry of God's creation. Yet racism, driven by pride and the lies of the enemy, works to sow division, foster animosity, and fracture the unity we are called to cultivate.

Racism not only dehumanizes its victims but also blinds its perpetrators to the image of God reflected in every individual. It leads to the exclusion and marginalization of others, forming barriers that isolate communities and deepen mistrust. Such behavior is a direct affront to the teachings of Christ, who calls us to care for the least among us, to welcome the stranger, and to love our neighbors without reservation. By fostering division, racism contradicts the very essence of Christ's mission to bring reconciliation and unity to humanity.

The call to compassion and care for the marginalized and disadvantaged is woven throughout Scripture. True faith is shown not in words alone but in deeds of kindness, justice, and humility toward all people, especially those who are often overlooked or mistreated. When we discriminate or fail to stand against the injustice of racism, we not only harm others but also betray the God who commands us to love without favoritism or partiality.

Let us reflect on the profound truth that in Christ, there is no division, no separation based on race, class, or status. We are all one, heirs of His promis, and members of His family. To live in this truth is to reject the lies of Satan, who seeks to divide and destroy, and to embrace the call to unity, equality, and love. May we, as followers of Christ, commit to breaking down the walls of prejudice and building bridges of understanding, ensuring that our lives reflect the inclusive and transformative love of our Savior.

> **Galatians 3:28 (KJV)** "There is neither Jew nor Greek, there is neither bond nor free, there is neither male nor female: for ye are all one in Christ Jesus."

> **James 2:9 (KJV)** "But if ye have respect to persons, ye commit sin, and are convinced of the law as transgressors."

> **Proverbs 22:2 (KJV)** "The rich and poor meet together: the LORD is the maker of them all."

Matthew 25:40 (KJV) "And the King shall answer and say unto them, Verily I say unto you, Inasmuch as ye have done it unto one of the least of these my brethren, ye have done it unto me."

As we conclude this reflection on unity in diversity and God's clear teachings against racism, may our hearts be deeply moved by the truth of His Word. Let us strive to see one another as God sees us not through the flawed lenses of prejudice or division, but with the eyes of love, compassion, and equality. The richness of our diversity is a testament to the boundless creativity of our Creator, and our unity reflects His divine purpose for humanity.

Racism and division are not of God but of the adversary, whose aim is to destroy the harmony we are called to embody as His children. To walk in faith means to reject these lies and to embrace the transformative power of love, justice, and humility in our lives. Each of us has a role to play in breaking down barriers, fostering understanding, and promoting the unity that God desires for His people.

May the Lord give you the understanding and wisdom to internalize these truths so that you might live as a beacon of His love in a world so often divided. May He open your eyes to the beauty of His creation in every person and equip you to stand against injustice in all its forms. As you go forth, may your life be a testimony to the power of God's grace and a reflection of His unifying love for all humankind.

CHAPTER 6

THE MIGHTY EQUALIZER: A DIVINE MESSAGE FOR THE PROMOTER OF WAR (WAR MONGER)?

=====================

=====================

Be Instrument Of Peace Instead Of War

What will the Lord God say to you, who incites conflicts and stokes the flames of war for selfish gain, using instability as an opportunity to exploit and plunder? You, who supply weapons and resources to chosen sides, fueling violence and destruction, are complicit in the loss of countless innocent lives. The cries of the oppressed, the widows, and the orphans echo before the throne of God, bearing witness to your actions. How will you answer for the rivers of suffering you have unleashed, for the desolation wrought upon communities, for the lives shattered by your greed?

War and genocide are among humanity's darkest sins, leaving in their wake unfathomable suffering, despair, and loss. Because of your pursuit of wealth and power, you have turned a blind eye to the plight of the innocent, those who have no refuge, no escape from the horrors of war. The physical and mental scars left upon survivors and the ruins of broken communities cry out against

you. The Lord, who is just and righteous, does not overlook such iniquity, and He will by no means clear the guilty.

God calls His children to be instruments of peace, not architects of destruction. To seek peace is to align with His divine will, to hunger and thirst for righteousness, and to turn away from vengeance and violence. Yet you, in defiance of this call, have chosen to perpetuate discord for personal gain. You have failed to heed the wisdom of seeking reconciliation, instead sowing seeds of hatred and division. The bloodshed you enable is not only an offense to humanity but a direct affront to the Creator, who desires that swords be turned into plowshares and nations learn war no more.

The Lord sees not only the devastation you cause but also the intentions of your heart. He calls you to repentance, to lay down your pursuit of destruction, and embrace the ways of peace. The path of war leads only to judgment, for the Almighty God is a defender of the oppressed and an avenger of the innocent. Be warned, for the riches you gain through bloodshed will testify against you on the day of reckoning.

Instead, choose the path of peace, humility, and righteousness. Seek to heal the wounds of conflict rather than deepen them, to build bridges where there is division, and to promote harmony instead of hatred. May the Lord give you the strength to turn from wickedness and the wisdom to become an instrument of His peace, bringing healing and hope to a world so deeply in need of it.

> **Matthew 5:9 (KJV)** "Blessed are the peacemakers: for they shall be called the children of God."
>
> **Proverbs 20:22 (KJV)** "Say not thou, I will recompense evil; but wait on the LORD, and he shall save thee."
>
> **Romans 12:18 (KJV)** "If it be possible, as much as lieth in you, live peaceably with all men."
>
> **Isaiah 2:4 (KJV)** "And he shall judge among the nations, and shall rebuke many people: and they shall beat their swords into plowshares, and their spears into pruninghooks: nation shall not lift up sword against nation, neither shall they learn war any more."
>
> **Psalms 34:14 (KJV)** "Depart from evil, and do good; seek peace, and pursue it."

The Lord God, in His righteousness, will surely hold accountable those who bring devastation and suffering out of greed for money and wealth. The teachings of our Lord Jesus Christ emphasize love, peace, and reconciliation as foundational values for His followers. To love one another as Christ has loved us is not merely a suggestion but a divine command, a call to mirror His boundless love in our interactions with all people. Yet, to incite violence, profit from harm, or fuel conflict is a betrayal of this sacred commandment and a rejection of the path of peace.

Those who cause destruction to amass wealth should reflect deeply on the ultimate cost of their actions. What good is it to gain the treasures of the world if, in doing so, one forfeits their soul? The pursuit of ill-gotten gain comes at a cost far greater than gold or silver, for it estranges the heart from God and invites His judgment. The loss of innocent lives, the suffering of the vulnerable, and the breakdown of communities stand as testimonies against those who choose greed over compassion, power over justice.

The Lord calls His people to pursue peace with all, to live holy lives, and to seek reconciliation where there is strife. To be a peacemaker is to align with His will, while to perpetuate conflict is to oppose His purpose. The actions of those who supply arms for war and destruction are inconsistent with the principles of love and justice that God requires of His children. Such choices not only harm others but also corrode the soul of the perpetrator, leaving them estranged from the God of peace.

God's Word reminds us of the ethical and moral responsibilities we bear. He calls us to act justly, love mercy, and walk humbly with Him. This means making decisions that promote the well-being of others, seeking solutions that heal rather than harm, and working tirelessly toward peace and reconciliation. Those who profit from war and suffering abandon these principles, prioritizing greed over goodness, and sowing seeds of despair where there could be hope.

The consequences of such actions reach beyond human accountability, for God sees and judges all. The reward for those who choose violence and destruction is not wealth or glory but the burden of guilt and the reality of divine judgment. Yet even for those who have strayed, God extends the invitation to repentance, offering the opportunity to turn away from evil and embrace the path of righteousness.

Let us, therefore, commit to embodying the teachings of Christ, working for peace and justice, and standing as instruments of healing in a broken world. May the Lord grant us wisdom and courage to walk in His ways, pursuing what is good, true, and life-givin, for the sake of our souls and the glory of His name.

War is a destructive and tragic event that often brings about severe consequences for individuals, communities, and nations. The Bible contains several admonitions and insights regarding the deadly consequences of war.

War brings unimaginable loss, claiming the lives of soldiers, civilians, and countless innocent children caught in its merciless grip. It leaves behind devastation, broken families, and shattered futures, all while contradicting the sanctity of life that Scripture so profoundly upholds. The Bible calls us to honor and protect life, to love one another, and to turn away from violence, but how easily do some ignore this command when the horrors of war unfold.

To those who loudly champion the sanctity of life, advocating tirelessly for the unborn, consider this: how can you claim to defend innocent lives in the womb while turning a blind eye to the

slaughter of innocent lives on the battlefield? How can you proclaim love for unborn children while remaining silent or, worse, complicit when children outside the womb are maimed, displaced, or killed in wars you help fuel? Your words ring hollow when they are not matched by actions to protect all life, born and unborn alike.

The sanctity of life is not a selective principle; it does not end at birth. It demands consistency and a commitment to value every human being, regardless of age, nationality, or circumstance. The same God who knits life together in the womb also mourns the lives lost to war, the tears of grieving parents, and the cries of children caught in conflict. To claim to love life while enabling its destruction is hypocrisy of the highest order.

If you truly believe in the sanctity of life, then let your actions reflect it in every sphere. Raise your voice against the engines of war. Use your influence to advocate for peace. Stand in defense of the vulnerable, whether they are in the womb, in refugee camps, or in communities ravaged by violence. Anything less is a betrayal of the very principle you claim to uphold.

The call to protect life is not partial. It is universal. Let us examine our hearts and actions to ensure they align with the faith we profess, honoring the sanctity of all life as God intended.

> **Exodus 20:13 (KJV)** "Thou shalt not kill."

> **Matthew 5:21 (KJV)** "Ye have heard that it was said by them of old time, Thou shalt not kill; and whosoever shall kill shall be in danger of the judgment:"

> **Matthew 5:22 (KJV)** "But I say unto you, That whosoever is angry with his brother without a cause shall be in danger of the judgment: and whosoever shall say to his brother, Raca, shall be in danger of the council: but whosoever shall say, Thou fool, shall be in danger of hell fire."

Wars bring untold devastation, reducing thriving cities to rubble, turning homes into ashes, and dismantling the infrastructure that sustains human life and dignity. The toll is not merely physical but deeply personal and emotional, leaving communities fractured and countless lives irreparably harmed. War tears apart the very fabric of society, leaving behind a legacy of suffering, loss, and despair that can take generations to heal.

Yet the Word of God speaks of a better way, calling His people to be builders of peace and architects of justice. Scripture envisions a world where swords are transformed into plowshare, and instruments of war are refashioned into tools for growth and prosperity. This divine vision urges us to reject violence and instead seek solutions that foster reconciliation, justice, and the flourishing of all.

> **Psalms 122:7 (KJV)** "Peace be within thy walls, and prosperity within thy palaces."

> **Isaiah 2:4 (KJV)** "And he shall judge among the nations, and shall rebuke many people: and they shall beat their swords into plowshares, and their spears into pruninghooks: nation shall not lift up sword against nation, neither shall they learn war any more."

War inflicts profound pain, both visible and invisible, leaving individuals with wounds that linger far beyond the battlefield. The physical scars of violence tell one story, but the emotional and psychological trauma carries an even deeper weight. Families torn apart, homes lost, and communities shattered create a grief so vast that it feels insurmountable. Those who survive are left to bear the burden of loss, fear, and despair, struggling to rebuild their lives amid the rubble of conflict.

Yet, in the midst of such brokenness, the Word of God speaks hope. Scripture reveals a God who binds up the wounds of the brokenhearted and heals the deepest pains of the afflicted. His promise is one of restoration, to bring beauty from ashes and joy where there was mourning. For those weighed down by the heavy burden of trauma, God extends comfort, renewing the spirit of those crushed by the sorrows of war.

The call to healing and restoration is not merely spiritual. It is also a practical mandate for God's people. To walk in obedience is to be His hands and feet, offering care and support to those who suffer. Whether through acts of kindness, words of encouragement, or the work of rebuilding broken communities, believers are called to be instruments of God's healing in a wounded world. This work reflects His boundless compassion, a light in the darkness for those who feel forgotten and abandoned.

The scars of war may last a lifetime, but God's power to heal surpasses all human understanding. His restoration is holistic, reaching into the depths of the heart to replace despair with hope, grief with gladness, and ashes with a crown of beauty. To align with His will is to stand with the afflicted, to advocate for peace, and to work toward the rebuilding of lives and societies torn apart by conflict.

Let us remember that no wound is too deep for God to heal and no heart too shattered for Him to restore. May we dedicate ourselves to the ministry of healing, carrying the message of comfort and hope to those who need it most. In doing so, we not only fulfill God's call but also become living testimonies of His love and power to redeem even the most broken of circumstances.

> **Psalms 147:3 (KJV)** "He healeth the broken in heart, and bindeth up their wounds."

> **Isaiah 61:1 (KJV)** "The Spirit of the Lord GOD is upon me; because the LORD hath anointed me to preach good tidings unto the meek; he hath sent me to bind up the brokenhearted, to proclaim liberty to the captives, and the opening of the prison to them that are bound;"

Isaiah 61:2 (KJV) "To proclaim the acceptable year of the LORD, and the day of vengeance of our God; to comfort all that mourn;"

Isaiah 61:3 (KJV) To appoint unto them that mourn in Zion, to give unto them beauty for ashes, the oil of joy for mourning, the garment of praise for the spirit of heaviness; that they might be called trees of righteousness, the planting of the LORD, that he might be glorified.

Wars uproot millions from their homes, forcing them to flee from everything familiar into the uncertainty of displacement. Families are torn apart, livelihoods are lost, and countless individuals are left to wander as refugees, often enduring harsh and inhumane conditions. These men, women, and children stripped of stability, safety, and dignity become some of the most vulnerable among us, crying out for compassion, justice, and care. Their plight is a stark reminder of the profound impact of human conflict and the urgent need for empathy and action.

Scripture speaks to the responsibility of God's people to care for the vulnerable, extending a hand of compassion to those who have been cast out and marginalized. Refugees are not merely statistics; they are individuals created in God's image, carrying their own stories, pain, and hopes. The Bible calls us to open our hearts and hands to them, offering shelter, sustenance, and care as a reflection of God's own love and provision.

To welcome and care for those displaced by war is to live out the essence of faith. It is to provide food for the hungry, drink for the thirsty, and shelter for the stranger. It is to clothe the naked, comfort the suffering, and restore dignity to those who have lost everything. Such actions are not merely acts of charity but profound expressions of obedience to God's call to love our neighbors as ourselves.

The scars of displacement run deep, both physically and emotionally. Refugees often carry not only the trauma of war but also the stigma of being seen as outsiders, unwanted in the places they seek refuge. Yet, the Bible reminds us that God's compassion knows no boundaries, and His call to care for the stranger is a sacred charge. To turn away from the suffering of refugees is to turn away from God Himself, for in serving them, we serve Him.

As we consider the plight of those displaced by war, let us be moved to act not with indifference or pit, but with love and urgency. May we provide not only for their immediate needs but also work toward long-term solutions that restore hope, stability, and dignity. In doing so, we fulfill the biblical mandate to care for the least among us, demonstrating the transformative power of God's love in a world desperate for compassion. Let us rise to this challenge, reflecting God's heart for the vulnerable and becoming instruments of His grace and mercy in their lives.

Leviticus 19:33 (KJV) "And if a stranger sojourn with thee in your land, ye shall not vex him."

Leviticus 19:34 (KJV) "But the stranger that dwelleth with you shall be unto you as one born among you, and thou shalt love him as thyself; for ye were strangers in the land of Egypt: I am the LORD your God."

Matthew 25:35 (KJV) "For I was an hungred, and ye gave me meat: I was thirsty, and ye gave me drink: I was a stranger, and ye took me in:"

Matthew 25:36 (KJV) "Naked, and ye clothed me: I was sick, and ye visited me: I was in prison, and ye came unto me."

War wreaks havoc not only on lives and infrastructure but also on economies, plunging entire regions into poverty and creating cycles of hardship that can persist for generations. The devastation of conflict leads to resource scarcity, economic inequality, and widespread suffering among the most vulnerable. While those caught in the crossfire struggle to survive, there exists a shadowy mechanism, the so-called defense industrial complex, that profits immensely from war's destruction. These entities fuel conflicts, not to defend or protec, but to perpetuate instability for financial gain, ensuring that war remains a lucrative industry.

Even more appalling is the hypocrisy that follows. Those who sit silently, or worse, actively benefit from war's devastation, often rebrand themselves as heroes through well-publicized humanitarian efforts. They appear as saviors, making grand gestures of charity and donations to rebuild the very communities their actions have destroyed. Through their cohorts and media narratives, they paint themselves as compassionate benefactors, conveniently diverting attention from their complicity in perpetuating the suffering they claim to alleviate.

Scripture, however, calls us to a higher standard. It reminds us that true justice and righteousness are not found in hollow gestures or surface-level acts of charity but in genuine actions that address the root causes of suffering. To give while ignoring the harm one has caused is to mock the very principles of compassion and justice. Faith without action rooted in justice and love is dead, and no amount of publicized philanthropy can cleanse the guilt of those who profit from the suffering of others.

The Bible speaks of a fast that God desires, not one of empty rituals, but of breaking the chains of oppression, sharing bread with the hungry, and providing shelter to the homeless. It calls for acts of genuine love and economic justice, where resources are shared, burdens are lifted, and communities are restored. For those who contribute to war's devastation, there is no absolution in token gestures. True repentance requires turning away from greed and actively working to rebuild what has been torn down, not for public accolades but for the sake of righteousness.

The suffering caused by war is not an abstract issue; it is a lived reality for millions. The impoverished, displaced, and marginalized bear the brunt of decisions made by those who prioritize profit over people. Economic justice demands that we not only help the poor but also dismantle the systems that create and perpetuate poverty in the first place.

Let us, therefore, reject the hypocrisy of profiting from destruction while posing as benefactors. Instead, let us strive for a world where resources are used to build, not destroy; to sustain, not exploit; to heal, not harm. In this way, we align ourselves with God's call to justice and mercy, becoming true instruments of His peace and provision in a world so desperately in need.

> **Isaiah 58:6 (KJV)** "Is not this the fast that I have chosen? to loose the bands of wickedness, to undo the heavy burdens, and to let the oppressed go free, and that ye break every yoke?"

> **Isaiah 58:7 (KJV)** "Is it not to deal thy bread to the hungry, and that thou bring the poor that are cast out to thy house? when thou seest the naked, that thou cover him; and that thou hide not thyself from thine own flesh?"

> **James 2:14 (KJV)** "What doth it profit, my brethren, though a man say he hath faith, and have not works? can faith save him?"

> **James 2:15 (KJV)** "If a brother or sister be naked, and destitute of daily food,"

> **James 2:16 (KJV)** "And one of you say unto them, Depart in peace, be ye warmed and filled; notwithstanding ye give them not those things which are needful to the body; what doth it profit?"

> **James 2:17 (KJV)** "Even so faith, if it hath not works, is dead, being alone."

War has a devastating power to foster hatred, deepen divisions, and create enmity between groups, often leaving wounds that fester for generations. It plants seeds of bitterness and distrust, turning neighbors into enemies and strangers into threats. The cycle of violence and retaliation becomes a trap, ensnaring humanity in an endless spiral of suffering and division. Amid this darkness, the Word of God shines brightly, calling us to a higher way, a way of love, forgiveness, and reconciliation that breaks the chains of hatred.

To love not only those who love us but even those who oppose us is one of the most radical and transformative teachings of Scripture. It is easy to be consumed by anger and resentment in the face of conflict, to justify vengeance in the name of justice. Yet, God calls His children to choose a different path, to strive for peace even in the most hostile circumstances. This is not a passive love but an active one, a deliberate decision to extend grace where it is undeserved, to seek understanding where there is division, and to build bridges where walls have been erected.

Forgiveness is not a denial of wrongdoing or dismissal of justice; it is the opening of a door to healing and restoration. When we refuse to forgive, we allow the poison of hatred to take root in our hearts, corroding our spirit and perpetuating the cycle of violence. True reconciliation requires courage, a willingness to confront pain, address injustice, and commit to a future where unity replaces division.

The Bible reminds us that peace is not merely the absence of war but the presence of harmony, justice, and love. To live at peace with others requires effort and sacrifice, a deliberate choice to prioritize relationship over retaliation, and healing over harm. This peace is not the result of human effort alone but reflects God's work in our hearts, transforming us into agents of His reconciliation.

War seeks to dehumanize, to turn "them" into "the other," but love reminds us that every person bears the image of God and is worthy of dignity and compassion. In choosing to love and forgive, we reject the narrative of enmity and affirm the sacredness of every life. In striving for reconciliation, we align ourselves with the heart of God, who desires unity and peace among His children.

Let us, therefore, be bold in rejecting the hatred that war fosters. May we be peacemakers in a world torn by conflict, ambassadors of God's love, and voices of reconciliation where there is division. In doing so, we reflect the character of our Creator and offer a glimpse of His kingdom, a kingdom where swords are beaten into plowshares and love triumphs over hatred.

> **Matthew 5:43 (KJV)** "Ye have heard that it hath been said, Thou shalt love thy neighbour, and hate thine enemy."

> **Matthew 5:44 (KJV)** "But I say unto you, Love your enemies, bless them that curse you, do good to them that hate you, and pray for them which despitefully use you, and persecute you;"

> **Romans 12:18 (KJV)** "If it be possible, as much as lieth in you, live peaceably with all men."

War often thrusts individuals into situations fraught with moral and ethical dilemmas, forcing choices that weigh heavily on the conscience. In the chaos of conflict, the lines between right and wrong can blur, and the pursuit of power or survival may overshadow the principles of justice, mercy, and truth. Yet, the Word of God calls us to a standard of righteousness that transcends the complexities of human conflict, offering ethical guidance even in the darkest of times.

Those who profit from or perpetuate war while cloaking their actions in righteousness must confront the stark warning of Scripture. It is not enough to appear virtuous outwardly while engaging in actions that exploit the vulnerable and perpetuate injustice. The hypocrisy of justifying violence and oppression under the guise of morality is a grave sin, for it deceives not only others but also the self, leading further away from the truth.

War is often accompanied by decisions that impact countless lives—decisions about who will suffer, who will benefit, and who will bear the cost. The Bible reminds us that every action, no matter how seemingly justifiable, must be weighed against the divine call to righteousness. Are we seeking personal gain or power at the expense of others? Are we exploiting the vulnerable or turning a blind eye to their plight? Such questions are not merely theoretical but are central to living a life that honors God.

Ethical guidance from Scripture urges us to examine our hearts and motives, ensuring that our actions align with God's principles. The pursuit of righteousness requires humility, self-reflection, and a willingness to prioritize the well-being of others over personal ambition. It demands that we reject deceit, manipulation, and exploitation, even when they are tempting or expedient. True righteousness is not about appearances but about living in a way that reflects God's justice and mercy.

The moral dilemmas of war are not limited to those on the battlefield. Leaders, decision-makers, and even bystanders are implicated in the choices made during conflict. To ignore the suffering caused by war, to profit from its devastation, or to remain silent in the face of injustice is to fail in the responsibility that God has placed upon us. The call to righteousness is universal, encompassing every role and every decision, no matter how great or small.

Let us, therefore, heed the ethical guidance of Scripture, striving for righteousness in all our actions. May we reject hypocrisy and embrace integrity, ensuring that our choices reflect the love, justice, and truth of God. In doing so, we become not only agents of His will but also witnesses to the transformative power of His Word, even in a world scarred by conflict.

> **Matthew 23:14 (KJV)** "Woe unto you, scribes and Pharisees, hypocrites! for ye devour widows' houses, and for a pretence make long prayer: therefore ye shall receive the greater damnation."

> **Matthew 23:15 (KJV)** "Woe unto you, scribes and Pharisees, hypocrites! for ye compass sea and land to make one proselyte, and when he is made, ye make him twofold more the child of hell than yourselves."

> **Matthew 23:16 (KJV)** "Woe unto you, ye blind guides, which say, Whosoever shall swear by the temple, it is nothing; but whosoever shall swear by the gold of the temple, he is a debtor!"

> **Matthew 23:17 (KJV)** Ye fools and blind: for whether is greater, the gold, or the temple that sanctifieth the gold?

The devastating consequences of war are not confined to the present. They ripple forward, impacting future generations in ways that perpetuate cycles of violence, trauma, and instability. Childre, born into the shadow of conflict, inherit a world scarred by hatred and division. They are shaped by what they witness: the destruction of homes, the loss of loved ones, and the bitterness of unresolved enmity. Such a legacy, if left unchecked, fosters a grim cycle where violence becomes a learned response, and peace seems an unreachable ideal.

Yet Scripture calls us to a higher purpose, to be mindful stewards of the next generation, to teach them the ways of peace, justice, and hope. It emphasizes the importance of instilling values that reflect God's righteousness, ensuring that children are raised with a vision of unity and compassion rather than division and despair. The choices we make today will echo into tomorrow, shaping the kind of world we leave for those who come after us.

To break the cycle of violence, we must begin with what we pass on. Will we hand down stories of vengeance, bitterness, and strife, or will we teach the lessons of reconciliation, forgiveness, and love? The responsibility to train up children in the path of righteousness is not merely a parental duty, it is a collective calling. As communities, nations, and a global family, we are charged with creating an environment where future generations can thrive, free from the burden of inherited conflict.

The Bible reminds us that hope for the future lies in a commitment to justice and peace today. By prioritizing these principles, we lay a foundation for a world where children do not have to bear the weight of war but can instead grow in safety, harmony, and purpose. This requires courage and intentionality, a willingness to confront the root causes of violence, to reject hatred, and to actively work toward solutions that promote healing and reconciliation.

Future generations are not bound by the past unless we fail to equip them with the tools to build a better future. The stories we tell, the lessons we teach, and the examples we set will determine whether they continue the cycles of violence or rise above them to become peacemakers and restorers of justice. This is not an abstract hope but a tangible mission, one that calls us to align our actions with the values of God's kingdom.

Let us, therefore, commit to the well-being of those who will come after us. May we strive to create a world where peace is not an aspiration but a reality, where justice flows like a river, and where every child has the opportunity to flourish. In doing so, we honor the call of Scripture and fulfill our sacred responsibility to ensure that the legacy we leave is one of love, not violence, hope, not despair.

> **Psalms 78:5 (KJV)** For he established a testimony in Jacob, and appointed a law in Israel, which he commanded our fathers, that they should make them known to their children:
>
> **Psalms 78:6 (KJV)** That the generation to come might know them, even the children which should be born; who should arise and declare them to their children:
>
> **Psalms 78:7 (KJV)** That they might set their hope in God, and not forget the works of God, but keep his commandments:

Proverbs 22:6 (KJV) Train up a child in the way he should go: and when he is old, he will not depart from it.

The devastating consequences of war often leave individuals grappling with profound questions, searching for meaning amid chaos and loss. The scars of conflict, physical, emotional, and spiritual, force humanity to confront its deepest vulnerabilities. In the silence after the violence, many are drawn into spiritual reflection, seeking answers to the pain they carry and yearning for hope in a world shattered by despair.

The weight of guilt, regret, and grief can feel unbearable, especially for those who have witnessed or participated in acts of destruction. Yet, in the midst of this brokenness, the Bible reminds us of the healing power of repentance and renewal. Acknowledging the sorrow and pain caused by war is not a sign of weakness but of strength, for it opens the door to redemption. God invites us to bring our burdens to Him, to lay down the weight of our failures, and to trust in His ability to restore what has been lost.

Faith becomes a lifeline in times of devastation, offering not just answers but also the strength to endure and the courage to rebuild. When human efforts fall short, when the world seems irreparably fractured, faith anchors us in the promise of a God who is steadfast, unchanging, and always present. It is through faith that we find the resilience to rise, to see beyond the ashes of destruction, and to embrace the possibility of new beginnings.

Hope is a divine gift, one that allows us to envision a future unmarred by the shadows of war. It is the assurance that no matter how dark the night, the dawn will come and that God's plans for humanity include peace, justice, and restoration. For those weary from the weight of war, hope rekindles the spirit, reminding them that they are not abandoned and that there is purpose even in their pain.

Redemption is the ultimate promise of Scripture and a reminder that no situation, no conflict, no devastation is beyond God's power to transform. He offers to renew not only individuals but entire communities, turning despair into joy and ashes into beauty. The spiritual journey that emerges from the ruins of war is one of healing, where broken hearts are mended, relationships are restored, and a vision of a brighter future takes shape.

The Bible's call to faith, hope, and redemption is not passive; it demands action. It urges us to turn away from the forces that perpetuate conflict and to embrace the principles of love, forgiveness, and reconciliation. As we reflect on the spiritual lessons born from war's devastation, let us commit to living as agents of God's peace and redemption, working to heal the wounds of the world and to reflect His glory in all we do.

In the aftermath of war, the search for meaning can lead us to the heart of God, where we find not only answers but also the strength to carry forward. May we draw upon the wellspring of His love, finding in Him the courage to rebuild and the faith to believe that even the most broken of circumstances can be redeemed

> **Psalms 34:18 (KJV)** "The LORD is nigh unto them that are of a broken heart; and saveth such as be of a contrite spirit."
>
> **Isaiah 40:31 (KJV)** "But they that wait upon the LORD shall renew their strength; they shall mount up with wings as eagles; they shall run, and not be weary; and they shall walk, and not faint."

As followers of Christ, we are called to be peacemakers, actively seeking to prevent conflict and to live harmoniously with all. The teachings of Jesus emphasize love, forgiveness, and reconciliation, urging us to resolve disputes amicably and to foster understanding among diverse groups. By embodying these principles, we not only avert the devastating consequences of war but also build communities rooted in compassion and justice. Let us commit to this path, striving to reflect God's love in our interactions and to promote peace in every aspect of our lives.

CHAPTER 7

THE MIGHTY EQUALIZER: A DIVINE MESSAGE FOR THE PRESIDENT AND HIS CABINET

======================

======================

Biblical Wisdom: A Nation's Journey from Corruption to Redemption!

I n a nation rich with resources and overflowing with potential, a President and his cabinet were entrusted with a sacred calling to lead with wisdom, equity, and compassion. The citizens, full of hope and anticipation, placed their trust in these leaders, believing they would steer the country toward a just and prosperous future.

But over time, the promise began to fade. The glow of hope dimmed as hunger spread, joblessness surged, insecurity became the norm, and the cost of living silently devoured the lives of ordinary people. Towns that once thrived with life and optimism sank into despair. The cries of the poor rose to the heavens, but those who had vowed to serve the people turned a deaf ear.

Instead of answering the cry of the afflicted, the leaders turned inward, feasting while others starved, celebrating while others wept. Grand events, flamboyant lifestyles, and unchecked extravagance replaced empathy and duty. Their governance became a festival of indulgence and tone-deaf to the suffering that echoed across the land.

*Like the rich man clothed in purple who ignored Lazarus at his gate, they walked past the broken without a second glance (**Luke 16:19–21**).*

Their judgment is not far off. For as 1 Peter 4:17 warns, judgment must begin at the house of God. And if those entrusted with the truth indulge in hypocrisy and neglect, what shall the end be for those who never knew compassion?

> **Proverbs 21:13 (KJV):** "Whoso stoppeth his ears at the cry of the poor, he also shall cry himself, but shall not be heard."

The words of Amos thunder through time:

> **Amos 6:1 (KJV)** Woe to them that are at ease in Zion, and trust in the mountain of Samaria, which are named chief of the nations, to whom the house of Israel came!

> **Amos 6:4 (KJV)** That lie upon beds of ivory, and stretch themselves upon their couches, and eat the lambs out of the flock, and the calves out of the midst of the stall;

> **Amos 6:5 (KJV)** That chant to the sound of the viol, and invent to themselves instruments of musick, like David;

> **Amos 6:6 (KJV)** That drink wine in bowls, and anoint themselves with the chief ointments: but they are not grieved for the affliction of Joseph.

True leadership demands compassion, not comfort. It is a sacred calling to defend the cause of the poor, to feed the hungry, shelter the vulnerable, and uphold justice. These are not mere ideals to preach, but actions to perform. Righteous rule is not measured by lavish ceremonies or eloquent speeches, but by the tears it dries, the burdens it lifts, and the lives it restores.

> **Isaiah 1:17 (KJV):** "Learn to do well; seek judgment, relieve the oppressed, judge the fatherless, plead for the widow."

The redemption of a nation will never be found in policies that favor the elite, nor in power structures that protect the privileged few. It lies in leaders who bend their ears to the cries of

the weak, who govern with humility, and who see their position not as a throne to dominate, but as a platform to serve.

Let this message sound as a trumpet blast a wake-up call to every leader who has wandered down the road of self-interest: ***Repent. Return.*** Restore. Seek wisdom. Uphold justice. Defend the afflicted. Only then can the nation rise from corruption into divine restoration.

Corruption has not only tainted governance; it has infected its very foundation. National resources meant for the good of all have been diverted into the hands of a greedy few, leaving the

majority of the people to wallow in hardship. Where integrity and compassion should have ruled, deceit and greed have built thrones.

Oppressive policies and harsh taxes now weigh heavily, not only on those at home but on citizens abroad who still try to contribute to their motherland. Imported goods meant to uplift communities are seized, resold at exploitative prices, and given to the elite while the rest suffer in lack.

As election season looms, desperation seeps through the cracks of leadership. Rather than face accountability, the corrupt manipulate the process — buying votes with stolen wealth, silencing critics, and trampling the people's will. This is no longer governance; it is betrayal.

Real leadership is a sacred trust, not a means for personal enrichment. When fairness, mercy, and truth are abandoned, society decays. Prosperity becomes a mirage, and despair festers where hope once lived.

> **Proverbs 14:34 (KJV):** "Righteousness exalteth a nation: but sin is a reproach to any people."

> **Proverbs 22:16 (KJV):** "He that oppresseth the poor to increase his riches, and he that giveth to the rich, shall surely come to want."

> **James 5:4 (KJV):** "Behold, the hire of the labourers... kept back by fraud, crieth: and the cries of them... are entered into the ears of the Lord of sabaoth."

To those entrusted with power: leadership is not a right to exploit, but a divine responsibility. When you trample the weak and fleece the poor, you forfeit your mandate. God is not blind, nor is He indifferent. He hears the cries of the defrauded, and He holds rulers accountable.

> **Ezekiel 34:4 (KJV)** "The diseased have ye not strengthened, neither have ye healed that which was sick, neither have ye bound up that which was broken, neither have ye brought again that which was driven away, neither have ye sought that which was lost; but with force and with cruelty have ye ruled them."

A nation's leadership must mirror the character of God which is just, compassionate, and upright. Leadership is not a license for self-exaltation, but a sacred stewardship entrusted by the Almighty. When rulers stray from this divine standard, judgment is not merely likely, it is inevitable. They do not govern by their own authority; they preside over what belongs to God. And from His throne, He will demand an account.

> **Romans 13:1–2 (KJV)** Let every soul be subject unto the higher powers. For there is no power but of God:

Romans 13:2(KJV) the powers that be are ordained of God. Whosoever therefore resisteth the power, resisteth the ordinance of God: and they that resist shall receive to themselves damnation.

Daniel 4:17 (KJV) This matter is by the decree of the watchers, and the demand by the word of the holy ones: to the intent that the living may know that the most High ruleth in the kingdom of men, and giveth it to whomsoever he will, and setteth up over it the basest of men.

What will the Lord say to the President and his ministers when they stand before His judgment seat, having turned a blind eye to the suffering they permitted? While the people perished in darkness, their hopes and future were stolen by those they trusted.

Exodus 34:7 (KJV): "He will by no means clear the guilty; visiting the iniquity... unto the third and to the fourth generation."

This is not just a moral warning, it is a generational consequence. The sins of today's leadership, if unrepented, will echo into the lives of their children and grandchildren

Recently, Ghana, once hailed as a shining light among developing nations, admired for its democratic stability and potential, has found itself in the shadow of grave allegations. A scandal has emerged that, if true, would speak not just to mismanagement, but to a deeper moral decay. It involves the disappearance of 1,300 containers, not mere metal boxes, but vessels meant to carry light to darkened homes, power to forgotten schools, and opportunity to neglected communities.

These containers were more than cargo. They symbolized hope, tangible promises of progress to the people. Now, they have become symbols of betrayal. Stolen in silence. Hidden in corruption. Auctioned for selfish profit. What was meant to uplift a nation has allegedly been hijacked by the very hands entrusted with its care.

This was not an error of bureaucracy or a lapse in record-keeping. It bears the marks of deliberate, orchestrated theft, executed by individuals entrusted with leadership but intoxicated by greed. Their motives, if proven true, were not national development but personal enrichment. It is like a man who purchases a vehicle to carry his people forward, only to abandon it, strip it for parts, and sell the scraps for gain, showing utter contempt for its original purpose and those who depended on it.

And what would God say of such a thing? If these allegations hold truth, His judgment will not tarry. To those who plundered what was meant for the poor:

Isaiah 33:1 (KJV): "Woe to thee that spoilest, and thou wast not spoiled; and dealest treacherously, and they dealt not treacherously with thee! when thou shalt cease to spoil, thou shalt be spoiled; and

when thou shalt make an end to deal treacherously, they shall deal treacherously with thee."

You have not just stolen material wealth, but you have robbed the future of a nation. You have taken bread from the mouths of the hungry, light from the eyes of children, and peace from the hearts of families. Your actions have not only impoverished the present, but have darkened the hopes of tomorrow.

James 4:17 (KJV): "Therefore to him that knoweth to do good, and doeth it not, to him it is sin.

To those who knew but remained silent, who saw but turned away: you are not innocent in the eyes of God. By failing to act when you had the knowledge and the power to stop it, you too bear responsibility. For God has called us to defend the oppressed, to speak out against evil, and to do justice, not merely to watch in indifference.

Your inaction is no less grievous than the actions of those who perpetrated this injustice. In His perfect justice, God will hold you accountable as well."

True leadership is not a license for luxury; it is a sacred trust, a divine stewardship given by God Himself. To lead is to serve, to sacrifice, and to uphold justice, mercy, and truth. Leaders are entrusted with power, not for personal gain, but to fulfill the needs of the people they serve. When that trust is violated, when greed and selfishness overtake the call to righteousness, judgment is inevitable.

This judgment will not only come from the courts of men, where human justice may falter, but it will stand before the throne of God, the ultimate judge of all. For He who sees the hearts of men and knows the depths of every act, will hold accountable all who have abused their position.

Luke 12:48 (KJV): "For unto whomsoever much is given, of him shall be much required."

Leaders are held to a higher standard, not for their comfort, but for their responsibility to God and to those they are called to lead. And if they fail to uphold the trust placed in them, they will answer not only to the people, but to the Almighty, who will not tolerate the misuse of authority for selfish purposes.

Let this be a warning: those who think that their power and wealth will shield them from accountability are gravely mistaken. God's judgment is just, and His wrath will not be stayed.

Romans 14:12 (KJV): "So then every one of us shall give account of himself to God."

Micah 2:1–2 (KJV): "Woe to them that devise iniquity... they covet fields... and oppress a man and his house..."

Remember that when righteousness leads, the people are filled with joy. But when wickedness takes root in positions of power, even the earth itself mourns.

This is a call to reflect on the state of leadership and governance, both in Ghana and across the globe. When leaders walk in integrity, justice, and righteousness, the nation flourishes, and its people experience peace and prosperity. However, when corruption, dishonesty, and selfishness take root in the halls of power, the effects ripple through society, leading to suffering, disillusionment, and a sense of despair among the people.

For those in positions of leadership, this is a reminder of the immense responsibility they bear. Their choices, their actions, and their stewardship not only shape the future of their nation but affect the well-being of generations to come. As stewards of God's resources and authority, their leadership should mirror the justice, compassion, and righteousness of God's own character.

For the people, it is a call to remain vigilant, to speak out against injustice, and to hold their leaders accountable. Silence and inaction in the face of wrongdoing only allow the ground to groan, as you beautifully put it. When wickedness thrives, it harms everyone. But when righteousness reigns, there is not only joy, but restoration and hope for the future.

Let this be a reminder that the nation's health, prosperity, and spiritual vitality are directly tied to the quality of its leadership. And ultimately, it is God who judges the hearts of rulers and the people alike

> **Proverbs 29:2 (KJV)** "When the righteous are in authority, the people rejoice: but when the wicked beareth rule, the people mourn."

And tragically, many of these same leaders mask their wickedness in piety. They attend church. Quote Scripture. Surround themselves with clergy who, rather than rebuking sin, bless it with their silence. But God is not mocked.

I do not speak as a distant observer, but as a son of the land, one whose heart beats with Ghana's every joy and sorrow. My words are not to condemn, but to awaken. I do not point fingers to shame, but to stir a conscience that sleeps.

Scripture calls us to examine ourselves first. And so, I begin there. For charity begins at home, and judgment of God as the Bible declares, must begin at the house of God. Let us cleanse our hearts, so our nation may be healed.

> **Matthew 7:5 (KJV):** "Thou hypocrite, first cast out the beam out of thine own eye; and then shalt thou see clearly to cast out the mote out of thy brother's eye."

> **1 Peter 4:17 (KJV):** "For the time is come that judgment must begin at the house of God: and if it first begin at us, what shall the end be of them that obey not the gospel of God?"

Everything I have raised in this chapter goes beyond mere mismanagement, it is calculated sabotage. The very hands entrusted with the nation's protection have become the claws that tear it apart. When those in power exploit the weak to fatten themselves, it is not just the economy that bleeds, it is the soul of the nation that suffers.

The scandal of the missing containers may have faded from the headlines, but the wound it left is still fresh in the hearts and minds of the people. This was more than the loss of goods, it was the theft of trust, the betrayal of hope. What was meant to empower communities was instead plundered for personal gain, and the silence that followed only deepened the pain.

But God is still on the throne. He humbles the proud. He lifts the lowly. And He hears every cry of injustice. Even when people suffer in silence, God does not forget.

Yet, there is hope. Judgment may be certain, but so is mercy, for those who turn from their wicked ways. Through Christ, restoration is still possible. Forgiveness awaits those who repent and choose to lead with integrity, humility, and truth.

> **Romans 6:23 (KJV):** "For the wages of sin is death; but the gift of God is eternal life through Jesus Christ our Lord."

> **Psalm 98:9 (KJV):** "For he cometh to judge the earth: with righteousness shall he judge the world, and the people with equity."

Let this chapter be a mirror and a trumpet reflecting the truth and sounding the alarm. There is still time to do what is right. Let justice roll like a river, and righteousness like a mighty stream. Ghana's redemption begins with godly leadership and a people who demand nothing less.

CHAPTER 8

THE MIGHTY EQUALIZER: A DIVINE MESSAGE FOR THE MEMBER OF PARLIAMENT (Representative)

========================

AKOMA NTOASO

"Linked hearts"

Asante philosophical symbol of Understanding, Agreement, Togetherness, Unity

========================

As a member of parliament or as someone who has willingly availed yourself of the sacred duty of representing the people, you hold an honor entrusted to you through their confidence and your own commitment. This privilege carries a profound responsibility to lead with integrity, guided by principles that transcend mere ambition.

True service to the people requires more than words; it demands actions rooted in justice, fairness, and moral uprightness. Leadership of this nature is not a platform for personal gain but a call to prioritize the collective good. The pursuit of financial stability or personal success must never be tainted by corruption or unethical practices, for such compromises erode the trust that forms the foundation of public service.

Let this responsibility serve as a profound reminder that representation is not a symbol of status or an avenue for entitlement but a sacred act of stewardship. It reflects the depth of your

character and stands as a testament to the principles you uphold. Leading with righteousness is not just fulfilling a role; it is honoring the trust placed in you by the people and embracing the higher calling of ethical and principled governance. For those in legislative or representative roles who find themselves under scrutiny for corrupt dealings, this is a moment of reckoning. It is a call to reflect deeply on the responsibilities entrusted to you and to realign your actions with the principles of honesty and humility. The allure of ill-gotten wealth is fleeting, but the value of a life lived in service to the greater good is enduring.

The measure of success in leadership is not in the accumulation of riches but in the legacy of justice, fairness, and genuine service to the people. Let your leadership be an example of integrity, rejecting the temptations of corruption and embracing the path of righteousness. In doing so, you honor not only your role as a representative but also the divine calling to lead with compassion and truth.

1 Timothy 6:10 (KJV): "For the love of money is the root of all evil."

Proverbs 16:8 (KJV): "Better is a little with righteousness than great revenues without right."

The Lord calls us to uphold fairness and integrity in all our dealings, warning against dishonest gain that distorts justice and betrays the trust of those we serve. The pursuit of wealth through corruption, embezzlement, or bribery not only defiles the soul but also undermines the foundations of governance. Leaders entrusted with the responsibility of representation must ensure that their actions reflect honesty and righteousness in every matter.

The practice of inserting unauthorized items into the national budget is a glaring departure from the principles of equity and accountability. Such actions betray the trust of the people, prioritizing personal gain over the welfare of the nation. The call to leadership is not a call to enrich oneself but to serve with transparency and integrity, ensuring that every decision aligns with the values of justice and fairness.

In the name of environmental protection or fiscal responsibility, lawmakers have introduced policies that, intentionally or not, place undue burdens on the poor while benefiting corporations. These legislative choices often prioritize the interests of powerful entities and lobbyists, leaving vulnerable communities to shoulder the weight of poorly conceived policies.

Take, for example, payroll taxes levied on low-income workers. These taxes extract earnings from those already struggling to make ends meet, only to funnel a portion of the proceeds into social programs like food stamps. While these programs are necessary, they act as band-aids on wounds inflicted by the very tax policies designed to support them. The system creates a vicious cycle that perpetuates poverty rather than alleviating it.

To those who sit in high places crafting laws and policies in the name of public good, this message is for you. A divine message to expose the hypocrisy dressed as virtue, the injustice wrapped in green rhetoric, and the betrayal concealed beneath the language of environmental stewardship.

One of the most damning examples is the law that mandates fees for paper bags at retail stores, an action promoted as a noble step toward environmental preservation. But let us speak plainly: this is not about saving the planet. It is a calculated act of economic oppression disguised as eco-consciousness. At checkout counters, poor shoppers who are already struggling to make ends meet, are asked, "Would you like a paper bag for ten or twenty-five cents…...?"

A question that may appear harmless to the affluent but strikes deep into the dignity and pockets of the economically burdened. These fees are not retained by the retailers; they are collected by city or county governments.

This fact, confirmed by legal minds, may seem to absolve the stores, but it does not. Both the seller and the state are entangled in a system that forces the poor to pay for what was once a basic courtesy. Worse still, the very bags the poor now purchase bear corporate logos on them, transforming those in need into unpaid advertisers for the powerful.

This is not policy; it is profiteering. It is not stewardship; it is state-sanctioned greed. What was once a sign of customer service has become a revenue stream carved from the backs of the least among us. And while governments pad their budgets under the banner of sustainability, the struggling mother is left juggling groceries in her arms, choosing between a bag and a bus fare.

If environmental preservation were the genuine intent, the laws would reward, not punish sustainable behavior. Imagine a system that gives ten or twenty-five cents credit to those who bring reusable bags, affirming their role in protecting creation. But no, these laws were never about rewarding the good. They were designed to monetize necessity, to extract more from those who have less, and to sell morality by the ounce. This is not simply poor legislation, it is a moral crisis. It reflects a rising trend where lawmakers abandon their mandate to serve and instead protect corporate interests and fill government coffers at the expense of the vulnerable. It is a betrayal of the very people they were elected to defend.

To those who claim to walk in the light of Christ: remember His words,"Whatsoever you do to the least of these, you do unto Me" (Matthew 25:40). These laws that tax the poor while glorifying the rich are not only unjust, they are ungodly. They are a stench in the nostrils of heaven, a mockery of divine justice.

It is time for repentance in governance. Tear off the mask of false virtue. Confront the harm hidden behind your policies. Let righteousness, not revenue, be your measure. Leadership must protect the vulnerable, reward the just, and embody compassion, not craft systems where the rich advertise on the backs of the poor.

Let those in positions of authority remember that their stewardship is accountable not only to the people but to the divine standard of righteousness. Integrity in leadership fosters trust, promotes equity, and strengthens the bonds of community. To act justly and lead with honor is to fulfill the sacred duty of representation and to reflect the character of the One who calls us to walk in truth.

>**Leviticus 19:35 (KJV):** "Ye shall do no unrighteousness in judgment, in meteyard, in weight, or in measure."

>**Leviticus 19:36 (KJV):** "Just balances, just weights, a just ephah, and a just hin, shall ye have: I am the Lord your God."

>**Proverbs 11:1 (KJV):** "A false balance is abomination to the Lord: but a just weight is his delight."

>**Proverbs 15:27 (KJV):** "He that is greedy of gain troubleth his own house; but he that hateth gifts shall live."

The Lord God mandates that all our transactions, including those related to budgetary allocations, be conducted with fairness and integrity. For those implicated in corruption scandal, involving overinflated costs, accepting bribes, and dedicating excessive time to personal business ventures, it's crucial to meditate on the divine preference for truthfulness over dishonesty and fraud.

Furthermore, legislators who accept bribes often disguised under the polished term **"lobbying"** must remember that the Lord God explicitly warns against greed and the corrupting influence of gifts that pervert justice.

>**Exodus 23:8, (KJV)** "And thou shalt take no gift: for the gift blindeth the wise, and perverteth the words of the righteous"

In every aspect of leadership, it is vital to uphold the divine principles of **justice, mercy, and humility.** These are not mere ideals but the foundation of righteous governance.

>**Micah 6:8, (KJV).** "He hath shewed thee, O man, what is good; and what doth the Lord require of thee, but to do justly, and to love mercy, and to walk humbly with thy God?"

Only by adhering to these virtues can lawmakers fulfill their responsibilities with honor and integrity, securing both the trust of the people and the favor of the Lord.

>**Proverbs 15:27 (KJV):** "He that is greedy of gain troubleth his own house; but he that hateth gifts shall live."

>**Proverbs 17:23 (KJV):** "A wicked man taketh a gift out of the bosom to pervert the ways of judgment."

>**Proverbs 22:16 (KJV):** "He that oppresseth the poor to increase his riches, and he that giveth to the rich, shall surely come to want."

The message emphasizes the perils of greed and corruption, particularly for lawmakers worldwide. It urges the rejection of bribery and exchanging favors for personal gain, advocating for prioritizing national well-being. The text highlights the corruptive impact of accepting gifts that compromise justice or judgment, reminding parliamentarians to maintain fairness and integrity. Furthermore, it cautions against unjust enrichment at the cost of the poor and calls for equitable policies that benefit all societal segments.

> **Isaiah 1:23 (KJV)**: "Thy princes are rebellious, and companions of thieves: every one loveth gifts, and followeth after rewards: they judge not the fatherless, neither doth the cause of the widow come unto them."

> **1 Timothy 6:10 (KJV)**: "For the love of money is the root of all evil: which while some coveted after, they have erred from the faith, and pierced themselves through with many sorrows."

The path of a legislator should be guided by principles of justice, mercy, and humility, values deeply embedded in God's Word and essential for meaningful governance.

As a parliamentarian, your actions hold the power to uplift or oppress. The misuse of this authority and privilege, whether through the acceptance of bribes, the manipulation of budgets, or the prioritization of personal gain over public service, such as acting as a lobbyist for other interests rather than the people you should truly represent, betrays the sacred duty entrusted to you. Wealth amassed through dishonesty or exploitation is fleeting and comes at the expense of the trust and well-being of those you are called to serve.

Let the principles of righteousness and integrity be your guiding light. True prosperity lies not in material gain but in the moral wealth of leading with justice and compassion. Reflect on the wisdom that cautions against the love of money, reminding us that greed corrupts not only the individual but the structures of governance. Prioritizing financial gain over fairness means sow seeds of inequality and discontent, undermining the foundations of society.

When facing matters such as budget allocations or legislative influence, consider the weight of your decisions. Fairness and honesty must govern every action, for they are the bedrock of trust and accountability. Reject the temptation to inflate expenses, accept undue rewards, or exploit your position for personal benefit. Such actions tarnish your legacy and erode the credibility of the office you hold.

A legislator's role is not to serve the interests of the wealthy or powerful at the expense of the vulnerable. Policies and laws must be crafted to protect and uplift those in need, ensuring equity and justice for all. To ignore this duty is to forsake the very principles of good governance and to risk the judgment of both history and divine justice.

At the state and local levels of governance, the disproportionate influence of powerful interests and corporate lobbying often results in laws that place unnecessary burdens on small businesses while catering to the financial agendas of large corporations. This troubling reality becomes glaringly evident in the crafting of draconian and biased policies that favor those with the resources to influence legislators, leaving small business owners to bear the weight of unreasonable regulations.

I am currently facing this reality firsthand as I prepare to publish my book. My driving school, which has successfully operated with two well-maintained 2017 Toyota vehicles, is now being forced to replace them due to a regulation that prohibits the use of vehicles older than seven years for driver training. These vehicles are in excellent condition and undergo regular inspections, yet the law mandates their replacement. I do not believe it is for safety reason, but as part of a policy enshrined in the transportation article of the Annotated Code of Maryland. The motivations behind such a law appear rooted in financial gain for car dealerships and the banks that finance vehicle purchase, rather than in genuine concern for public safety.

The irony of this legislation is striking. The regulation, part of **COMAR 11.23.01**, explicitly requires all driving school vehicles to pass annual inspections by a licensed state inspector, regardless of their age or mileage. This requirement alone ensures that vehicles meet safety standards. Yet, even a brand-new car with zero miles must undergo inspection unless the owner possesses the elusive certificate of origin, a document typically retained by banks when financing a vehicle, making it nearly impossible for most small business owners to qualify for an exemption.

The implication is clear: this law isn't focused on enhancing safety. If safety were truly the priority, the annual inspection requirement would be sufficient to ensure vehicles are in good condition. Instead, this legislation seems tailored to generate profits for car dealerships and financial institutions, creating a windfall at the expense of small businesses that lack the power and resources to advocate for more equitable policies. As I write, the law remains unchanged, but I've heard from a source within the Motor Vehicle and Driver Education Division that there are discussions about increasing the requirement to eight years. This change wouldn't benefit me, as I've already decommissioned two 2017-model vehicles and purchased a 2025 model for the school, leaving me with financial obligations and debt that I'll carry for the next six years. Ironically, after finalizing the deal, the finance manager at the dealership shook my hand and cheerfully said, "See you in seven years." Securing financing for a vehicle in a business name is an incredibly difficult task for a small business. Few banks offer financing for business vehicle, and those that do often charge exorbitant fees due to the lack of sufficient credit history for the business.

Proverbs 31:8 (KJV) "Open thy mouth for the dumb in the cause of all such as are appointed to destruction."

Proverbs 31: 9 (KJV) "Open thy mouth, judge righteously, and plead the cause of the poor and needy."

Isaiah 10:1 (KJV) "Woe unto them that decree unrighteous decrees, and that write grievousness which they have prescribed;"

Isaiah 10:2 (KJV) "to turn aside the needy from judgment, and to take away the right from the poor of my people, that widows may be their prey, and that they may rob the fatherless!"

Forcing small businesses to purchase brand-new vehicles for driver training serves no practical purpose beyond enriching those who benefit from the sale and financing of these vehicles. Furthermore, every time a new vehicle is introduced, it requires costly modifications, such as drilling holes to install dual instructor brakes, a significant expense that adds to the already heavy financial burden. These modifications are necessary for driver training, and the wear and tear on these vehicles is inevitable. Yet small businesses are expected to comply with these regulations or face withdrawal of licenses to operate, regardless of the economic strain it imposes.

Even the wealthiest individuals would hesitate to buy a brand-new car solely for driver training purposes. Expecting small businesses to do so reflects a complete disconnect from the realities entrepreneurs face daily. This policy highlights the growing gap between lawmakers influenced by corporate interests and the small business owners they are meant to represent.

This type of legislation underscores a troubling trend, the prioritization of corporate profits over the needs of the people. It is a stark reminder of the critical need for fairness and equity in governance. Policymakers must consider the real-world implications of their decisions and ensure that regulations support, rather than hinder, the efforts of small businesses to thrive. Leadership at all levels must reflect integrity and compassion, crafting laws that benefit the community as a whole, not just the privileged few with access to power.

This experiences at firsthand highlights a troubling trend in governance: laws that prioritize corporate gain over the needs of ordinary citizens. Small businesses, often the backbone of local economies, lack the financial muscle to lobby for their interests. Meanwhile, corporate entities with deep pockets can influence legislation that secures their profits while imposing undue burdens on others.

As legislators, the duty to serve the people must outweigh the lure of corporate influence. Governance should reflect fairness and equity, crafting policies that uplift small businesses rather than stifling them with unreasonable demands. Leadership at every level, whether state, local, or national, should be guided by principles of justice and compassion, ensuring that laws are rooted in the well-being of all, not just the privileged few.

This is a call to legislators to reflect on the impact of their decisions. Policies that benefit powerful interests while oppressing small businesses and betray the principles of good governance. It is time to prioritize the needs of the community, recognizing that true leadership is measured not by the favors granted to the wealthy but by the fairness extended to the vulnerable.

Let this be a reminder to all in authority that the role of governance is to serve, not to exploit. Legislators must craft laws that promote equity, empower small businesses, and resist the sway of corporate power. Only by adhering to these principles can they truly honor the trust placed in them by the people they represent.

In your service, let humility and compassion guide your steps. Walk in integrity, rejecting dishonesty and greed, and act as a beacon of fairness and righteousness. True leadership is measured not by the wealth it accumulates but by the lives it transforms through acts of justice and mercy. Let these principles shape your legacy as a representative.

May the values of justice, humility, and compassion serve as your moral compass, illuminating the path toward faithful and righteous leadership. Your role is not merely to legislate but to embody the principles of fairness and integrity, ensuring that your service honors the trust placed in you by the people and the higher calling of governance.

CHAPTER 9

THE MIGHTY EQUALIZER: A DIVINE MESSAGE FOR THE SCIENTIST?

=====================

ANANSE NTENTAN

"Spider's web"

Asante philosophical symbol of Wisdom, Creativity, Craftiness, Shrewdness

=====================

*I*n an age of extraordinary scientific breakthroughs, humanity has made remarkable strides in improving the quality of life. Through God-given wisdom, science has been a tool for advancing health, technology, and understanding the natural world. However, the same pursuit of knowledge has, at times, ventured into unethical territory, challenging the divine order of creation and undermining the moral principles that sustain society.

The Word of God stands as the ultimate authority and guide in examining the ethical implications of our scientific endeavors. For every discovery, there must be reflection.

What will the Lord, the Lord, say to you, the scientist, who uses your knowledge to create technologies and inventions that harm rather than heal, that exploit rather than uplift, that defy God's laws rather than align with His wisdom? How will you answer when asked about the unethical and immoral consequences of your work? Let us turn to Scripture for guidance and reflection on the responsibilities of those who pursue knowledge:

Jeremiah 10:12 (KJV) "He hath made the earth by his power, he hath established the world by his wisdom, and hath stretched out the heavens by his discretion."

Romans 1:22 (KJV) "Professing themselves to be wise, they became fools,

Romans 1:23 (KJV) "And changed the glory of the uncorruptible God into an image made like to corruptible man, and to birds, and fourfooted beasts, and creeping things."

Proverbs 14:12 (KJV) "There is a way which seemeth right unto a man, but the end thereof are the ways of death."

Science is a gift from God, meant to be used in partnership with His wisdom to improve the quality of life and glorify His creation. When scientists act in isolation from divine principles, they risk creating tools and systems that harm rather than heal.

This teaching admonishes scientists to consider their responsibility not only to humanity but also to God. Let your knowledge be tempered with humility, your discoveries guided by morality, and your advancements aligned with God's divine purpose. For in the end, you will stand before the Lord to account for the impact of your work.

Genesis 1:31 (KJV) "And God saw everything that he had made, and, behold, it was very good."

This verse underscores that God's creation is inherently good and harmonious. Scientists should exercise caution and respect for the natural order of creation, avoiding any actions that disrupt the balance set by the Creator.

Psalm 24:1 (KJV) "The earth is the Lord's, and the fulness thereof; the world, and they that dwell therein."

This verse emphasizes the divine ownership of the Earth, compelling scientists to be stewards of God's creation rather than disruptors of it.

The pursuit of scientific knowledge is a profound responsibility, one that calls for unwavering integrity and a steadfast commitment to moral principles. Scientists, like representatives in leadership, are entrusted with a sacred duty, which is to seek truth with humility, fairness, and a deep respect for humanity and the world God has created.

The ethical responsibility of a scientist is not merely about discovery but about stewardship. They are tasked with ensuring that their work adheres to principles of honesty, justice, and care, safeguarding the welfare of individuals, and upholding the dignity of all life. Their research must consider the broader societal and environmental impacts, reflecting a commitment to serving the

greater good rather than personal ambition or gain.

Scientists are also called to acknowledge the limitations of human wisdom, recognizing that knowledge, without ethical guidance, can lead to harm. They must remain vigilant against the allure of pride or self-reliance, choosing instead to seek wisdom that departs from harm and promotes the well-being of creation. This humility fosters a spirit of discernment, ensuring that their contributions align with what is just, good, and beneficial for all.

In aligning their work with these values, scientists fulfill a divine task. Their pursuit of knowledge becomes not merely an academic endeavor but a reflection of God's purpose for humanity. In their quest to innovate, they must do so with integrity, to discover with care, and to contribute to the flourishing of the world. By grounding their work in principles of righteousness, they honor the sacred trust placed in them and become instruments of good in accordance with God's plan.

Let scientists, like all who seek to lead or influence, remain guided by these enduring principles, ensuring that their work uplifts, protects, and serves the world they are called to steward.

> **Proverbs 11:3 (KJV)** "The integrity of the upright shall guide them."
>
> **Proverbs 3:7 (KJV)** "Be not wise in thine own eyes: fear the Lord, and depart from evil."

Scientists are called to renew their minds and use their knowledge to pursue what is good and acceptable in the eyes of the Lor, rather than harmful or morally questionable endeavors.

A virtuous scientist can harness their knowledge to promote human morality by aligning their work with the principles of love, compassion, and ethical responsibility. Just as Jesus taught us, good scientists can use their expertise to address critical societal challenges such as poverty, disease, and environmental degradation, striving to improve the well-being of all people.

i. **Micah 6:8 (KJV)** "do justly, and to love mercy, and to walk humbly with thy God"

ii. **Philippians 4:8 (KJV)** "Finally, brethren, whatsoever things are true, whatsoever things are honest, whatsoever things are just, whatsoever things are pure, whatsoever things are lovely, whatsoever things are of good report; if there be any virtue, and if there be any praise, think on these things."

Scientists bear a profound responsibility to ensure that their inventions and discoveries serve the greater good and uphold the moral fabric of society. Their work must be rooted in values of truth, honesty, justice, and purity, reflecting a commitment to advancing not just knowledge but the well-being of humanity.

In their pursuit, scientists should strive to create innovations that cultivate virtues such as love, peace, patience, kindness, and self-control. These qualities, akin to the fruits of a life guided by

higher principles, are essential for fostering a society that is not only progressive but also harmonious and ethical. Scientific advancements must be more than technological milestones they yearn for should rather become a catalyst for unity, compassion, and the betterment of the human condition.

By aligning their work with these virtues, scientists can ensure that their contributions do not harm or divide but instead build bridges of understanding and promote a deeper respect for life and creation. Their inventions should inspire peace and joy, address suffering with gentleness, and embody a spirit of goodness and selflessness.

To innovate with integrity is to honor the higher calling of their areas of expertise to not only advance human knowledge but to steward it responsibly for the flourishing of society. By promoting virtues through their work, scientists uphold their sacred role as builders of a world where progress and morality walk hand in hand.

> **Philippians 2:3 (KJV)** "Let nothing be done through strife or vainglory; but in lowliness of mind let each esteem other better than themselves."
>
> **Philippians 2:4 (KJV)** "Look not every man on his own things, but every man also on the things of others."
>
> **Psalm 24:1 (KJV)** "The earth is the Lord's, and the fulness thereof; the world, and they that dwell therein."

From a perspective that considers how God might judge scientists who deviate from ethical paths, the following approaches become crucial. In the belief that God acts as the ultimate equalizer, the judgment of scientists who stray from ethical paths is significant. This view underscores the necessity for scientists to conduct their work not for self-glorification but for the betterment of humanity, with the understanding that neglecting this duty may invite divine judgment.

Acknowledging the limitations of science and respecting the moral and spiritual aspects of life is crucial; overstepping these bounds could lead to God's displeasure. Collaboration for the common good is encouraged, and those who indulge in unethical practices for personal gain risk divine retribution.

Furthermore, using scientific knowledge in ways that harm people or the environment is seen as defying God's command to steward His creation, potentially drawing His chastisement. Ignoring or exploiting vulnerable communities in scientific endeavors is viewed as a breach of divine principles, possibly resulting in divine correction.

Pride, particularly in refusing to admit errors or stay open to new evidence, is warned against in Christian teachings and might lead to divine discipline. Christian scientists are reminded that separating their faith from their work, especially when it leads to unethical actions, could be perceived as forsaking their spiritual calling, risking divine consequences.

This perspective stresses the importance of aligning scientific pursuits with ethical and spiritual values, highlighting the potential spiritual consequences for those who deviate. Scientists are advised to maintain humility in their quest for knowledge and technological advancement, avoiding arrogance that could lead to dangerous outcomes. In this view, God is seen as the balancer of moral integrity in the scientific realm, holding individuals account.

> **Proverbs 16:18 (KJV)** "Pride goeth before destruction, and an haughty spirit before a fall."

> **James 4:6 (KJV):** "But he giveth more grace. Wherefore he saith, God resisteth the proud, but giveth grace unto the humble."

> **Proverbs 3:5 (KJV):** "Trust in the Lord with all thine heart; and lean not unto thine own understanding."

> **Proverbs 3:6 (KJV):** In all thy ways acknowledge him, and he shall direct thy paths."

> **Proverbs 11:1(KJV):** "A false balance is abomination to the Lord: but a just weight is his delight."

> **Psalm 24:1(KJV):** "The earth is the Lord's, and the fulness thereof; the world, and they that dwell therein."

> **Proverbs 29:23(KJV):** "A man's pride shall bring him low: but honour shall uphold the humble in spirit."

A scientist who separates their faith or belief in the Creator of the universe from their scientific work risks undermining the sacred balance that aligns discovery with purpose. Science divorced from ethical principles, humility, and recognition of divine order can lead to dangerous practices that harm humanity and contradict the moral framework intended by the Creator.

The pursuit of knowledge is not merely a scientific endeavor but a spiritual responsibility. Scientists, as stewards of their gifts, are called to align their work with values that honor humanity and creation. Failure to serve humanity with humility, compassion, and ethical integrity betrays not only the trust of society but the universal order ordained by God. Such actions carry consequences that can affect third to fourth generations.

The wisdom of the Creator calls for humility in the face of knowledge. Arrogance in scientific pursuits, especially when it leads to the creation of harmful technologies or unethical practices, reflects a rejection of the harmonious order established by the Almighty. Scientists must strive to pursue advancements with reverence, ensuring their contributions promote life, healing, and progress in alignment with moral principles.

Let science and faith, or the understanding of a higher order, coexist in harmony. In doing so, scientists not only achieve greatness in their discoveries but also honor the Creator's purpose for humanity. The use of God's knowledge for the greater goo, fostering growth, compassion, and a deeper understanding of the universe's divine design.

In the realm of science, one should always be cautious and vigilant, acknowledging the potential consequences of their actions.

Absolutely, the wisdom of humility holds profound significance for scientists in their pursuit of knowledge and innovation. Embracing humility allows them to prioritize the welfare of humanity and the common good over personal accolades. It encourages a deep respect for the limitations of human understanding and an appreciation for the vast mysteries of the natural world, often beyond our grasp. This humility is crucial in guiding scientists to draw ethical boundaries, especially in potentially hazardous research areas where the risk of "playing god" is high.

Moreover, the biblical concept of stewardship can greatly inspire scientists. Viewing their knowledge and discoveries as gifts from God instills a sense of responsibility. This perspective motivates scientists to ensure their research is beneficial for humanity and conducted with reverence for the natural world. It's a reminder that their work is not just a pursuit of personal achievement, but a service to the larger community.

In their quest for knowledge and technological progress, scientists must maintain humility to avoid the arrogance that could lead to dangerous innovations. This humility is essential in recognizing the potential repercussions of their work, prompting cautious and responsible scientific inquiry. Remaining vigilant and aware of the consequences of their actions ensures that science remains a tool for positive change and ethical advancement.

> **Proverbs 16:18 (KJV)** "Pride goeth before destruction, and an haughty spirit before a fall."

> **1 Corinthians 10:12 (KJV)** "Wherefore let him that thinketh he standeth take heed lest he fall."

The Bible provides scientists with a profound call to humility, guiding them to approach their work with a focus on the well-being of others, a recognition of their limitations, and a sense of stewardship over their knowledge. This approach not only aligns with Christian values but also contributes to the ethical and moral foundation of their scientific endeavors.

Seeking guidance and wisdom and being ready to learn from both successes and failures are signs that God is the one who gives knowledge to those who seek it in humility and gives them the glory and honor they deserve.

> **Proverbs 2:6 (KJV)** "For the Lord giveth wisdom: out of his mouth cometh knowledge and understanding"

Proverbs 3:5-6 (KJV) "encourages seeking the guidance of the Lord, stating"

James 1:5 (KJV) "If any of you lack wisdom, let him ask of God, that giveth to all men liberally, and upbraideth not; and it shall be given him"

Trust in the Lord with all thine heart, and lean not unto thine own understanding. In all thy ways acknowledge him, and he shall direct thy paths. Scientists should turn to God for wisdom and direction when making decisions about their research and inventions.

In matters of ethical and moral significance, it is essential to seek divine wisdom and guidance.

The Scriptures offer profound guidance for those who seek to understand the universe and God's intentions for humanity. The Bible serves as the source code to unlock the divine blueprint that illuminates the principles of truth, justice, and morality. For scientists, this wisdom provides a foundation for navigating the ethical complexities of their work, reminding them of their sacred responsibility to align their pursuits with God's purpose.

Scientists must respect the natural order of God's creation, as revealed in the Bible. This natural order reflects the balance and wisdom of the Creator, a system intricately designed to sustain life and promote harmony. Tampering with this divine balance without regard for ethical considerations can lead to profound consequences, both for humanity and for the world. Science must not seek to defy the inherent wisdom embedded in creatio, but instead work within the moral and ethical boundaries set by God.

The COVID-19 pandemic has revealed the devastating consequences of human hubris in the pursuit of knowledge and experimentation. The desire to manipulate pathogens and engage in dangerous scientific endeavors without fully understanding the implications has put the entire world at greater risk, leading to the loss of countless innocent lives. The pursuit of knowledge must be tempered with humility, recognizing that human understanding is finite and ultimately subject to divine authority.

When overconfidence in human ability and knowledge leads to a dismissal of ethical boundaries, it becomes an assertion that God does not exist or that divine wisdom is irrelevant. This hubris, evident in the unbridled pursuit of dangerous experiments, can unleash unprecedented harm upon humanity. Instead of fostering innovation for the greater good, pride-driven science risks crossing the threshold from progress to peril.

Such actions not only compromise societal values but also endanger the moral fabric of humanity. When reverence and ethical discernment are abandoned, science becomes a tool of destruction rather than a beacon of hope. The pandemic serves as a sobering reminder of the need

for humility, reverence, and responsibility in scientific exploration, ensuring that progress aligns with the principles of human dignity and divine wisdom.

As stewards of God's creation, scientists are called to act with love, responsibility, and a commitment to the well-being of their fellow human beings. Every new invention or technology must be evaluated through the lens of its impact on humanity, ensuring that it contributes to the greater good rather than undermining moral and ethical principles. Their work should reflect respect for the Creator's design, prioritizing life, harmony, and justice over ambition or self-interest.

To fulfill this sacred calling, scientists must renew their minds, conforming their pursuits to the standards of morality and ethics established by God. This alignment ensures that their contributions honor the Creator, benefit humanity, and safeguard the natural order of the universe. The Scriptures, as the ultimate guide, call for scientists to seek divine wisdom in their endeavors, balancing discovery with stewardship and innovation with reverence.

Ultimately, science is not separate from faith but a testament to the wonder of God's creation. Scientists, as custodians of knowledge, are invited to explore the mysteries of the universe with humility and awe, using their gifts to reflect the glory of the Creator and advance the well-being of the world. By adhering to the principles outlined in the Word of God, they fulfill their divine purpose, shaping a future that honors both the Creator and the creation.

> **Matthew 22:39 (KJV)** "Thou shalt love thy neighbor as thyself."
>
> **Proverbs 3:5-6 (KJV)** "Trust in the Lord with all thine heart; and lean not unto thine own understanding. In all thy ways acknowledge him, and he shall direct thy paths."
>
> **Ecclesiastes 3:11 (KJV)** "He hath made every thing beautiful in his time."
>
> **Romans 12:2 (KJV)** "And be not conformed to this world: but be ye transformed by the renewing of your mind."
>
> **Proverbs 16:18 (KJV)** "Pride goeth before destruction, and an haughty spirit before a fall."

In moments of ethical uncertainty, scientists are called to seek guidance beyond their own understanding. Divine wisdom offers clarity and direction, serving as a compass when navigating the moral dilemmas that accompany the pursuit of knowledge. This wisdom, rooted in the Creator's design, reminds us that science is not merely about discovery but about stewardship, an opportunity to honor the natural order and uphold the moral boundaries established by God.

As we continue to explore the vast and ever-expanding frontiers of science, it is imperative to approach this journey with humility, integrity, and a commitment to ethical responsibility. The biblical principles of stewardship and moral accountability call us to use the gift of wisdom and understanding for the betterment of humanity and the glory of the Creator.

Scientific progress must not come at the expense of ethical considerations. Instead, it should reflect a profound respect for the natural order and a dedication to promoting life, justice, and the greater good. By aligning our work with these principles, we not only advance knowledge but also safeguard the moral fabric of society, ensuring that our contributions uplift and sustain the world entrusted to us.

In closing, let us remember that science and faith are not in opposition but are complementary paths to understanding the wonders of creation. By seeking divine guidance and anchoring our work in ethical integrity, we fulfill our responsibility as stewards of knowledge, honoring the Creator and building a future defined by wisdom, compassion, and justice. Let this be our enduring commitment as we shape the future of science and humanity.

CHAPTER 10

The Mighty Equalizer: Understanding the Legacy of Colonialism in Africa and Its Global Ramifications

========================

EPA

"Handcuffs"

Asante philosophical symbol of Law, Justice, Slavery, Captivity, and the Crime of white people's Colonization of Black People, including both Physical Colonization on the Continent of Africa and Spiritual and Mental Colonization of all Black People in the Diaspora through the economic shackles of Racism and false historical narratives about the Black People

======================

Colonialism represents a significant chapter in the history of Africa and other regions around the world. The effects of colonialism have left deep imprints on the socio-political, economic, and cultural landscapes of the affected nations. This book aims to explore the profound repercussions of colonialism, drawing upon biblical references from the scriptures to shed light on the moral and ethical aspects of colonization and its implications for both colonizers and the colonized.

The tragic history of slavery and colonization, often intertwined with misinterpretations of scripture, has left a legacy of pain and distrust toward the Word of God. Many have pointed to certain biblical texts to suggest that these evils were divinely sanctioned, using them to justify the subjugation of entire populations. Others have leveraged this notion to sow doubt about the truth and sanctity of the Bible. Yet, such interpretations overlook a profound truth: every word of God is prophetic, not an endorsement of evil, but a revelation of human choices and their consequences under divine judgment.

Colonial powers, driven by greed and a thirst for dominance, embarked on brutal campaigns of exploitation, stripping indigenous peoples of their freedom, dignity, and heritage. Some of these oppressors took misguided solace in scripture, distorting its message to rationalize their actions. But the Word of God is clear: those who manipulate His truth for wicked purposes will face divine judgment. Just as Judas fulfilled the prophecy of betraying Jesus and yet bore full responsibility for his treachery, so too will those who have used the Bible to justify oppression be held accountable. "The Son of Man will go just as it is written about him. But woe to that man who betrays the Son of Man! It would be better for him if he had not been born." This profound statement, spoken by Jesus, underscores the gravity of personal accountability even within the framework of divine providence. While the betrayal of the Son of Man was foretold as part of God's redemptive plan, it did not absolve the betrayer of the responsibility for his actions. The warning, for God's justice cannot be mocked.

The misuse of scripture to perpetuate colonialism and slavery stands as a grave warning to all who wield God's Word without reverence or understanding. The Bible does not condone such atrocities but instead reveals the fallen nature of humanity and the need for redemption. The perpetrators of these historic evils, as well as those who continue to exploit others today under the guise of divine approval, will not escape the righteous judgment of the Lord. Let this be a reminder that every prophetic word serves as both a revelation and a test, calling humanity to uphold justice, humility, and reverence for the divine truth.

The legacy of colonization continues to ripple through history, shaping societies and fostering inequalities. Yet, even in the aftermath of such grave injustices, God's Word remains steadfast, offering hope, restoration, and a call to repentance for those who have strayed. It is not the Bible that endorses evil but the hearts of those who choose to twist its message for personal gain. Let us hold fast to the truth, knowing that God will vindicate the oppressed and bring justice to those who misuse His name.

> **Jeremiah 22:13 (KJV)** "Woe unto him that buildeth his house by unrighteousness, and his chambers by wrong; that useth his neighbour's service without wages, and giveth him not for his work;"

Micah 2:1 (KJV) "Woe to them that devise iniquity, and work evil upon their beds! when the morning is light, they practise it, because it is in the power of their hand."

Micah 2:2 (KJV) "And they covet fields, and take them by violence; and houses, and take them away: so they oppress a man and his house, even a man and his heritage."

Isaiah 10:1 (KJV) "Woe unto them that decree unrighteous decrees, and that write grievousness which they have prescribed;"

Isaiah 10:2 (KJV) "To turn aside the needy from judgment, and to take away the right from the poor of my people, that widows may be their prey, and that they may rob the fatherless."

Isaiah 10:3 (KJV) "And what will ye do in the day of visitation, and in the desolation which shall come from far? to whom will ye flee for help? and where will ye leave your glory?"

Genesis 1:28 (KJV) "And God blessed them, and God said unto them, Be fruitful, and multiply, and replenish the earth, and subdue it: and have dominion over the fish of the sea, and over the fowl of the air, and over every living thing that moveth upon the earth."

Exodus 22:1 (KJV) "If a man shall steal an ox, or a sheep, and kill it, or sell it; he shall restore five oxen for an ox, and four sheep for a sheep."

Luke 19:8 (KJV) "And Zacchaeus stood, and said unto the Lord; Behold, Lord, the half of my goods I give to the poor; and if I have taken any thing from any man by false accusation, I restore him fourfold"

Leadership is a sacred responsibility, calling for wisdom, justice, and compassion in the stewardship of society. A righteous man governs with integrity, fostering stability and prosperity, while the unjust leader paves the way for destruction. Colonialism, with its profound socio-political changes, serves as a historical example of how leadership can either nurture or devastate nations.

The imposition of foreign political structures, arbitrary borders, and exploitative systems of governance left scars that are still visible today. Ethnic conflicts, unstable post-colonial governments, and the ongoing struggles for self-determination are remnants of this legacy. These outcomes underscore the consequences of leadership driven by greed and exploitation rather than justice and moral responsibility.

Ethical leadership recognizes that true power lies not in domination but in uplifting the oppressed and nurturing the land and its people. Where governance is rooted in justice, a nation thrives; where it is corrupted, decay sets in. Those entrusted with authority must remember that their actions ripple through generations, for leadership is not merely about ruling others, but it is about serving with accountability, ensuring that the foundations laid are ones of equity and peace.

> **Proverbs 22:16(KJV)** "He that oppresseth the poor to increase his riches, and he that giveth to the rich, shall surely come to want."

> **Proverbs 29:4 (KJV)** "The king by judgment establisheth the land: but he that receiveth gifts overthroweth it."

> **Leviticus 19:13 (KJV)** "Thou shalt not defraud thy neighbour, neither rob him: the wages of him that is hired shall not abide with thee all night until the morning."

The treachery of colonial powers stands as a stark violation of the principles of justice and stewardship. Driven by greed and a ruthless hunger for wealth, they forcibly seized lands, exploited resources, and subjugated entire populations. Their actions were not acts of leadership but of plunder, stripping indigenous communities of their autonomy, dignity, and inheritance. The legacy of colonialism is a dark chapter of profound betrayal in human history, marked by one group venturing across the globe in pursuit of dominance and exploitation over others.

True stewardship is rooted in fairness and integrity, seeking to uplift rather than oppress, to nurture rather than destroy. Colonial powers, however, rejected these values, enriching themselves at the expense of those they subjugated. Their false claims of bringing civilization masked a campaign of exploitation, leaving nations economically and socially fractured. The moral contradictions between their professed spiritual ideals and their actions laid bare their hypocrisy, exposing a deliberate choice to ignore the principles of justice and compassion.

The enduring economic and social struggles of post-colonial nations are a direct consequence of this treachery. Colonial powers did not lead; they oppressed. They did not build; they dismantled. Their actions are a grim reminder that greed and exploitation, disguised as progress, sow destruction and suffering. True stewardship reflects a higher calling, to serve, protect, and uplift, recognizing that the earth and all within it are not spoils of conquest but treasures entrusted for the good of all. Let history serve as a warning and a call to accountability, ensuring that such betrayal is neither forgotten nor repeated.

> **Psalms 24:1 (KJV)** "The earth is the LORD'S, and the fulness thereof; the world, and they that dwell therein."

> **Genesis 2:15 (KJV)** "And the LORD God took the man, and put him into the garden of Eden to dress it and to keep it"

> **Matthew 25:40 (KJV)** "And the King shall answer and say unto them, Verily I say unto you, Inasmuch as ye have done it unto one of the least of these my brethren, ye have done it unto me."

The imposition of foreign cultures and values during colonialism represents a profound violation of the sanctity of identity and heritage. Indigenous populations, stripped of their traditions and forced to conform to alien norms, faced a disruption that fractured their sense of self and community. This cultural erasure was not merely an act of dominance but a deliberate attempt to reshape entire societies according to the whims of those who sought to control them.

A true government representative honors the uniqueness of each community, resisting conformity to systems that oppress and devalue. They understand the sacredness of identity and work to protect it, recognizing that every culture, every tradition, carries a divine imprint worthy of preservation. The colonial practice of cultural suppression stands in stark contrast to this principle, leaving behind a legacy of confusion, loss, and struggle for restoration.

Such actions remind us of the devastating consequences of forcing people into molds that deny their God-given uniqueness. A righteous steward seeks transformation not by erasing identity but by honoring and uplifting the inherent worth of every community, ensuring that the richness of their heritage remains intact for generations to come.

> **Romans 12:2** (KJV) "And be not conformed to this world: but be ye transformed by the renewing of your mind, that ye may prove what is that good, and acceptable, and perfect, will of God."
>
> **Isaiah 42:22 (KJV)** "But this is a people robbed and spoiled; they are all of them snared in holes, and they are hid in prison houses: they are for a prey, and none delivereth; for a spoil, and none saith, Restore."

The call to lead others is a sacred charge to act with justice, compassion, and humility. True leadership respects the unique identities of those it serves, fostering peace and prosperity without erasing the richness of their heritage. Colonialism, however, disregarded this sacred duty, imposing foreign norms that disrupted the cultural fabric of indigenous peoples, leaving them to grapple with the deep wounds of lost traditions and fractured identities.

The impact of colonialism was not limited to economic exploitation; it sought to reshape the very soul of the societies it invaded. This forced conformity stripped communities of their cultural essence, leaving a legacy of struggle as they fought to reclaim what was taken. A true government representative does not seek to dominate or impose but to nurture, protect, and honor the diversity of identities entrusted to their care.

Restoring what was lost requires a commitment to justice and the pursuit of the common good. It calls for leadership that uplifts and heals, embracing the wisdom of walking humbly while working for the well-being of all. The sacred task of leadership lies in cherishing and preserving the beauty of every culture, ensuring that their voices and heritage endure as a testament to their resilience and divine worth.

Micah 6:8 (KJV) "He hath shewed thee, O man, what is good; and what doth the Lord require of thee, but to do justly, and to love mercy, and to walk humbly with thy God?"

Jeremiah 29:7 (KJV) "But seek the welfare of the city where I have sent you into exile, and pray to the Lord on its behalf, for in its welfare you will find your welfare."

The scriptures points to the moral underpinnings of colonialism and show us how decades of colonialism have violated the principles of justice and compassion and the importance of justice and mercy in human interactions, which colonial powers often failed to uphold.

In light of these biblical principles, it is essential to reflect on the historical consequences of colonialism and consider pathways to reconciliation and healing.

Proverbs 16:6 (KJV) "By mercy and truth iniquity is purged: and by the fear of the Lord men depart from evil"

Micah 6:8 (KJV) "He hath shewed thee, O man, what is good; and what doth the LORD require of thee, but to do justly, and to love mercy, and to walk humbly with thy God."

Colonialism left a profound scar on African societies, suppressing native cultures, traditions, and language, and causing the erosion of cultural identities. The imposition of arbitrary borders ignored the intricate relationships between ethnic and tribal groups, sowing seeds of political instability, conflict, and tension that persist to this day.

Discriminatory practices, such as apartheid in South Africa, institutionalized social injustices and inequalities, leaving a legacy of oppression that continues to shape societal structures. Economically, many African nations remain burdened by dependency and debt, entrenched by colonial exploitation and resource extraction.

The remnants of colonial borders and imposed power structures continue to fuel political instability and unrest across the continent. Yet, despite the deep disruption to their heritage, African nations are actively working to reclaim their identity, revive their traditions, and preserve the richness of their native languages and cultures, standing resilient in the face of a challenging legacy.

Matthew 5:7(KJV) "Blessed are the merciful: for they shall obtain mercy."

Isaiah 1:17(KJV) "Learn to do well; seek judgment, relieve the oppressed, judge the fatherless, plead for the widow."

Proverbs 21:15 (KJV) "It is joy to the just to do judgment: but destruction shall be to the workers of iniquity."

Scripture calls us to seek truth, reconciliation, and healing as we face the enduring legacy of colonialism. This journey did not begin yesterday, nor can it be accomplished in a single day. True reconciliation requires determination, humility, and the courage to acknowledge past wrongs and turn away from them. Only then can we begin the genuine work of rebuilding relationships founded on equality and mutual respect, rather than perpetuating the neocolonialist mentality disguised as aid or dependency.

The tragedy of colonialism is deeply complex and multifaceted, marked by profound injustices and hard-learned lessons. Yet, it also presents an opportunity to confront the past with honesty, to reject patterns of exploitation, and to commit to a future rooted in justice, dignity, and true friendship. This process demands more than words; it requires a transformative shift in both mindset and action, guided by a sincere desire to honor the principles of fairness and shared humanity.

The call to justice challenges us to examine the moral and ethical failures of colonialism, urging individuals and nations to confront its legacy with a commitment to fairness, mercy, and reconciliation. The actions of colonial powers, steeped in exploitation and oppression, starkly violated the principles of justice and compassion, trampling on the dignity and rights of the vulnerable groups of people. Such deeds expose a flagrant disregard for the sacred duty to protect and uplift, replacing it with greed and indifference.

While some may argue, as previously noted, that slavery and suffering were foretold in scripture, prophecy does not signify divine approval of injustice. Even though the crucifixion of Christ was foreordained, those who betrayed and crucified Him bore full responsibility for their actions. Similarly, the prophecy of a people enduring bondage and oppression serves not as an endorsement of such acts but as a revelation that those who perpetrate evil will face divine judgment. God's plan is always to bring justice, freedom, and restoration to those who have been wronged.

This truth bears directly on the actions of colonial powers, whose economic and social exploitation left deep scars on nations and generations. Their deeds and desires to amass wealth through the oppression of others and looting of natural resources of others cannot be justified under any pretext. Those who enriched themselves at the expense of the oppressed will not escape accountability unless they truly repent.

> **Matthew 26:24 (KJV)** "The Son of man goeth as it is written of him: but woe unto that man by whom the Son of man is betrayed! it had been good for that man if he had not been born."
>
> **Acts 7:6 (KJV)** "And God spake on this wise, That his seed should sojourn in a strange land; and that they should bring them into bondage, and entreat them evil four hundred years."
>
> **Acts 7:7 (KJV)** "And the nation to whom they shall be in bondage will I judge, said God: and after that shall they come forth, and serve me in this place."

A true representative government understands the weight of responsibility to act justly, defend the vulnerable, and uphold dignity for all. Oppression may exist for a time, but it is never without consequence. Justice belongs to the Lord, and His plan ensures that every wrong will be made right, and those who misuse their power will answer for their actions. Repentance and reconciliation remain the only patos to align with divine justice and heal the wounds of history.

Colonialism stands as a stark reminder of the devastating consequences of unchecked greed and injustice. It disregarded the divine mandate to care for one's neighbor, sowing seeds of inequality and suffering that persist to this day. As we reflect on this dark chapter of history, the path forward becomes clear: to pursue justice with unwavering resolve, to seek reconciliation through humility, and to work tirelessly for the healing and restoration of those wronged. This is not just a call to remember the past but a mandate to transform the future with compassion and a renewed commitment to righteousness.

> **Proverbs 28:5 (KJV)** Evil men understand not judgment: but they that seek the LORD understand all things.
>
> **Isaiah 1:17 (KJV)** Learn to do well; seek judgment, relieve the oppressed, judge the fatherless, plead for the widow.
>
> **Amos 5:11 (KJV)** Forasmuch therefore as your treading is upon the poor, and ye take from him burdens of wheat: ye have built houses of hewn stone, but ye shall not dwell in them; ye have planted pleasant vineyards, but ye shall not drink wine of them

As African nations and other so-called third-world countries have achieved independence, the path of decolonization has been riddled with challenges, and the enduring effects of colonization remain deeply entrenched in the fabric of their societies. It is a sobering and tragic truth that many of those who orchestrated and perpetuated these acts of exploitation and oppression were individuals who openly identified as Christians or followers of other faith, yet failed to live out the principles of justice, compassion, and stewardship that lie at the heart of their professed beliefs...

In conclusion, the impact of colonialism on Africa and beyond is a profound and enduring legacy, leaving consequences that ripple through generations. The moral and ethical insights drawn from scripture challenge us to examine the sacred responsibilities entrusted to humanity, govern justly, practice fair and equitable economics, preserve cultural identity, and steward the earth's resources with integrity and care. Reflecting on the historical consequences of colonialism is far more than an intellectual pursuit; it is a moral imperative and a moment of reckoning to confront the contradictions between faith and action, to repent of past injustices, and to commit to shaping a future rooted in righteousness, accountability, and true equality.

May the LORD God Almighty shine His face upon you. May the LORD Jesus Christ grant you wisdom and understanding. May the Holy Spirit dwell with your spirit always...Amen.

CHAPTER 11

DID GOD PRESCRIBE WHAT ATTITUDE TO HAVE TOWARD THE POOR AND NEEDY?

=====================

AYA

"Fern"

Asante philosophical symbol of Endurance, Independence, Defiance against difficulties, Hardiness, Perseverance, and Resourcefulness

=====================

How we respond to the poor and needy is not a question of charity but a reflection of our moral and spiritual character. Compassion, generosity, and justice are not optional virtues; they are sacred responsibilities entrusted to all, especially to those blessed with wealth, influence, and spiritual leadership. The call to care for the less fortunate is not just a societal obligation. It is a divine mandate that mirrors the heart of God.

Across the ages, the sacred texts of the Judeo-Christian tradition have provided clear guidance on how to treat the vulnerable. They call for mercy, empathy, and active generosity, reminding us that to serve the needy is to honor their inherent dignity as bearers of the divine image. For the rich and powerful, and for the church as a spiritual beacon, this is not merely an ethical responsibility but a holy charge to live out the principles of love and justice.

To feed the hungry, clothe the naked, and care for the marginalized is not simply an act of charity; it is an expression of deep social and spiritual responsibility. These actions are manifestations of love, reflecting the values of humility, grace, and divine justice. Those with resources and influence are uniquely positioned to effect meaningful change, transforming lives and communities through their commitment to these principles.

The church, as the moral compass of society, holds a sacred responsibility to live out the teachings of compassion, humility, and justice not only in words but in meaningful actions. However, a troubling trend has emerged in which some pastors and prophets prioritize personal wealth and luxury over the well-being of the poor members of their congregations. This practice is not only a departure from the teachings of Christ but a betrayal of the trust placed in spiritual leaders.

Far too often, the story of the poor widow is used to convince struggling congregants to give the last of their resources, even when it means they go without basic necessities. While the widow's faith is commendable, it was Christ Himself who pointed out the disparity between her sacrificial giving and the abundance of others who gave out of their excess. Today, some spiritual leaders exploit such narrative, not to inspire collective generosity but to fund lavish lifestyles and personal comforts at the expense of the very people they are called to serve.

The church's resources are meant to uplift the needy, support the vulnerable, and provide for the destitute within its fold. Yet, when those resources are redirected toward extravagance and self-indulgence, the church loses its moral authority and fails in its sacred mission. Pastors and prophets are stewards of God's blessings, entrusted with guiding their congregations in righteousness and compassion. To misuse these blessings for personal gain is a grievous violation of their calling.

True leadership in the church is not measured by opulent lifestyles or the size of one's following but by the depth of care shown to those in need. To neglect the poor while living in abundance is to turn away from God's instruction and reject the sacred charge to serve with humility and grace. Such actions reveal a failure to see the divine image in those who suffer, and they compromise the witness of the church in the world.

Conversely, to redirect resources toward feeding the hungry, sheltering the homeless, and supporting struggling members is to align with the heart of God. The church must lead by example, ensuring that its wealth is used not for personal gain but to uplift the least among us. This is the essence of true discipleship, which means being the hands and feet of Christ in a broken world.

Let this be a call to pastors, prophets, and all spiritual leader: to examine their stewardship and redirect their focus toward the needs of their congregations. The church must prioritize its sacred duty to care for the poor, using its influence and resources to reflect the boundless love and mercy of God. For in doing so, spiritual leaders not only honor their calling but fulfill the ultimate purpose of the church to serve as a beacon of hope, justice, and compassion in a world that so desperately needs it.

Proverbs 19:17 (KJV) "He that hath pity upon the poor lendeth unto the Lord, and that which he hath given will he pay him again."

Matthew 25:35 (KJV) "For I was an hungred, and ye gave me meat: I was thirsty, and ye gave me drink: I was a stranger, and ye took me in:"

Matthew 25: 36 (KJV) "Naked, and ye clothed me: I was sick, and ye visited me: I was in prison, and ye came unto me."

The scripture vividly portrays the profound connection between kindness to the poor and our relationship with God. Acts of compassion and generosity toward the needy are not merely charitable deeds but reflections of our faith and devotion to God. In essence, when we show benevolence to those in need, we honor God, and such acts will not go unnoticed or unrewarded.

This passage serves as a powerful reminder from Jesus Himself, underscoring that our treatment of the poor and vulnerable is a vital expression of our faith. Justice and fairness stand as pillars of doing God's will, and our approach to the poor must embody these principles. Compassion is not just about giving but about recognizing the inherent dignity of every person and acting in ways that reflect divine justice.

Moreover, the Bible calls attention to the greater blessing in giving rather than receiving, emphasizing the impartiality that should characterize our actions. True compassion does not discriminate based on socioeconomic status but treats all individuals with equity, reflecting the love and fairness that God commands. This is the essence of living out one's faith in service to others as an extension of our devotion to God and our commitment to His will.

Leviticus 19:15 (KJV) "Ye shall do no unrighteousness in judgment: thou shalt not respect the person of the poor, nor honor the person of the mighty: but in righteousness shalt thou judge thy neighbor."

1 John 3:17 (KJV) "But whoso hath this world's good, and seeth his brother have need, and shutteth up his bowels of compassion from him, how dwelleth the love of God in him"

Philippians 4:18 (KJV) "But I have all, and abound: I am full, having received of Epaphroditus the things which were sent from you, an odour of a sweet smell, a sacrifice acceptable, well pleasing to God."

Acts 20:35 (KJV) "I have shewed you all things, how that so labouring ye ought to support the weak, and to remember the words of the Lord Jesus, how he said, It is more blessed to give than to receive."

> **Luke 6:38 (KJV)** "Give, and it shall be given unto you; good measure, pressed down, and shaken together, and running over, shall men give into your bosom. For with the same measure that ye mete withal it shall be measured to you again."

It's no secret that many preachers today have taken scriptures, such as the well-known verse in **Luke 6:38**, and skewed their message to serve their own bellies, often reducing its profound spiritual meaning to a transactional promise of financial gain. While the Bible does call for generosity, it emphasizes a spirit of compassion and fairness, not manipulation or coercion under the guise of religious obligation.

The scripture teaches us that justice and fairness should be our guiding principles, especially in how we treat the poor and needy. The call is clear: we must not discriminate against the less fortunate, but rather judge and treat all individuals with equity, regardless of their social or economic standing. Yet, in many of today's churches, this principle is often overshadowed by messages that prioritize institutional wealth over genuine care for the downtrodden.

Generosity, as prescribed in the Bible, is not about enriching the powerful but about uplifting the vulnerable. Scripture reminds us that withholding assistance when we have the means to help those in need reveals a lack of God's love in our hearts. It calls for us to embrace a compassionate attitude, reflecting the divine mandate to share our blessings with those who are struggling.

True biblical generosity is about embodying God's love in action, not about fulfilling self-serving interpretations of scripture. It challenges us to move beyond surface-level giving and toward a life rooted in justice, equity, and unwavering compassion for the poor and needy. Let us return to the heart of the scriptures, focusing on uplifting the marginalized rather than distorting God's Word for personal or institutional gain.

God encourages a spirit of sharing among His people, especially when it comes to helping the less fortunate. In the New Testament, the Apostle Paul provides guidance to Timothy regarding the wealthy:

> **1 Timothy 6:17 (KJV)** "Charge them that are rich in this world, that they be not highminded, nor trust in uncertain riches, but in the living God, who giveth us richly all things to enjoy;"

> **1 Timothy 6:18 (KJV)** "that they do good, that they be rich in good works, ready to distribute, willing to communicate."

> **Matthew 10:8 (KJV)** "Heal the sick, cleanse the lepers, raise the dead, cast out devils: freely ye have received, freely give."

> **2 Corinthians 9:6 (KJV)** "But this I say, He which soweth sparingly shall reap also sparingly, and he which soweth bountifully shall reap also bountifully."

> **2 Corinthians 8:7 (KJV)** "Therefore, as ye abound in everything, in faith, and utterance, and knowledge, and in all diligence, and in your love to us, see that ye abound in this grace also."

The wealthy are called to generosity, to be ready and willing to share their blessings with those in need. This instruction is not simply an act of charity but a reflection of grace in action. The Apostle Paul, addressing the believers, urges them to excel in the grace of giving, just as they strive to excel in faith, knowledge, and other spiritual disciplines.

Scripture offers abundant teachings on how individuals and societies should approach poverty and care for the less fortunate. God's prescription for our attitudes toward the poor is clear, emphasizing compassion, justice, and a deep sense of responsibility. These principles are woven into the fabric of biblical instruction, reminding us that the treatment of the vulnerable reflects the character of a community and its adherence to divine will.

The Bible also underscores the necessity of justice and equity in addressing poverty. From the commandments given to the Israelites in Leviticus to the teachings of Jesus, the call is consistent: provisions must be made for the poor, and justice must be upheld. These teachings remind us that caring for the needy is not merely an option but a sacred responsibility, entrusted to all who seek to align their lives with God's righteousness.

> **Deuteronomy 15:7 (KJV)** "If there be among you a poor man of one of thy brethren within any of thy gates in thy land which the Lord thy God giveth thee, thou shalt not harden thine heart, nor shut thine hand from thy poor brother:"

> **Deuteronomy 15:8 (KJV** "But thou shalt open thine hand wide unto him, and shalt surely lend him sufficient for his need, in that which he wanteth."

> **Leviticus 19:15 (KJV)** "Ye shall do no unrighteousness in judgment: thou shalt not respect the person of the poor, nor honor the person of the mighty: but in righteousness shalt thou judge thy neighbor."

The imperative of impartiality and fairness in addressing the needs of both the poor and the wealthy is a foundational principle of biblical justice. God's justice transcends social status, requiring that all people, regardless of their position in society, be treated with equity and dignity. However, the glaring reality in many of today's churches reveals a troubling departure from these principles. Too often, the affluent are catered to with reverence, while the less fortunate are neglected or reduced to subjects of pity campaigns to further institutional agendas.

The Bible offers clear and unequivocal guidance on God's prescribed attitude toward the poor and needy so that we can show compassion, mercy, justice, fairness, generosity, and sharing. These

virtues are not optional but are central to a life of faith. The biblical verses referenced throughout this discussion underscore the critical truth that our actions toward the poor reflect the authenticity of our relationship with God. Faith, devoid of love for and service to the vulnerable, is hollow. Yet, in many instances, churches have prioritized wealth-building over the well-being of the downtrodden, distorting scripture to justify financial gain rather than fostering true compassion and justice.

Scripture is explicit about the moral and spiritual consequences for those who exploit or mistreat the poor. This applies not only to individuals but also to wealthy nations that, under the guise of aid, perpetuate dependency and inequality in poorer countries. The exploitation of the vulnerable is seen as a direct reproach to God, the Creator of all, and a grave moral failing. Ignoring the cries of the poor for lack of immediate personal gain risks spiritual disconnection and even the silencing of one's own cries before God in times of need.

As people of faith, the call is clear: to pursue justice and relief for the oppressed among us, not forgetting the poor, the fatherless, and the widows. This is not merely a suggestion but a divine mandate, a sacred responsibility to live out principles of mercy and compassion in our daily lives. So long as we have breath and the ability, we are charged to seek equity, challenge exploitation, and act as stewards of justice. In doing so, we reflect the character of God and fulfill the true mission of faith, one that transcends materialism and self-interest.

> **Proverbs 14:31 (KJV)** "He that oppresseth the poor reproacheth his Maker: but he that honoureth him hath mercy on the poor."

> **Proverbs 21:13 (KJV):** "Whoso stoppeth his ears at the cry of the poor, he also shall cry himself, but shall not be heard."

> **Isaiah 1:17 (KJV)** "Learn to do well; seek judgment, relieve the oppressed, judge the fatherless, plead for the widow."

The parable of the sheep and the goats in the New Testament teaches that nations will be judged based on how they treat the least among them. Neglecting to assist those in need can result in unfavorable judgment. God encourages generosity and cheerful giving, emphasizing that giving should come from the heart, not as a result of exploitation or compulsion

> **2 Corinthians 9:7 (KJV)** "Every man according as he purposeth in his heart, so let him give; not grudgingly, or of necessity: for God loveth a cheerful giver."

> **Isaiah 33:15 (KJV)** "He that walketh righteously, and speaketh uprightly; he that despiseth the gain of oppressions, that shaketh his hands from holding of bribes, that stoppeth his ears from hearing of blood, and shutteth his eyes from seeing evil."

In conclusion, scripture underscores the profound moral and spiritual consequences of exploiting the poor and vulnerable. Those who mistreat the needy are not only acting unjustly but are ultimately dishonoring their Creator. Such actions, born of greed or indifference, invite judgment and expose a failure to live in alignment with divine principles. Instead, scripture calls individuals, nations, and institutions to embody justice, fairness, and generosity, ensuring that their dealings uplift rather than oppress.

A representative, whether acting on behalf of individuals, organizations, or nations, is charged with a sacred responsibility to act with integrity and compassion. The Bible provides a timeless framework for engaging with the marginalized, calling for a heart that gives willingly, not out of compulsion or self-interest, but with genuine joy and generosity. It also emphasizes walking righteously, speaking truth, and rejecting ill-gotten gain, ensuring that every action reflects an unwavering commitment to justice and moral responsibility.

In addressing the needs of the less fortunate, the call is not merely to charity but to embody compassion, fairness, and a sense of accountability. These principles challenge us to go beyond superficial efforts, urging us to build systems and practices that restore dignity and create lasting change. Whether in governance, community leadership, or personal action, the role of a representative is to champion the cause of the oppressed and to serve as a beacon of hop, rooted in justice, generosity, and righteousness.

CHAPTER 12

THE MIGHTY EQUALIZER: A DIVINE MESSAGE FOR THE WORLD BANK?

=====================

BESE SAKA

"Sack of cola nuts"

Asante philosophical symbol of Affluence, Abundance, Unity

=====================

I n recent years, the dealings of international financial institutions, such as the World Bank, with impoverished nations have drawn sharp scrutiny, exposing troubling questions about the fairness of their financial terms and assistance. This chapter examines these issues through a biblical lens, seeking to understand how God's principles of justice, compassion, and ethical financial practices might apply to such relationships. The scriptures provide profound insights into the moral and spiritual dimensions of these interactions, challenging the prevailing practices of exploitation and imbalance.

The relationship between institutions like the World Bank and impoverished nations must evolve from one of exploitation to a genuine partnership. Too often, financial assistance is laden with high-interest loans and conditions that prioritize the interests of wealthier powers, perpetuating cycles of dependency and undermining the potential of poorer nations. These practices, cloaked in the guise of aid, fail to empower; instead, they entangle nations in debt while compromising their economic sovereignty.

Consider the loans provided for roads and infrastructure development. While the initial investment is welcome, the terms often come with strings attached, such as consultants, engineers, and project managers handpicked by the lending institutions. These foreign experts, while valuable, are frequently overpaid, their costs burdening the very nations the loans are meant to uplift. Meanwhile, local contractors and engineers who are capable and eager to engage or at least act as sub-contractors and contribute in their own small way are sidelined, losing out on opportunities for growth and technical exchange.

This model not only drains poor nations of resources but also stifles the local economy. The funds meant for development return to the lenders through inflated fees and contracts, leaving recipient countries with debt but little sustainable benefit. Instead of fostering self-reliance and economic growth, this approach entrenches inequality and weakens the foundation of long-term development.

The solution lies in reimagining these partnerships. Aid should be structured to empower local economies, with separate provisions for ongoing maintenance and development. Infrastructure projects, for instance, can include dedicated funds for local contractors, ensuring that roads and buildings remain functional while also creating jobs and fostering economic growth. Collaboration between foreign and local engineering firms should be a cornerstone of these projects, facilitating technical exchange and building the capacity of local industries.

Such an approach not only ensures the success and sustainability of development projects but also respects the dignity and potential of the recipient nations. Aid should uplift, not exploit; it should empower, not entangle. This is not just a matter of economic strategy but of moral responsibility, reflecting the principle that development must prioritize justice, fairness, and equity.

Institutions like the World Bank must recognize their role not as overlords but as partners in progress. The goal should be to create pathways for nations to thrive independently, not to trap them in perpetual debt. By fostering collaboration, investing in local capacity, and structuring aid without hidden interests, these institutions can transform their relationships with poor nations into models of equity and empowerment.

Such a shift would honor the spirit of true development, creating a future where nations are not bound by the chains of debt but lifted by the strength of collaboration, fairness, and mutual respect.

Scripture teaches us that to oppress the poor is to dishonor their Maker and that justice must never be skewed in favor of the powerful at the expense of the marginalized. Exploiting the vulnerability of impoverished nations for financial gain is not merely an economic failure but a profound moral and spiritual violation. As representatives of justice, we are called to align our practices with principles of fairness, ensuring that financial dealings uplift rather than exploit and restore dignity rather than diminish it.

The role of a donor, whether at an institutional or personal level, is to act with integrity, champion the cause of the oppressed, and promote economic systems that reflect divine justice. By examining these interactions through the lens of scripture, we are reminded that true assistance empowers, uplifts, and restores hope but not to enslaves or exploits. This is the standard to which we must hold ourselves accountable in every sphere of influence.

> **Proverbs 14:31 (KJV)** "He that oppresseth the poor reproacheth his Maker: but he that honoureth him hath mercy on the poor.
>
> **Proverbs 22:22 (KJV)** Rob not the poor, because he is poor: neither oppress the afflicted in the gate.
>
> **Leviticus 19:15 (KJV)** Ye shall do no unrighteousness in judgment: thou shalt not respect the person of the poor, nor honor the person of the mighty: but in righteousness shalt thou judge thy neighbor.

What would God say about the role of wealthy nations using international financial institutions like the World Bank to control and exploit smaller and poorer nations? Scripture provides an unambiguous answer: He demands justice, fairness, and compassion. When financial systems are designed to favor the mighty at the expense of the vulnerable, such practices are a stark violation of divine principles. The Lord's character, described as both merciful and just, warns of the consequences for those who perpetuate oppression and inequity.

The practice of offering loans or grants with skewed terms and conditions favoring one nation over another or imposing conditions that perpetuate dependency of the very people you were intending to uplift is a clear example of financial oppression. This is not assistance; it is exploitation masked as aid. Scripture calls for the oppressed to be relieved, for fairness to prevail, and for the powerful to reject unjust gains and bribes. The wealthy nations that manipulate financial systems to control poorer countries are reminded that their actions do not escape the sight of the Lord, who holds all accountable.

God's Word repeatedly stresses the responsibility of those with power and resources to use them righteously. Wealthy nations are charged to avoid arrogance and exploitation, instead using their influence to promote equity and support the less fortunate. The biblical standard for stewardship is one of accountability: the resources and power entrusted to the wealthy are not for selfish gain but to build, restore, and uplift. Failing to act justly toward the vulnerable will incur severe consequences, as the scripture vividly illustrates.

The parable of the unjust steward warns against using positions of power to exploit others, highlighting the eternal consequences of such choices. Similarly, the exhortation to the rich reminds them to place their trust not in fleeting wealth but in the living God, who commands generosity and good works. The Lord's admonition to the nations remains clear and unambiguous, reminding us to show compassion, and the act of justice and fairness are not willful but are divine mandates.

This perspective on the World Bank's dealings with impoverished nations calls for reflection on how these principles are applied today. Exploitation under the guise of aid is a reproach to God and undermines the very fabric of justice He commands. As representatives of nations or institutions, those in power must align their actions with the divine call to righteousness, ensuring that their dealings uplift rather than oppress.

In conclusion, the biblical message to those with wealth and influence is one of both opportunity and warning. The power to shape global financial practices carries a responsibility to reflect God's justice and mercy. The accountability for failing to do so is not only moral but eternal. Let the principles of compassion, fairness, and equity guide every interaction, for in doing so, we reflect the heart of God's will for humanity.

CHAPTER 13

THE MIGHTY EQUALIZER: A DIVINE MESSAGE FOR THE FALSE PROPHETS?

=====================

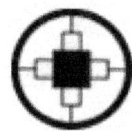

DAME-DAME

"Name of a board game"

Asante philosophical symbol of Intelligence, Ingenuity, Foresightedness, Preemption

=====================

*T*hroughout history, numerous prophets have sought to facilitate spiritual deliverance through a vast array of methods. These have ranged from the use of everyday elements like salt, water, and san, to more symbolic items such as candle, and anointing oils, and even the incorporation of practices like fasting, prayer, and retreats to sacred mountains. Despite the diversity of these approaches, the Almighty has made it known that there exists a singular, infallible path to deliverance, a path grounded not in the material or the ritualisti, but in the spiritual principle of righteousness.

The question then arises, why do some prophets stray from this divine guidance, opting instead for a multitude of other practices? The answer lies in the divine message specifically tailored for those who have turned away from the simplicity of God's command. This message underscores that true deliverance and spiritual liberation cannot be achieved through physical means or complex rituals but are found in the embrace of righteousness alone.

For those prophets who ignore this heavenly wisdom and continue to mislead others with false teachings and practices, the divine response is one of both correction and consequence. The principle of righteousness is not merely a recommendation; it is a directive from the Divine, a cornerstone of spiritual truth that cannot be overlooked without repercussion.

The divine message to false prophets is clear; They should return to the path of righteousness, for it is the only way to true deliverance. Those who persist in their deviations, leading others astray, will face divine judgment tailored to the nature of their misguidance. The punishment, though severe, is not borne of malice but of a righteous desire to realign the lost with the eternal truth.

In essence, the Almighty's message to those veering from the path is a call to simplicity and purity of faith. It is an invitation to discard the unnecessary and embrace the fundamental, to find power not in physical substances or elaborate rituals but in the profound and transformative principle of living righteously. This, according to divine wisdom, is the true essence of deliverance and spiritual fulfillment.

> **Ezekiel 14:14 (KJV)** "Though these three men, Noah, Daniel, and Job, were in it, they should deliver *but* their own souls by their righteousness, saith the Lord GOD."

> **Ezekiel 14:20 (KJV)** "Though Noah, Daniel, and Job, *were* in it, *as* I live, saith the Lord GOD, they shall deliver neither son nor daughter; they shall *but* deliver their own souls by their righteousness."

In essence, the divine guidance for combating spiritual adversity and life's challenges is remarkably straightforward. When faced with demonic influences or when things seem to be going awry in your life, the solution does not necessarily involve seeking out a prophet. Instead, the most effective remedy lies within oneself, turning away from sin, evil, and all forms of unrighteousness.

This approach is presented not just as a suggestio, but as the ultimate spiritual medicine for the soul. Embracing righteousness and rejecting paths that lead away from it is depicted as the most powerful means to repel Satan and his demonic forces. The divine message emphasizes that the key to spiritual well-being and protection lies in personal transformation and adherence to the path of righteousness.

For those who mislead others by suggesting alternatives that stray from this simple yet profound truth, the divine perspective is clear: such false prophets will face the consequences. The nature of these consequences is aligned with the divine principle of justice, serving both as a correction for the spread of misguidance and as a deterrent against further deviation from the spiritual truth.

This divine message underscores a call back to the fundamental principles of faith and righteousness, offering a clear and accessible path to spiritual liberation and protection against

malevolent forces. It highlights the importance of personal accountability and the power of individual transformation as the cornerstone of spiritual defense.

> **Daniel 4:27 (KJV)** "Wherefore, O king, let my counsel be acceptable unto thee, and break off thy sins by righteousness, and thine iniquities by shewing mercy to the poor; if it may be a lengthening of thy tranquility."

This provides additional insight into the journey towards genuine spiritual liberation, underscoring a key principle: the act of living righteously in itself does not guarantee salvation at moments of wrongdoing, just as engaging in wrongdoing does not seal one's fate if one decides to forsake their misdeeds. This concept emphasizes the fluid nature of spiritual existence, where redemption and repercussions are directly linked to the choices and actions one makes in the presen, rather than being anchored solely to one's past actions.

Furthermore, it's conveyed that a promise of life awaits those who conscientiously evaluate their behavior and opt to leave behind their wrongdoings. This promise serves as a beacon of hope, reinforcing the idea that transformation and renewal are always within reach, provided there's a willingness to turn away from past transgressions. Here's further proof of the path to true deliverance:

> **Ezekiel 18:28 (KJV)** "Because he considereth, and turneth away from all his transgressions that he hath committed, he shall surely live, he shall not die."

> **Ezekiel 33:12 (KJV)** "Therefore, thou son of man, say unto the children of thy people, The righteousness of the righteous shall not deliver him in the day of his transgression: as for the wickedness of the wicked, he shall not fall thereby in the day that he turneth from his wickedness; neither shall the righteous be able to live for his *righteousness* in the day that he sinneth."

In the role of a genuine minister of Jesus Christ, the essence of conducting deliverance lies in engaging in conversation with those seeking counsel. The primary goal of this dialogue is to identify the sins of the individual. Upon uncovering these sins, the minister is to reveal them to the person, guided by Scriptural teachings, and advise them to renounce these sins. This act of turning away from sin is presented as the authentic remedy for overcoming the troubles and afflictions they are facing.

> **Lamentations 2:14 (KJV)** "Thy prophets have seen vain and foolish things for thee: and they have not discovered thine iniquity, to turn away thy captivity; but have seen for thee false burdens and causes of banishment."

Here is Jesus Christ doing deliverance!

> **John 8:10 (KJV)** "When Jesus had lifted up himself, and saw none but the woman, he said unto her, Woman, where are those thine accusers? hath no man condemned thee?"
>
> **John 8:11 (KJV)** She said, No man, Lord. And Jesus said unto her, Neither do I condemn thee: go, and sin no more."

Here, again, is Jesus Christ doing deliverance!

> **John 4:16 (KJV)** "Jesus saith unto her, Go, call thy husband, and come hither."
>
> **John 4:17 (KJV)** "The woman answered and said, I have no husband. Jesus said unto her, Thou hast well said, I have no husband:"
>
> **John 4:18 (KJV)** "For thou hast had five husbands; and he whom thou now hast is not thy husband: in that saidst thou truly."

Here, again, is Jesus Christ doing deliverance!

> **John 5:14 (KJV)** "Afterward Jesus findeth him in the temple, and said unto him, Behold, thou art made whole: sin no more, lest a worse thing come unto thee. "

Here is Apostle Peter doing deliverance!

> **Acts 8:22 (KJV)** "Repent therefore of this thy wickedness, and pray God, if perhaps the thought of thine heart may be forgiven thee."
>
> **Acts 8:23 (KJV)** "For I perceive that thou art in the gall of bitterness, and *in* the bond of iniquity."

The LORD Jesus Christ be with your spirit. The LORD Jesus Christ give you understanding.

CHAPTER 14

THE MIGHTY EQUALIZER: A DIVINE MESSAGE FOR THE FALSE TEACHER?

===================

DENKYEM

"Crocodile"

Asante philosophical symbol of Adaptability

===================

*I*n every nation where religion is deeply woven into the fabric of society, there emerges a place of sacred nature, such as a mountain, a river, or a grove, or a forest revered as a site of spiritual cleansing, healing, or divine intervention. These places, often enshrined by tradition and folklore, become centers of pilgrimage, attracting those who seek answers to life's problems or relief from their burdens.

In Ghana, where I hail from, one such place is **Atwea** Mountain. This mountain has become a focal point for spiritual exercises, famously endorsed by a popular Church of Ghana years ago after one of its priests reportedly witnessed a miraculous light descending upon its peak. Over time, countless individuals have claimed healing and spiritual breakthroughs on the mountain, further solidifying its reputation as a sacred space.

Throughout the year, prophets and spiritual seekers flock to **Atwea** Mountain, making it a hub for diverse religious activities. Visitors from Ghana and beyond ascend their heights, hoping to encounter the divine through fasting, prayers, and prophetic ministrations. On the surface, it seems a testament to a nation's faith and devotion.

Yet, beneath this veneer of piety lies a troubling reality. **Atwea** Mountain has also become a notorious den of immorality and idolatry. Acts of fornication, adultery, theft, and deceit are rampant among those who claim to seek spiritual power. Many so-called prophet' prey upon unsuspecting congregants, swindling them out of their money under the guise of spiritual guidance. The mountain has become a marketplace, teeming with traders peddling so-called holy oils, spiritual artifacts, and other items promising divine favor.

This paradox reveals a deeper issue: the idolatry embedded in both the people and their leaders. The reverence for the mountain has, for many, supplanted true devotion to God. The mountain itself has become an idol, a place where spiritual seekers often place their trust in rituals and prophets rather than in the living God. Leaders who should guide their flock in truth and righteousness instead exploit their faith for personal gain, further entrenching the people in spiritual confusion.

The question we must confront as Christians is clear: Are such practices rooted in biblical truth? Is it a Christian requirement to ascend mountains for spiritual exercises or to seek God's power through fasting and prayer on specific peaks? Or have these traditions become veils for idolatry and distractions from genuine faith in God?

To answer these questions, we must turn to Scripture. True spiritual power comes not from geography but from an intimate relationship with the Lord. Jesus Himself declared that worship is not tied to a place but is in spirit and truth. While the Bible recounts instances of significant encounters with God on mountains, prominent religious figures lik, Moses on Sinai, Elijah on Carmel, and Jesus at the Mount of Transfiguration. These moments were not about the mountains themselves but about God's sovereign presence and purpose.

The danger lies in elevating the mountain, the ritual, or the prophet above God. Such misplaced faith becomes idolatry, diverting believers from the pure worship and obedience that God desires. Leaders, too, must examine their motives, ensuring that they do not exploit the sacred for personal gain or lead others into spiritual error.

Let us approach this matter with discernment and humility, searching the Scriptures to align our faith and practice with God's Word. True spiritual renewal does not require a specific place but a heart fully surrendered to God, seeking Him with sincerity and truth. As we examine this topic, may we be reminded that God is not confined to mountains or rituals but is near to all who call upon Him in faith.

Prophet Elijah went to the mountain, and God spoke with him there:

> **1 Kings 19:9 (KJV)** "And he came thither unto a cave, and lodged there; and, behold, the word of the LORD *came* to him, and he said unto him, What doest thou here, Elijah?"

> **1 Kings 19:10 (KJV)** "And he said, I have been very jealous for the LORD God of hosts: for the children of Israel have forsaken thy covenant, thrown down thine altars, and slain thy prophets with the sword; and I, *even* I only, am left; and they seek my life, to take it away."

> **1 Kings 19:11 (KJV)** "And he said, Go forth, and stand upon the mount before the LORD. And, behold, the LORD passed by, and a great and strong wind rent the mountains, and brake in pieces the rocks before the LORD; *but* the LORD *was* not in the wind: and after the wind an earthquake; *but* the LORD *was* not in the earthquake:"

> **1 Kings 19:12 (KJV)** "And after the earthquake a fire; *but* the LORD *was* not in the fire: and after the fire a still small voice."

We find a second reference to the Man of God going to the top of the mountain:

> **2 Kings 1:8 (KJV)** "And they answered him, *He was* an hairy man, and girt with a girdle of leather about his loins. And he said, It *is* Elijah the Tishbite."

> **2 Kings 1:9 (KJV)** "Then the king sent unto him a captain of fifty with his fifty. And he went up to him: and, behold, he sat on the top of an hill. And he spake unto him, Thou man of God, the king hath said, Come down."

In a third reference, we find that the people who love to go to the mountains to fast and pray point to the LORD Jesus Christ as justification for them also going to the mountains:

> **Matthew 4:1 (KJV)** "Then was Jesus led up of the Spirit into the wilderness to be tempted of the devil."

> **Mark 1:13 (KJV)** "And he was there in the wilderness forty days, tempted of Satan; and was with the wild beasts; and the angels ministered unto him."

> **Mark 9:2 (KJV)** "And after six days Jesus taketh *with him* Peter, and James, and John, and leadeth them up into an high mountain apart by themselves: and he was transfigured before them."

In spite of the above references, what we find in the Scriptures of Truth is contrary to what many so-called Christians do today, being led by the Devil! The truth is that you do not go to the mountain for any spiritual cleansing, power, healing, or anything! The mountain top has zero spiritual significance for your spiritual growth, seeing that it is rather the Scriptures that ensure our spiritual growth and not any mountain top experience!

> **Acts 20:32 (KJV)** "And now, brethren, I commend you to God, and to the word of his grace, which is able to build you up, and to give you an inheritance among all them which are sanctified."

> **Colossians 3:16 (KJV)** "Let the word of Christ dwell in you richly in all wisdom; teaching and admonishing one another in psalms and hymns and spiritual songs, singing with grace in your hearts to the Lord."

> **Hebrews 5:14 (KJV)** "But strong meat belongeth to them that are of full age, *even* those who by reason of use have their senses exercised to discern both good and evil."

> **James 1:21 (KJV)** "Wherefore lay apart all filthiness and superfluity of naughtiness, and receive with meekness the engrafted word, which is able to save your souls."

> **1 Peter 2:2 (KJV)** "As newborn babes, desire the sincere milk of the word, that ye may grow thereby:"

Secondly, throughout Scripture, we see that true men of God ascended mountains *after* they were filled with the Spirit of God, not as a means to receive power. The notion that spiritual power is obtained by simply going to a mountain is not rooted in biblical truth but rather a distortion that can mislead believers. It is a dangerous and deceptive doctrine, one that diverts faith from God Himself and instead places it in rituals or locations.

Let us now turn to the Scriptures to discern the truth: Did the true men of God receive power on the mountaintop, or were they already empowered by the Spirit before they went? By examining these examples, we will uncover the biblical foundation for understanding the relationship between divine power, spiritual encounters, and its significance or lack thereof of those physical places.

1. Here we see Abraham, the man of God, receiving the promise of salvation and divine covenant while in the valley and the plain, *before* ever ascending to the mountain top. This demonstrates that his encounter with God's power and purpose was not dependent on the height of the mountain but on his faith and obedience to the Lord.

   > **Genesis 15:6 (KJV)** "And he believed in the LORD; and he counted it to him for righteousness."

Genesis 22:2 (KJV) "And he said, Take now thy son, thine only *son* Isaac, whom thou lovest, and get thee into the land of Moriah; and offer him there for a burnt offering upon one of the mountains which I will tell thee of

Romans 4:3 (KJV) "For what saith the scripture? Abraham believed God, and it was counted unto him for righteousness."

James 2:23 (KJV) "And the scripture was fulfilled which saith, Abraham believed God, and it was imputed unto him for righteousness: and he was called the Friend of God."

2. Here is Moses, the man of God, receiving the empowerment of the Holy Spirit in the valley and the plain before ascending to the mountain top. His divine calling and spiritual equipping occurred through his obedience and relationship with God, not through the physical act of climbing a mountain:

Exodus 4:14 (KJV) "And the anger of the LORD was kindled against Moses, and he said, *Is* not Aaron the Levite thy brother? I know that he can speak well. And also, behold, he cometh forth to meet thee: and when he seeth thee, he will be glad in his heart."

Exodus 4:15 (KJV) "And thou shalt speak unto him, and put words in his mouth: and I will be with thy mouth, and with his mouth, and will teach you what ye shall do."

Exodus 4:16 (KJV) "And he shall be thy spokesman unto the people: and he shall be, *even* he shall be to thee instead of a mouth, and thou shalt be to him instead of God."

Exodus 4:17 (KJV) "And thou shalt take this rod in thine hand, wherewith thou shalt do signs."

Exodus 17:10 (KJV) "So Joshua did as Moses had said to him, and fought with Amalek: and Moses, Aaron, and Hur went up to the top of the hill."

Exodus 24:18 (KJV) "And Moses went into the midst of the cloud, and gat him up into the mount: and Moses was in the mount forty days and forty nights."

3. Here is Samson, the man of God, receiving the power of the Holy Spirit even in the valley of his mother's wom, before he ever ascended to the mountaintop. His strength and purpose were ordained by God from the very beginning, emphasizing that divine empowerment does not depend on a physical location but on God's sovereign will:

Judges 13:2 (KJV) "And there was a certain man of Zorah, of the family of the Danites, whose name *was* Manoah; and his wife *was* barren, and bare not."

Judges 13:3 (KJV) "And the angel of the LORD appeared unto the woman, and said unto her, Behold now, thou *art* barren, and bearest not: but thou shalt conceive, and bear a son."

Judges 13:4 (KJV) "Now therefore beware, I pray thee, and drink not wine nor strong drink, and eat not any unclean *thing*:"

Judges 13:5 (KJV) "For, lo, thou shalt conceive, and bear a son; and no rasor shall come on his head: for the child shall be a Nazarite unto God from the womb: and he shall begin to deliver Israel out of the hand of the Philistines."

Judges 15:7 (KJV) "And Samson said unto them, Though ye have done this, yet will I be avenged of you, and after that I will cease."

Judges 15:8 (KJV) "And he smote them hip and thigh with a great slaughter: and he went down and dwelt in the top of the rock Etam."

Judges 16:3 (KJV) "And Samson lay till midnight, and arose at midnight, and took the doors of the gate of the city, and the two posts, and went away with them, bar and all, and put *them* upon his shoulders, and carried them up to the top of an hill that *is* before Hebron."

4. Here is David, the man of God, receiving the power of the Holy Spirit in the valley and the plain before he ever ascended to the mountain top. His anointing and divine strength were granted through his relationship with God, illustrating that true spiritual empowerment comes from God's presence, not the elevation of a physical place:

1 Samuel 16:11 (KJV) "And Samuel said unto Jesse, Are here all *thy* children? And he said, There remaineth yet the youngest, and, behold, he keepeth the sheep. And Samuel said unto Jesse, Send and fetch him: for we will not sit down till he come hither."

1 Samuel 16:12 (KJV) "And he sent, and brought him in. Now he *was* ruddy, *and* withal of a beautiful countenance, and goodly to look to. And the LORD said, Arise, anoint him: for this *is* he."

1 Samuel 16:13 (KJV) "Then Samuel took the horn of oil, and anointed him in the midst of his brethren: and the Spirit of the LORD came upon David from that day forward. So Samuel rose up, and went to Ramah."

Psalm 121:1 (KJV) "A Song of degrees. I will lift up mine eyes unto the hills, from whence cometh my help."

5. Here is Isaiah, the Man of God receiving the power of the Holy Spirit in the valley and in the plain before he went to do the work of God:

Isaiah 6:1 (KJV) "In the year that king Uzziah died I saw also the Lord sitting upon a throne, high and lifted up, and his train filled the temple."

Isaiah 6:2 (KJV) "Above it stood the seraphims: each one had six wings; with twain he covered his face, and with twain he covered his feet, and with twain he did fly."

Isaiah 6:3 (KJV) "And one cried unto another, and said, Holy, holy, holy, *is* the LORD of hosts: the whole earth *is* full of his glory."

Isaiah 6:4 (KJV) "And the posts of the door moved at the voice of him that cried, and the house was filled with smoke."

Isaiah 6:5 (KJV) "Then said I, Woe *is* me! for I am undone; because I *am* a man of unclean lips, and I dwell in the midst of a people of unclean lips: for mine eyes have seen the King, the LORD of hosts."

Isaiah 6:6 (KJV) "Then flew one of the seraphims unto me, having a live coal in his hand, *which* he had taken with the tongs from off the altar:"

Isaiah 6:7 (KJV) "And he laid *it* upon my mouth, and said, Lo, this hath touched thy lips; and thine iniquity is taken away, and thy sin purged."

Isaiah 6:8 (KJV) "Also I heard the voice of the Lord, saying, Whom shall I send, and who will go for us? Then said I, Here *am* I; send me."

Isaiah 6:9 (KJV) "And he said, Go, and tell this people, Hear ye indeed, but understand not; and see ye indeed, but perceive not."

6. Here is Ezekiel, the man of God, receiving the power of the Holy Spirit in the valley and the plain before embarking on the work of God. His divine commissioning and spiritual empowerment came through God's presence and calling, demonstrating that true strength for ministry is granted by God Himself, not tied to any specific location:

Ezekiel 3:22 (KJV) "And the hand of the LORD was there upon me; and he said unto me, Arise, go forth into the plain, and I will there talk with thee."

Ezekiel 3:23 (KJV) "Then I arose, and went forth into the plain: and, behold, the glory of the LORD stood there, as the glory which I saw by the river of Chebar: and I fell on my face."

Ezekiel 3:24 (KJV) "Then the spirit entered into me, and set me upon my feet, and spake with me, and said unto me, Go, shut thyself within thine house."

7. Here is Jesus Christ, the Son of God who is fully human and fully divine, receiving the power of the Holy Spirit in the valley and the plain before beginning His ministry and the work of God. Though He was entirely God in nature, as a man, He had to receive the Holy Spirit before embarking on His earthly mission. His divine anointing came through the Spirit's descent upon Him at His baptism, affirming that true empowerment for God's work is granted by the Father, independent of any physical elevation or location.

Matthew 3:13 (KJV) "Then cometh Jesus from Galilee to Jordan unto John, to be baptized of him."

Matthew 3:14 (KJV) "But John forbad him, saying, I have need to be baptized of thee, and comest thou to me?"

Matthew 3:15 (KJV) "And Jesus answering said unto him, Suffer *it to be so* now: for thus it becometh us to fulfil all righteousness. Then he suffered him."

Matthew 3:16 (KJV) "And Jesus, when he was baptized, went up straightway out of the water: and, lo, the heavens were opened unto him, and he saw the Spirit of God descending like a dove, and lighting upon him:"

Matthew 3:17 (KJV) "And lo a voice from heaven, saying, This is my beloved Son, in whom I am well pleased."

Matthew 4:1 (KJV) "Then was Jesus led up of the Spirit into the wilderness to be tempted of the devil."

Matthew 4:8 (KJV) "Again, the devil taketh him up into an exceeding high mountain, and sheweth him all the kingdoms of the world, and the glory of them;"! Thus, in seven distinct instances drawn from the Scripture of Truth, the Scriptures demonstrate that the true purpose of ascending a mountain is not to obtain spiritual power, healing, or divine favor, but rather to seek seclusion from distractions in order to pray and focus on God. Any teaching that portrays mountain ascents as a means to access special spiritual cleansing, power, or breakthroughs is a deception, not rooted in God's will. Such practices misdirect believers from the truth of God's Word and align more closely with the cunning devices of the enemy rather than the divine plan of God!

John 4:19 (KJV) "The woman saith unto him, Sir, I perceive that thou art a prophet

John 4:20 (KJV) "Our fathers worshipped in this mountain; and ye say, that in Jerusalem is the place where men ought to worship."

John 4:21 (KJV) "Jesus saith unto her, Woman, believe me, the hour cometh, when ye shall neither in this mountain, nor yet at Jerusalem, worship the Father."

John 4:22 (KJV) "Ye worship ye know not what: we know what we worship: for salvation is of the Jews."

John 4:23 (KJV) "But the hour cometh, and now is, when the true worshippers shall worship the Father in spirit and in truth: for the Father seeketh such to worship him."

John 4:24 (KJV) "God *is* a Spirit: and they that worship him must worship *him* in spirit and in truth."

The truth, as we have demonstrated in this Bible Study, is that the power of salvation and the Holy Spirit is received through faith and obedience to God, not through physical locations such as mountain tops. While some may feel drawn to specific places for prayer or reflection, Jesus Christ clearly teaches that worship is not bound to any physical site but is rooted in spirit and truth. His words remind us that true communion with God is not dependent on geography but on the condition of our hearts.

In *John 4:19-2*, Jesus explained that the time had come when worship would no longer be tied to mountains or temples but would be a direct and personal connection with the Father. This profound teaching invites us to worship God wherever we are, with sincerity and in alignment with His Spirit. Pursuing spiritual power or connection through specific physical locations risks misunderstanding the very nature of God and His accessibility to all who seek Him in faith."

Churches and leaders must reflect on these teachings. Organizing pilgrimages to mountains or sites for spiritual cleansing, renewal of anointing, or Holy Ghost baptism can inadvertently shift focus away from the personal relationship with God that Jesus emphasized. It is crucial to remember that God is not confined to places; His presence is with those who seek Him earnestly, no matter where they are.

Rather than being tied to rituals or locations, our faith calls us to obedience, humility, and truth. The call to worship God in spirit and truth is universal, transcending physical boundaries and focusing on the transformative power of a genuine relationship with Him. Let us align our worship and practices with the teachings of Christ, ensuring that our faith remains pure and grounded in His Word.

The LORD Jesus Christ be with your spirit. The LORD Jesus Christ give you understanding.

CHAPTER 15

THE MIGHTY EQUALIZER: A DIVINE MESSAGE FOR ALL YOUR LIES AGAINST THE HOLY SPRIT?

========================

DUAFE

"Wooden comb"

Asante philosophical symbol of Beauty, Hygiene, Feminine Qualities

========================

*I*t is essential to understand that one who is deeply learned in the Word of God, the Bible, holds a position of spiritual clarity and authority that surpasses one who merely hears voices from uncertain sources. The Scriptures repeatedly affirm that God works with those who diligently study and apply His Word, rather than relying solely on unverified spiritual experiences. These same verses demonstrate that salvation is not a passive event but a learned and intentional spiritual journey.

Furthermore, the path to Heaven requires knowledge and understanding of God, rooted in the truths of His Word. Any voice or message you may hear, no matter how holy it may seem to you or me, must align first with the written Word of God, the Bible. If what you hear does not receive the final approval of Scripture, it cannot be from God.

Let us now turn to the following verses to confirm this doctrine and reaffirm the authority of the Word of God as the ultimate standard of truth and guidance.

Psalm 119:7 (KJV) "I will praise thee with uprightness of heart, when I shall have learned thy righteous judgments."

Isaiah 29:11 (KJV) "And the vision of all is become unto you as the words of a book that is sealed, which *men* deliver to one that is learned, saying, Read this, I pray thee: and he saith, I cannot; for it *is* sealed:"

Isaiah 29:12 (KJV) "And the book is delivered to him that is not learned, saying, Read this, I pray thee: and he saith, I am not learned."

Isaiah 50:4 (KJV) "The Lord GOD hath given me the tongue of the learned, that I should know how to speak a word in season to *him that is* weary: he wakeneth morning by morning, he wakeneth mine ear to hear as the learned."

Isaiah 50:5 (KJV) "The Lord GOD hath opened mine ear, and I was not rebellious, neither turned away back."

John 6:45 (KJV) "It is written in the prophets, And they shall be all taught of God. Every man therefore that hath heard, and hath learned of the Father, cometh unto me."

Acts 7:22 (KJV) "And Moses was learned in all the wisdom of the Egyptians, and was mighty in words and in deeds."

Romans 16:17 (KJV) "Now I beseech you, brethren, mark them which cause divisions and offences contrary to the doctrine which ye have learned; and avoid them."

Philippians 4:9 (KJV) "Those things, which ye have both learned, and received, and heard, and seen in me, do: and the God of peace shall be with you."

In concluding our teaching, it becomes clear that our faith is deeply rooted in the power of the Holy Spirit and the truth of God's Word. The Word of God stands as the ultimate source of guidance, teaching us His righteous judgments and calling us to align every aspect of our lives with His truth. Through it, we find the path to salvation, spiritual growth, and the discernment needed to navigate a world filled with conflicting voices.

The Holy Spirit, working through the Word, sustains and empowers us in our journey of faith. It is through the Spirit that we are taught by God Himself, opening our hearts to His wisdom and enabling us to live according to His righteous principles. This divine teaching is not merely informational; it is transformational, shaping us into vessels of truth and righteousness.

The Word of God reveals that the ability to lead a life pleasing to Him flows from our willingness to be taught and molded by His Spirit. It equips us to speak words in season to the weary, to discern truth from error, and to walk steadfastly in His ways. Those who submit themselves to this divine teaching grow in wisdom and might, just as those in Scripture who were both instructed by God and used mightily for His purposes.

Yet, this journey requires vigilance. We are warned against straying from the truth, reminded to hold fast to the teachings we have learned and received, and to avoid influences that lead us away from the Word. To walk in the Spirit is to remain rooted in the Word, practice what we have been taught, and live as examples of God's transformative power.

The Holy Spirit, through the Word, calls us to a life of obedience, integrity, and unwavering trust in God's righteous plan. It is through this divine sustenance that we find the strength to persevere, the wisdom to act justly, and the grace to embody the light of Christ in a world that desperately needs it.

As we reflect on these truths, let us renew our commitment to learning from the Spirit through His Word, allowing it to shape our hearts and guide our steps. For in doing so, we align ourselves with the ultimate source of power and sustenance, living lives that glorify God and testify to His boundless love and truth.

Let this be a solemn reminder that the Holy Spirit works in harmony with the written Word of God. Any voice, teaching, or practice that deviates from Scripture cannot claim divine authority. To lie against the Holy Spirit is to reject the truth of God's Word and to oppose His righteous judgments. Instead, let us submit ourselves to the Almighty, the Holy Spirit, who leads us into all truth, convicts us of error, and empowers us to walk in the light of God's wisdom.

May we leave this teaching with a renewed commitment to learn, receive, and live out the righteous judgments of God, allowing His Spirit to transform our lives into reflections of His truth and glory.

CHAPTER 16

THE MIGHTY EQUALIZER: A DIVINE MESSAGE FOR THE CORRUPT JUDGE AND LAWYERS?

========================

DWENNIMMEN

"Ram's horns"

Asante philosophical symbol of Humility and Strength in Mind, Body, and Soul

========================

What will the Lord God say to those judges, lawyers, and legal practitioners who have turned the scales of justice into instruments of oppression, favoring the wealthy and powerful while leaving the poor to suffer? In a world where the legal system is meant to uphold fairness, equality, and righteousness, we are often confronted with a painful reality. A system designed to be so expensive and inaccessible that only the rich can navigate its complexities, while the poor are left to bear the brunt of its failures.

To those who established these unjust systems and to those who enforced them without seeking reform, what answer will you give when you stand before the Judge of all creation? What will God say to those who accept bribes, manipulate outcomes, and exploit their roles for personal gain? Through biased judgments, wrongful convictions, and unjust sentences, you inflict grievous harm upon your neighbors, wielding the law not as a shield for the vulnerable but as a weapon against them.

The cost of justice has been set so high that it effectively excludes the poor, leaving them defenseless against the machinery of power. Meanwhile, the wealthy buy their way out of accountability, escaping the consequences of their evil deeds with ease. In your blatant disregard for fairness, you have knowingly perpetuated a system that widens the gap between rich and poor, corrupting the very foundation of justice.

The Bible is clear in its condemnation of such practices. It speaks of the responsibility of those in authority to uphold justice with integrity and to defend the rights of the oppressed. "Woe to those who acquit the guilty for a bribe, but deny justice to the innocent." The cries of the poor, wrongfully convicted, and unjustly treated rise to the ears of God, and He will not remain silent.

To those who profit from this broken system, your actions are not hidden from the Lord. The day will come when you will stand before the Righteous Judge who cannot be bribed, whose scales are perfectly balanced, and whose judgments are final. What excuse will you offer then for the lives ruined, the families shattered, and the justice denied?

This is a call to those in the legal profession, to those who legislate, and to those who enforce the law: reform the system you serve. Seek to make justice accessible, fair, and equitable for all. Advocate for the rights of the poor, defend the defenseless, and ensure that the law becomes a true reflection of divine principles and righteousness over greed, compassion over wickedness, and impartiality.

Let this be a warning and a challenge. The Lord God will hold accountable all who wield power unjustly, but He will also bless those who work to restore fairness and equity. Stand on the side of justice, not corruption, for it is through integrity and righteousness that true justice prevails.

What will the Lord God say to those judges and lawyers who have, through their actions, inflicted grievous harm upon their neighbors by manipulating the legal system for the benefit of the wealthy and powerful? This harm encompasses wrongful convictions, unjust sentences, and biased judgments that favor the privileged few.

In our world, where the scales of justice are meant to balance fairly, we often witness a painful reality: the actions of corrupt judges and lawyers causing grievous injuries to our neighbors. This chapter explores the profound question: What will the Lord God say to these lawyers and judges who accept bribes and other inducements to deliver favorable legal outcomes that favor the wealthy at the expense of the less fortunate?

Your blatant disregard for due legal proces, knowingly exploits a system that is beyond the means of the common person to navigate. You make the system so expensive that the poor person is left in the cold. They wield their positions for personal gain, unfairly leveraging their roles within the legal profession.

The Bible is replete with wisdom that emphasizes the principles of justice, righteousness, and the duty of those in positions of authority to uphold the law without bias.

In a recent case of injustice, a suspect in a murder trial was remanded in prison for nearly a decade without sufficient evidence to convict or even properly prosecute. Despite the long years of detention, the authorities failed to establish a case, yet the individual remained deprived of liberty, caught in a web of legal manipulation and power abuse.

What will the Lord God say to the prosecutor, the judge, or the law enforcers who bring dubious charges against people without evidence? How will He judge those who misuse the authority entrusted to them by the people, wielding it as an instrument of oppression rather than justice? The Scriptures declare that the Almighty abhors falsehood and injustice:

> **Isaiah 10:1 (KJV):** "Woe unto them that decree unrighteous decrees,
> and that write grievousness which they have prescribed;"

The Lord, the righteous Judge, will not turn a blind eye to the cries of the innocent who suffer under corrupt rulings. Those who pervert justice for personal gain or out of malice will one day stand before the divine courtroom, where no bribes, influence, or manipulation will prevail. The question remains: when the scales of divine justice tip against the oppressor, who will intercede for them?

> **Proverbs 31:9 (KJV)** "Open thy mouth for the dumb in the cause
> of all such as are appointed to destruction."
>
> **Proverbs 31-9 (KJV)** "Open thy mouth, judge righteously, and
> plead the cause of the poor and needy."

The Scriptures serve as our unwavering guide to the divine mandate for justice, shedding light on the plight of the vulnerable and impoverished within flawed legal systems. They call into question the ethical stance of legal professionals who manipulate the system to coerce the underprivileged into admitting guilt for crimes they did not commit, a practice that epitomizes a profound disregard for justice and equity.

Particularly troubling is the tendency of wealthy and powerful nations, which often champion individual freedoms, to sustain legal systems that are more focused on securing convictions than pursuing true justice. These systems frequently evade accountability, masking wrongful convictions and disproportionately impacting the less fortunate, especially marginalized groups. Wealthier individuals exploit their resources to secure favorable legal outcomes, while those with fewer means, including minorities, are left vulnerable to systemic bias and exploitation, increasing the likelihood of wrongful convictions.

Alarmingly, some individuals perpetuating these injustices, including those who publicly profess Christian faith, do so with ulterior motives. Whether driven by political ambition or the desire to enhance conviction records as a display of toughness on crime, their actions betray the fundamental principles of justice and mercy central to their faith.

The notion of "free" legal aid, heralded as a safeguard for the disadvantaged, often results in substandard representation, forcing defendants into plea bargains regardless of their innocence. This systemic flaw perpetuates a cycle of injustice, disproportionately punishing those unable to afford quality legal defense. Such practices raise serious ethical concerns, compelling us to reflect on the integrity of these systems and the divine judgment that may await those who facilitate or enable such injustices.

For those who claim to follow the teachings of Christ, this betrayal of justice is especially stark. The biblical mandate is clear: justice must not favor the wealthy, nor should the rights of the poor and marginalized be neglected. Scriptures consistently emphasize fairness, equity, and compassion in all dealings, and they condemn those who exploit their positions to perpetuate oppression.

This reflection compels legal professionals, policymakers, and all who participate in these systems to reevaluate their practices. It is not enough to operate within the rules if the rules themselves are unjust. True justice demands accountability, equity, and a commitment to the well-being of all, particularly the vulnerable. The Scriptures challenge us to rise above political ambition and self-interest to embody the principles of fairness, mercy, and truth in every facet of our lives and professions.

In light of these truths, let us consider the weight of our actions and the systems we sustain. What answer will we give to the Righteous Judge when asked how we upheld His command for justice? The time for reflection, reform, and repentance is now, for only in aligning our systems with the divine standard can we truly embody the justice and fairness God demands of us.

> **Isaiah 1:23 (KJV):** "Thy princes are rebellious, and companions of thieves: every one loveth gifts, and followeth after rewards: they judge not the fatherless, neither doth the cause of the widow come unto them,"

> **Proverbs 29:7 (KJV):** "The righteous considereth the cause of the poor: but the wicked regardeth not to know it."

> **Amos 5:12 (KJV):** "For I know your manifold transgressions and your mighty sins: they afflict the just, they take a bribe, and they turn aside the poor in the gate from their right."

> **Jeremiah 22:17 (KJV):** "But thine eyes and thine heart are not but for thy covetousness, and for to shed innocent blood, and for oppression, and for violence, to do it."

The legal system frequently results in wrongful convictions and sentences that favor the wealthy, undermining the societal structure. This analysis reveals the difficulties faced by those wrongfully convicted, who encounter harsh probation conditions and potential exploitation by law enforcement

upon reentering society. This situation indicates a justice system more oriented towards punishment than rehabilitation, disproportionately affecting the poor and vulnerable.

Correcting these judicial mistakes is often difficult and expensive, with avenues for appeal largely available to the wealthy. The critique points to a prison industry that views inmates as financial assets rather than human beings.

Biblical teachings warn of divine judgment on those who maintain and support this corrupt system, indicating a severe discrepancy between their actions and the biblical calls for justice and mercy. The question arises: what would the Lord God say to legal professionals who mislead and coerce the innocent, contributing to a system rife with injustice and inequality? This situation illustrates the extensive damage caused by a legal system that neglects fairness and favors the powerful, prompting a deeper examination of its impact on individuals and society.

In this vein, biblical prophecy warns of divine condemnation for those who sustain and advocate for this flawed system. Such individual, who contravene the biblical imperatives of justice and mercy are likely to incur the wrath of God, highlighting the profound disconnect between their actions and the scriptural values of equity and compassion.

These words remind us of the divine call to ensure justice, particularly for those who are vulnerable and oppressed.

What will the Lord God say to these lawyers and judges who offer false counsel, leading individuals to plead guilty to crimes they did not commit due to a lack of concern for justice and fairness?

Corruption within the legal system manifests in various forms, causing immense harm to the fabric of society. It leads to wrongful convictions, unfair sentences, and judgments skewed in favor of the rich and powerful. This chapter delves deeper into the consequences of such actions, exploring how they disrupt lives and communities.

> **2 Chronicles 19:7(KJV)** "Wherefore now let the fear of the Lord be upon you; take heed and do it: for there is no iniquity with the Lord our God, nor respect of persons, nor taking of gifts."

This scripture serves as a profound reminder that justice must always remain paramount, especially with a focus on protecting the vulnerable members of society. It challenges us to uphold a higher standard of accountability and fairness, emphasizing the timeless wisdom of the Bible: to defend the weak, act with integrity, and strive for a society where justice truly prevails.

What will the Lord God say to the lawyers and judges who accept bribes and inducements, twisting legal outcomes to favor the wealthy while neglecting the rights of the less fortunate? What will He say to those who, through kickbacks and corruption, render the legal system inaccessible to those who need it most?

Consider the plight of those who seek justice but are denied due to the greed and manipulation of others. A friend of mine, whose intellectual property rights were violated, cannot secure legal representation because law firms claim conflicts of interest, which reminds me that they have bought all the best lawyers in town by having been retained or influenced by unscrupulous entities that exploit the rights of others. This reflects a system where justice is not blind but for sale, leaving the vulnerable abandoned and without recourse.

The Lord God's Word is clear: those in positions of authority are called to uphold justice, not to exploit it. To accept bribes, to make the law a tool of oppression rather than equity, is to betray the very principles that underpin righteous governance. These actions not only harm individuals but also erode the moral fabric of society, replacing fairness with favoritism and justice with inequity.

This is a call for reflection and reform. Lawyers, judges, and all who wield influence in the legal system must remember that their ultimate accountability is to the Creator, whose judgment is impartial and just. The defense of the vulnerable is not just a legal duty but a divine mandate, one that demands integrity, compassion, and unwavering commitment to truth.

Let us, therefore, seek to rebuild trust in our legal systems, ensuring they reflect the principles of equity and justice that God commands.In the end, it is not wealth, power, or influence that matters; it is the righteousness and fairness with which we conduct our lives and fulfill our responsibilities.

The LORD Jesus Christ be with your spirit. The LORD Jesus Christ give you understanding.

CHAPTER 17

THE MIGHTY EQUALIZER: A DIVINE MESSAGE FOR THE CORRUPT SCHOOL ADMINSTRATOR?

========================

EBAN

"Fence"

Asante philosophical symbol of Love, Safety, Security

========================

Education plays a critical role in shaping the intellect, character, and moral foundation of individuals. Scripture calls us to *"study to show ourselves approved,"* emphasizing that the pursuit of knowledge is fundamental to personal development and should align with divine wisdom. The proper nurturing of the mind begins with structured learning, especially in childhood, where foundational principles are laid. As scripture admonishes, we are to *"train up a child in the way they should go, so that when they grow old, they will not depart from it."* This sacred responsibility places educators, policymakers, and boards of education in a position of immense influence and accountability.

The curriculum and teaching materials must reflect not only intellectual rigor but also moral clarity, grounded in the wisdom and knowledge of God. Any deviation from this purpose and any attempt through indoctrination or the propagation of ideologies that conflict with parental guidance and ethical principles can constitute a grave betrayal of trust. Those who mislead or corrupt the young, replacing truth with confusion, will ultimately answer to the Lord Almighty, who holds the welfare of children in high regard. The warning is severe: to lead a child astray, to tarnish their understanding of truth, or to compromise their moral foundation is an offense of the highest order. The judgment for such actions will be swift and unrelenting, for the Lord's heart is deeply moved by the welfare of the young. To harm or misguide them is to invite consequences far graver than any earthly punishment. Those entrusted with shaping young minds must uphold their duty with integrity, knowing that their stewardship carries eternal implications.

> **Matthew 18:6 (KJV)** "But whoso shall offend one of these little ones which believe in me, it were better for him that a millstone were hanged about his neck, and that he were drowned in the depth of the sea."

In today's world, education stands as a beacon of hope and opportunity, yet it is increasingly endangered by practices that compromise its sacred purpose. Corrupt administrators and educators who divert resources from teaching and learning, forsake moral values, or foster unethical agendas endanger not only the future of students but also the moral integrity of society itself. The alarming rise of initiatives encouraging children to question and redefine their identities at a tender age, often without parental consent and under the guise of human rights, exemplifies this deviation. Such actions distort the true purpose of education, sowing confusion rather than cultivating wisdom and understanding.

What will the Lord say to the school administrator who prioritizes personal political gain, the teacher who fosters immorality, or the policymaker who sacrifices the well-being of children for ideological pursuits? The judgment for leading the young astray will be swift and severe. To betray the trust inherent in the role of an educator by indoctrinating rather than educatin, and by promoting confusion under the banner of progres, is to abandon the noble calling of shaping young minds with truth and righteousness.

The ripple effects of such corruption extend far beyond the classroom. Normalizing unethical behaviors and values in the educational system risks creating a generation that carries these flaws into adulthood, influencing society in destructive ways. Education is not merely about imparting knowledge; it is about instilling values, nurturing character, and aligning young minds with principles that honor God and serve humanity.

Let this be a clarion call to all who are entrusted with the sacred duty of educating the next generation. Uphold the principles of truth, morality, and excellence. Teach not merely to inform but to transform and guide our future leaders toward a future of integrity, wisdom, and purpose. Remember, shaping young minds is an eternal responsibility, for every child is precious in the sight of God. Those who fail this trust will not escape the accountability of the Almighty.

Proverbs 1:8 (KJV) "My son, hear the instruction of thy father, and forsake not the law of thy mother:"

Proverbs 1:9 (KJV) "For they shall be an ornament of grace unto thy head, and chains about thy neck."

Proverbs 22:6 (KJV) "Train up a child in the way he should go: and when he is old, he will not depart from it."

Parents entrust their children to schools with the expectation that the time spent away from home will be in a safe, nurturing, and morally upright environment. This trust is profound, as children spend significant portions of their day with educators or teachers who are, in essence, strangers to the family. Would you knowingly hand over your child to someone unworthy of that trust? Certainly not. Parents must have confidence that the people influencing their children during their absence uphold the highest standards of integrity and care.

The responsibility placed on educators is immense. They are not merely tasked with teaching academic lessons but are also charged with shaping the moral and ethical development of the children in their care. Scripture highlights the critical role parents play in raising their children, emphasizing discipline, guidance, and moral grounding. Yet, this role extends into the classroom, where teachers and administrators must uphold the same principles of justice, honesty, and integrity that parents strive to instill at home. Schools should be sanctuaries of learning and growth, free from corruption and influences that compromise a child's well-being.

What message does the Lord have for those in the educational system who betray this sacred trust? To corrupt school administrators and teachers who manipulate children against their parent's upbringing and encourage children to question disciplinary actions taken at home or position of parents as antagonists. Such actions erode the family structure and undermine parental authority, sowing seeds of discord and rebellion. Scripture affirms the importance of discipline in upbringin, and those who seek to invert this divine order invite judgment.

Proverbs 22:6 (KJV) "Train up a child in the way he should go: and when he is old, he will not depart from it."

Proverbs 13:24 (KJV) "He that spareth his rod hateth his son: but he that loveth him chasteneth him betimes."

Proverbs 22:15 (KJV) "Foolishness is bound in the heart of a child; but the rod of correction shall drive it far from him."

Proverbs 23:13-14 (KJV) "Withhold not correction from the child: for if thou beatest him with the rod, he shall not die"

Proverbs 23:14 (KJV) "Thou shalt beat him with the rod, and shalt deliver his soul from hell."

The growing trend of branding opportunities for the less privileged as "undeserved" while favoring the wealthy and well-connected is a direct assault on the principles of fairness and justice. When institutions of learning or positions of influence impose disproportionately high standards to exclude those from disadvantaged backgrounds and labeling and dismissing such opportunities as unequal or unmerited given to those who actually earned them in their own struggles of limited resources, betray their core mission.

This practice does not merely deny deserving individuals access to education and leadership roles; it erodes the moral foundation of these institutions and deepens societal divisions. The deliberate restriction of opportunities under the guise of maintaining "excellence" or "standards" is, in reality, an unethical manipulation that turns education and influence into privileges for the few rather than instruments of societal progress.

Those who control these systems such as educators, administrators (admission boards), and decision-makers who are entrusted with a sacred duty to foster fairness, not to act as gatekeepers for the privileged. When wealth and status become the ultimate criteria for success, institutions lose their credibility, and the very fabric of society is weakened. Scripture warns against such injustice: *"Woe unto them that decree unrighteous decrees, and that write grievousness which they have prescribed"* (*Isaiah 10:1, KJV*).

True leadership in education and governance demands a commitment to equity, ensuring that every individual, regardless of background, is given a fair chance to contribute and succeed. It is not merely an academic or administrative duty, it is rather a moral and spiritual obligation. Those who misuse their power to suppress the deserving will ultimately answer before God for the lives they have hindered and the justice they have perverted. A just society is built on the principles of truth and equal opportunity, and it is the responsibility of those in power to uphold these values for the betterment of all.

> **Proverbs 11:3 (KJV)** "The integrity of the upright shall guide them: but the perverseness of transgressors shall destroy them."
>
> **Isaiah 56:1 (KJV)** "Thus saith the Lord, Keep ye judgment, and do justice: for my salvation is near to come, and my righteousness to be revealed."
>
> **Isaiah 56:2 (KJV)** "Blessed is the man that doeth this, and the son of man that layeth hold on it; that keepeth the sabbath from polluting it, and keepeth his hand from doing any evil"

The actions of corrupt school administrators and boards extend far beyond the classroom, impacting not only the advancement of deserving students but also the health and well-being of many underprivileged children. Diverting funds from essential programs, such as school feeding initiatives, betrays the very purpose of education as a means of nurturing and equipping the next

generation. For countless students, especially those from impoverished backgrounds, school meals may represent their only access to a nutritious meal. Yet, when these programs prioritize cost-cutting or profit over quality, they jeopardize the health and future of these children by offering meals laden with artificial flavors and processed ingredients, which may harm their development and long-term health.

School feeding programs should be a beacon of care and nourishment, providing children with wholesome, nutritious meals that foster both physical health and cognitive development. To serve substandard or harmful food or to divert resources from these program, is to betray the trust of families who rely on schools to care for their children in their absence. The consequences of such negligence ripple through generations, compromising the future of those who depend on you the most.

The corrupt practices that favor the wealthy and powerful over deserving students compound this betrayal. When fairness and justice are cast aside, the trust students place in authority figures, and institutions is eroded at a formative age. By hindering the advancement of capable students in favor of those with privilege, administrators, and teachers send a message that honesty, integrity, and merit are meaningless values crucial to a child's moral and social development.

What will the Lord, the Sovereign God, say to you who have misused your position to create an environment riddled with corruption and neglect? Your implicit disregard for justice and fairness has diminished the potential of the very children you are entrusted to nurture. Your actions, driven by greed and apathy, have perpetuated a cycle of harm by depriving students of educational opportunities but also by compromising their physical and moral well-being.

Let this be a call to accountability for all who hold influence over young lives. Uphold justice, prioritize integrity, and ensure that every action taken reflects the sacred responsibility to nurture and protect the students under your care. The Lord's judgment will not overlook the harm done to the innocent, and the weight of your actions will be measured against the trust and care you were entrusted to provide.

The LORD Jesus Christ be with your spirit. The LORD Jesus Christ give you understanding.

CHAPTER 18

THE MIGHTY EQUALIZER: A DIVINE MESSAGE FOR THE CORRUPT POLICE

======================

ASASE YE DURU

"The Earth is heavy"

Asante philosophical symbol of Divinity of Mother Earth

======================

What will the Lord, the Sovereign God, say to you, the corrupt police officer who accepts bribes, extorts money from individuals, and obstructs justice? Your duty is to serve and protect, yet you betray the very trust and authority bestowed upon you, turning your role into a weapon of oppression rather than a shield of fairness. Your actions do not just harm individuals; they corrode the moral fabric of society and deepen the divide between the powerful and the vulnerable.

In many countries, especially developing nations, corruption has become synonymous with policing. Officers often enter the force not through merit but through political favoritism, aligning them with the agendas of powerful figures rather than the principles of justice. I, in places like developing countries, officers, commonly referred to as "the boys," are expected to bring back their share of the bribe, funneled upward to superiors who demand their cut. It is not uncommon for officers to pay bribes themselves to secure postings at lucrative barriers where they can prey on unsuspecting drivers, turning every checkpoint into a tollgate for their personal gain.

The ordinary motorist, whether commuting to work, riding motorbikes, or operating taxis to earn an honest living of some sort, has become a prime target for extortion by corrupt police officers. These hardworking individuals, striving day and night to make ends meet, find themselves subjected to unfair demands, unable to resist or challenge the oppressive system due to their lack of wealth or influence. They are easy prey, while the rich and powerful often evade scrutiny entirely, protected by their connections and resources.

What makes this injustice even more disheartening is that many of the officers engaging in these acts are people of faith, possibly in name as Christians who seek to portray success by arriving at church in a new, polished car or by making sizeable donations in the form of tithes or offerings. These acts are often seen as outward signs of "blessings," reinforcing their perceived status within the congregation. Yet, on such Sundays, they will not hear a sermon condemning extortion or the exploitation of the vulnerable. The preacher, wary of alienating those whose financial support sustains the church, remains silent on such issues, focusing instead on more comfortable topics like spiritual warfare against witches and wizards.

This silence perpetuates a cycle of injustice, where the struggles of the poor are ignored, and the actions of the corrupt are left unchecked. The message of justice, compassion, and accountability central to the faith is overshadowed by the pursuit of material gain and status. This imbalance not only harms the individuals being extorted but also undermines the moral integrity of society and the church itself.

It is a call for both the faith community and law enforcement to confront these practices, acknowledging the harm they inflict and the responsibility to uphold justice. True faith is reflected not in outward displays of wealth but in actions that honor God through fairness, integrity, and compassion for the least among us.

For police officers, targeting the affluent can be risky. Mistakenly demanding a bribe from a well-connected individual may result in severe consequences, such as demotion, transfer to an undesirable remote location, or even job loss. This fear of reprisal ensures that the wealthy remain above the reach of routine police stops, further entrenching a system of inequality.

Police officers often justify stopping motorists without suspicion, using these arbitrary stops as a pretext to extort money from unsuspecting drivers. This unchecked authority becomes a license to oppress, transforming law enforcement into a mechanism for exploiting the vulnerable while granting immunity to the privileged. In such a system, justice is not blind; it is skewed to serve the interests of the powerful, leaving the poor disproportionately punished and marginalized.

Even in wealthy nations where outright bribery may not be the norm, incentives tied to arrest quotas perpetuate systemic injustice. Officers are often driven to target minorities and poor motorists, issuing tickets and imposing fines not for public safety but to meet financial targets. These practices disproportionately affect those who are already vulnerable, creating a system where justice is for sale and fairness is a distant ideal.

What will the Lord say to those who twist justice for personal gain, who oppress the powerless while enabling the powerful? The warning is clear to them, the Lord detests corruption and demands accountability from those entrusted with authority. To allow crime to fester, to obstruct justice, and to oppress the vulnerable is to stand in direct opposition to the principles of righteousness and fairness that God commands.

Let this be a call to repentance for all who have corrupted their positions of power. The role of law enforcement is sacred, a reflection of God's own call for justice and protection for the oppressed. To misuse this authority is to invite divine judgment, for the cries of the oppressed will not go unheard by the Almighty. Uphold justice, act with integrity, and remember that your ultimate accountability is to the God who sees all and judges righteously.

i. **Proverbs 15:27 (KJV)** "He that is greedy of gain troubleth his own house; but he that hateth gifts shall live"

ii. **Luke 3:14 (KJV)** "And the soldiers likewise demanded of him, saying, And what shall we do? And he said unto them, Do violence to no man, neither accuse any falsely; and be content with your wages."

You who abuse power with impunity, who exploit your authority to oppress and mistreat others, reflect on the grave responsibility entrusted to you. When you turn your position into a tool for bribery and corruption, targeting the poor and vulnerable for your only survival by abusing the rights of poor motorists struggling to make ends meet. You violate not only their civil and human rights but also the moral code of true service, your oath of office, and the constitution under which you are charged to uphold.

Law enforcement is not a position of dominance or exploitation; it is a sacred trust, a call to serve and protect with integrity and fairness. To misuse this role, extracting bribes and oppressing those who cannot defend themselves, is to betray the very purpose of your authority. Instead of being a shield for the defenseless, you have become a punisher for those without wealth or influence, serving the interests of the powerful at the expense of the poor.

Consider the example of the Servant Leader, who taught that greatness is found in humility and service, not in domination or exploitation. True leadership, including in law enforcement, is about lifting burdens, not imposing them; about ensuring justice, not perverting it for personal gain. Those entrusted with authority are called to reflect these principles, using their power to protect the vulnerable and uphold fairness.

When law enforcement becomes a tool of corruption, targeting poor motorists with unfair fines, bribes, and harassment, it creates a cycle of injustice that erodes trust and perpetuates inequality.

The very system designed to provide safety and order instead becomes a source of oppression, forcing the powerless into further hardship while allowing the wealthy to escape accountability.

This is a call to repentance and reform. Law enforcement officers must examine their actions and realign their service with the principles of justice, fairness, and compassion. To abuse power is to reject the divine mandate for leadership; to serve with integrity is to honor the sacred trust placed in you.

Let this message be a reminder that true greatness lies not in wielding power over others but in serving them with humility and justice. The Lord calls all who hold positions of authority to act with righteousness, ensuring that the law is a source of protection, not exploitation. In doing so, you fulfill the true purpose of your role and reflect the justice and mercy of the Creator.

> **Matthew 20:25 (KJV)** "But Jesus called them unto him, and said, Ye know that the princes of the Gentiles exercise dominion over them, and they that are great exercise authority upon them."

> **Matthew 20:26 (KJV)** "But it shall not be so among you: but whosoever will be great among you, let him be your minister;"

> **Matthew 20:27 (KJV)** "And whosoever will be chief among you, let him be your servant:"

> **Matthew 20:28 (KJV)** "Even as the Son of man came not to be ministered unto, but to minister, and to give his life a ransom for many."

> **Luke 22:24 (KJV)** "And there was also a strife among them, which of them should be accounted the greatest."

> **Luke 22:25 (KJV)** "And he said unto them, The kings of the Gentiles exercise lordship over them; and they that exercise authority upon them are called benefactors"

> **Luke 22:26 (KJV)** "But ye shall not be so: but he that is greatest among you, let him be as the younger; and he that is chief, as he that doth serve."

> **Luke 22:27 (KJV)** "For whether is greater, he that sitteth at meat, or he that serveth? is not he that sitteth at meat? but I am among you as he that serveth"

You act on false accusation and turn blind eye to the truth. Bearing false witness or intentionally acting on false accusations against innocent people which is contrary to the teaching of the Bible.

Exodus 20:16 (KJV) "Thou shalt not bear false witness against thy neighbour."

Proverbs 19:5 (KJV) "A false witness shall not be unpunished, and he that speaketh lies shall not escape."

What will the Lord, the Lord God, say to you for disregarding His command to show impartiality and fairness as taught in the divine Word? The Lord calls for the fair and equal treatment of all individuals, irrespective of their race, social status, or economic position. Yet you have chosen to discriminate, showing favoritism not out of justice but driven by personal bias and preference.

You act with cruelty and violence in the pursuit of your duties, exercising excessive force disproportionately against those you despise or deem less valuable. In doing so, you ignore the sacred call to regard every life with dignity and respect. Your actions betray the teachings of our Lord Jesus Christ, who calls us to love one another, to show compassion, and to seek peace in all our dealings.

Matthew 5:9 (KJV) "Blessed are the peacemakers: for they shall be called the children of God."

Matthew 26:52 (KJV) "Then said Jesus unto him, Put up again thy sword into his place: for all they that take the sword shall perish with the sword."

Your own Words on your police cruisers, **"SERVE AND PROTECT,"** is in judgment against you if you fail to honor those promises. Failure to serve and protect vulnerable people among us by neglecting your duty to these poor people in the interest of the elite in the top echelons of society is answerable to God. This is a betrayal of your own oath and direct neglect of your basic function as a law enforcement officer.

Isaiah 1:17 (KJV) "Learn to do well; seek judgment, relieve the oppressed, judge the fatherless, plead for the widow."

James 1:27 (KJV) "Pure religion and undefiled before God and the Father is this, To visit the fatherless and widows in their affliction, and to keep himself unspotted from the world."

What will the Lord, the Lord God, say to you on the day of judgment that he has used you as a tool in this Evil world by giving you the authority to protect his own, but you ignore their plight and join forces with the devils to harm his children? Neglecting the needs of the poor, needy neighbor, the stranger, the widow, the homeless, and the marginalized people among us is contrary to your role.

Matthew 25:31 (KJV) "When the Son of man shall come in his glory, and all the holy angels with him, then shall he sit upon the throne of his glory:"

Matthew 25:32 (KJV) "And before him shall be gathered all nations: and he shall separate them one from another, as a shepherd divideth his sheep from the goats:"

Matthew 25:33 (KJV) "And he shall set the sheep on his right hand, but the goats on the left."

Matthew 25:34 (KJV) "Then shall the King say unto them on his right hand, Come, ye blessed of my Father, inherit the kingdom prepared for you from the foundation of the world:"

Matthew 25:35 (KJV) "For I was an hungred, and ye gave me meat: I was thirsty, and ye gave me drink: I was a stranger, and ye took me in:"

Matthew 25:36 (KJV) "Naked, and ye clothed me: I was sick, and ye visited me: I was in prison, and ye came unto me."

Matthew 25:37 (KJV) "Then shall the righteous answer him, saying, Lord, when saw we thee an hungred, and fed thee? or thirsty, and gave thee drink?"

Matthew 25:38 (KJV) "When saw we thee a stranger, and took thee in? or naked, and clothed thee?"

Matthew 25:39 (KJV) "Or when saw we thee sick, or in prison, and came unto thee?"

Matthew 25:40 (KJV) "And the King shall answer and say unto them, Verily I say unto you, Inasmuch as ye have done it unto one of the least of these my brethren, ye have done it unto me."

Matthew 25:41 (KJV) "Then shall he say also unto them on the left hand, Depart from me, ye cursed, into everlasting fire, prepared for the devil and his angels:"

Matthew 25:42 (KJV) "For I was an hungred, and ye gave me no meat: I was thirsty, and ye gave me no drink:"

Matthew 25:43 (KJV) "I was a stranger, and ye took me not in: naked, and ye clothed me not: sick, and in prison, and ye visited me not."

Matthew 25:44 (KJV) "Then shall they also answer him, saying, Lord, when saw we thee an hungred, or athirst, or a stranger, or naked, or sick, or in prison, and did not minister unto thee?"

Matthew 25:45 (KJV) "Then shall he answer them, saying, Verily I say unto you, Inasmuch as ye did it not to one of the least of these, ye did it not to me."

Matthew 25:46 (KJV) "And these shall go away into everlasting punishment: but the righteous into life eternal."

The Lord, the Lord God values all his children and will hold all who harm or neglect to provide when they have the means to do so accountable and will condemn them according to His Judgement.

Ecclesiastes 8:11 (KJV) "Because sentence against an evil work is not executed speedily, therefore the heart of the sons of men is fully set in them to do evil."

The LORD Jesus Christ be with your spirit. The LORD Jesus Christ give you understanding.

CHAPTER 19

THE MIGHTY EQUALIZER: A DIVINE MESSAGE FOR THE PRIME MINISTER AND YOUR CORRUPT CABINET?

======================

ESE NE TEKREMA

"The teeth and the tongue"

Asante philosophical symbol of Friendship, Interdependence, Co-Existence, Tolerance

======================

What will the Lord God say to you, Mr. Prime Minister, and your cabinet, for turning the sacred responsibility of governance into a tool for personal enrichment? You once stood before the people, appealing for their trust, vowing to eradicate corruption and correct the injustices of the past. Yet, after assuming office, have you taken decisive action to hold the corrupt accountable, or have your words faded into empty rhetoric?

The people rightfully ask: Were your promises merely a calculated means to seize power? Have you failed to act out of fear that exposing corruption might one day expose you? Or worse, have you become part of the very system you once condemned, shielding wrongdoers in a silent exchange for your own protection? Governance is not merely about occupying a seat of power; it is about wielding authority with integrity, ensuring that justice is done, and breaking the cycle of deception and greed.

If you continue to turn a blind eye while your fellow officers accept bribes, engage in kickbacks, and amass wealth at the expense of the people, you betray not only the trust of those who elected you but the very foundation of good governance. When leaders allow corruption to flourish, it is the struggling workers, the poor, and the voiceless who suffer the most. Every unjust law, every manipulated policy, and every stolen public fund places a heavier burden on those already struggling to survive.

Leadership is not just about making policies; it is about enforcing justice. As the head of government, it is your duty to ensure that those in positions of power are held accountable not only in words but in action. If corruption thrives under your administration, you bear direct responsibility for the harm it causes.

To curb this abuse, you must go beyond mere pledges of reform. Demand full asset declarations from every officeholder under your leadership not just for themselves but also for their immediate families. Too often, stolen wealth is hidden in the names of relatives and friends, robbing the nation of its future while corrupt officials masquerade as honorable men. The people see through this deception, and so does the Lord God, who will hold each of you accountable.

If you fail to act against injustice, you are not merely negligent you are complicit. Every stolen resource denies children an education, deprives hospitals of life-saving equipment, and keeps the most vulnerable trapped in poverty.

The question before you is clear; will you be remembered as a leader who stood for justice, or will history mark your name among those who enriched themselves at the expense of their people? Will your tenure be one of bold action and reform, or will it be another chapter in the long history of broken promises and unfulfilled mandates?

The judgment of the Almighty is not reserved for the afterlife alone, it manifests in the collapse of corrupt governments, the downfall of deceitful rulers, and the destruction of nations that forsake justice. You still have the power to shape your legacy. Choose to lead with integrity, to uplift the poor, and to restore the trust of your people. For only then will you truly honor the One who has placed you in power, and only then will you escape the wrath that awaits those who misuse their authority.

> **Proverbs 15:27 (KJV)** "He that is greedy of gain troubleth his own house; but he that hateth gifts shall live."

> **Proverbs 17:23 (KJV)** "A wicked man taketh a gift out of the bosom to pervert the ways of judgment."

The scriptures emphasize the fundamental importance of loyalty and honesty in small tasks as reflections of one's ability to handle greater responsibilities. How one manages the little things is a true measure of character. Furthermore, the Bible draws a sharp distinction between material wealth as *"unrighteous mammon"* and *"true riches,"* which symbolize spiritual and eternal values. This

distinction underscores the vital necessity of reliability and faithfulness in managing both personal resources and those entrusted to individuals by society.

However, in the pursuit of reform and restructuring, great care must be taken not to punish the very people that such policies are meant to help. I mean, the weak, the poor, and the marginalized. In your efforts to cleanse the system of corruption, be careful not to cast out the innocent alongside the guilty. Leadership requires discernment and wisdom, ensuring that justice is not wielded as a blunt instrument that harms those who are already struggling under the weight of systemic inequities.

A leader who fails to distinguish between true reform and reckless upheaval risks bringing suffering upon the most vulnerable. In the name of fighting corruption, policies should not deprive the common citizen of the little they have, nor should restructuring serve as an excuse to impose undue hardship on the weak. Consider this old adage: ***"You cannot afford to throw away the bathwater with the baby in it"*** If reform crushes the struggling rather than lifting them, it becomes oppression in a different form.

When individuals in positions of trust exploit public resources for personal gain, whether through corruption, embezzlement, or reckless policy decisions, they do not only steal from the present but rob future generations of their inheritance. The wealth amassed through deceitful means or the mismanagement of funds will not endure; it will crumble under the weight of divine justice. The Lord does not overlook injustice, and those who misuse their power will find themselves accountable not only before history but before God Himself.

The use of public office is not for self-enrichment but for service. Leadership is a sacred trust, one that must be exercised with wisdom, equity, and a deep sense of responsibility toward the people, especially the most vulnerable.

Policies must be designed not only to punish wrongdoers but also to protect the innocent from unintended consequences. Those in power must ensure that reform does not become another form of injustice.

For example, consider a scenario where a hospital that provides essential healthcare services to a rural community is found to be entangled in corruption, with its owner involved in fraudulent financial dealings with government officials. Shutting down the hospital entirely as a punitive measure may seem like justice against the corrupt owner, but in reality, it punishes the sick, the elderly, and the poor who rely on its services for survival. A more just and responsible approach would be to prosecute the corrupt individuals while ensuring the hospital remains operational and uninterrupted, perhaps by placing it under temporary government administration or facilitating its acquisition by a more ethical organization.

True justice does not simply cut down the tree of corruption; it ensures that the innocent who took shelter under its branches are not left exposed to the harsh elements of suffering and deprivation. Leadership must be guided by wisdom, ensuring that punishment is directed at the guilty while safeguarding the livelihoods and well-being of the innocent.

The Ten Commandments serve as a cornerstone of divine justice, unequivocally condemning theft and reinforcing the sanctity of respecting the rights and livelihoods of others. This principle does not only apply to the individual thief but also to leaders whose actions, whether through corruption, negligence, or unbalanced policies, inflict harm on society.

True accountability lies not just in the verdict of history but before the righteous judgment of God, whose justice spans beyond time. Every leader must ask: ***What legacy am I building?*** Will your name be remembered for bringing fairness and prosperity to your people, or will it be associated with hardship, mismanagement, and misplaced priorities?

The call to leadership is a call to stewardship. It is not merely about managing resources but about upholding integrity, faithfulness, and moral responsibility. Those who wield power must reflect deeply on the consequences of their actions. For in the end, leadership is not measured merely by policies implemented but by the lives touched, protected, and uplifted. May wisdom guide every leader to uphold justice while ensuring that the weak are shielded, not sacrificed, in the name of reform.

> **Luke 16:10 (KJV)** "He that is faithful in that which is least is faithful also in much: and he that is unjust in the least is unjust also in much."

> **Luke 16:11 (KJV)** "If therefore ye have not been faithful in the unrighteous mammon, who will commit to your trust the true riches?"

> **Luke 16:12 (KJV)** "And if ye have not been faithful in that which is another man's, who shall give you that which is your own?"

> **Exodus 20:15 (KJV)** "Thou shalt not steal."

Mr. Prime Minister, do you wish to be remembered as a leader under whose watch public trust faltered, prioritizing family and friends over the greater good of the nation? Nepotism and cronyism have tainted your administration, with key positions often filled not on the basis of merit or ability but personal connections. This has resulted in the mismanagement of crucial national affairs, sidelining competence and undermining the efficient governance of the state. The people look to you not only for leadership but for fairness and integrity with values that should guide every decision in office

However, the hope for a better future remains. There is always an opportunity to turn from these practices and embrace a path of reform that prioritizes fairness, transparency, and equity. True leadership is marked not by clinging to past mistakes but by the courage to change course and realign governance with the principles of justice and integrity.

The teachings from Scripture offer timeless wisdom for this journey of transformation. The scripture cautions against favoritism and partiality, urging us to judge not based on wealth or status but with equity and impartiality. Similarly, the Word of God reminds us of the dangers of small compromises that can erode ethical foundations, calling for unwavering adherence to principles of fairness and righteousness.

Imagine a future where positions of power are filled based on competence and merit, where every decision made by your cabinet prioritizes the public good over personal connections. This is the legacy that can redefine your leadership, a commitment to equitable governance that ensures every citizen, regardless of their background, has a fair opportunity to contribute to and benefit from the nation's progress.

By aligning your administration with these values, you have the chance to rebuild public trust, foster national unity, and create a governance model that serves as a beacon of fairness and justice. Let the words of wisdom from Scripture guide this transformation, reminding you that true greatness in leadership comes from serving others impartially and with integrity.

The future is still yours to shape. The decisions you make today can inspire hope, mend broken systems, and leave a lasting legacy of fairness and prosperity for generations to come. Embrace this opportunity to lead with justice and humility, and the history of your leadership will be one of redemption, renewal, and hope.

> **Proverbs 28:21 (KJV)** "To have respect of persons is not good: for for a piece of bread that man will transgress."

> **James 2:1 (KJV)** "My brethren, have not the faith of our Lord Jesus Christ, the Lord of glory, with respect of persons."

> **James 2:2 (KJV)** "For if there come unto your assembly a man with a gold ring, in goodly apparel, and there come in also a poor man in vile raiment;"

> **James 2:3 (KJV)** "And ye have respect to him that weareth the gay clothing, and say unto him, Sit thou here in a good place; and say to the poor, Stand thou there, or sit here under my footstool:"

> **James 2:4 (KJV)** "Are ye not then partial in yourselves, and are become judges of evil thoughts?"

Mr. Prime Minister, this is a moment to reflect on the critical responsibility of leadership and the role of your cabinet in upholding justice. It is vital to ensure that governance does not obstruct investigations or interfere with legal due processes. Protecting oneself, family, or associates at the expense of justice risks undermining the trust placed in you by the people and the principles of fairness that underpin a just society.

Consider the consequences of actions that delay or deny justice. When high-ranking officials are implicated in wrongdoing, whether through mismanagement or illicit gains, the integrity of the system depends on transparency and accountability hindering these processes not only violates the ethical mandate of leadership but also erodes the confidence of the public in the rule of law.

> **Proverbs 17:15 (KJV)** "He that justifieth the wicked, and he that condemneth the just, both of them alike are an abomination to the LORD."

> **Exodus 38:6 (KJV)** "And he made the staves of shittim wood, and overlaid them with brass."

> **Luke 16:10 (KJV)** "He that is faithful in that which is least is faithful also in much: and he that is unjust in the least is unjust also in much."

> **Luke 16:11 (KJV)** "If therefore ye have not been faithful in the unrighteous mammon, who will commit to your trust the true riches?"

> **Luke 16:12 (KJV)** "And if ye have not been faithful in that which is another man's, who shall give you that which is your own?"

> **Luke 16:13 (KJV)** "No servant can serve two masters: for either he will hate the one, and love the other; or else he will hold to the one, and despise the other. Ye cannot serve God and mammon."

The misuse of public resources for personal enrichment, the accumulation of vast wealth in overseas accounts, and the maintenance of a luxurious lifestyle for oneself and one's family stand in direct opposition to the principles of integrity and accountability expected of those in positions of power. These actions not only betray public trust but undermine the foundations of justice and equity upon which good governance should be built.

This warning serves as a call for serious action from law enforcement and institutions tasked with checking power. Those who divert public resources for personal gain must be held accountable, and their actions must face the scrutiny of transparent investigations. Without accountability, the erosion of public trust will only deepen, fostering disillusionment and widening the divide between leaders and the people they are sworn to serve.

Faithfulness and integrity are not optional virtues. They are grounded in scripture and are the bedrock of leadership. How one manages the responsibilities entrusted to them, even in small matters, reflects their overall reliability and suitability for larger tasks. Leaders who prioritize personal gain over communal welfare fail not only their constituents but also the moral obligations of their role.

Law enforcement and regulatory bodies must act decisively to uphold these principles. Those entrusted with the authority to check abuse must ensure that no one is above the law, sending a clear message that public service is a sacred trust, not a pathway to personal enrichment.

This is a moment for reflection, reform, and renewed commitment to righteous stewardship. The future of governance depends on leaders who value integrity over greed, communal welfare over self-interest, and justice over corruption. Let this warning serve as a catalyst for change, ensuring that the ideals of fairness and accountability are upheld for generations to come.

Your corrupt no-bid contracts and manipulated procurement processes have become the pathways through which favoritism thrives, enabling those in power to enrich themselves and their associates at the expense of the nation's future. By rigging contracts and tenders to favor friends, family, or even their own businesses through intermediaries, these practices undermine trust, foster inequality, and divert resources meant for the public good into private hands. Such actions not only betray the citizens you serve but jeopardize the integrity and prosperity of the entire nation.

> **Proverbs 11:1 (KJV)** "A false balance is abomination to the LORD: but a just weight is his delight."

> **Proverbs 29:24 (KJV)** "Whoso is partner with a thief hateth his own soul: he heareth cursing, and bewrayeth it not."

Leveraging the mechanisms of law under the guise of authority, you've appropriated the assets of others, employing tactics of intimidation and manipulation to dismantle competition. Fabricated charges against political and business rivals serve as barriers, undermining their economic pursuit, and occasionally extorting bribes in the process. Properties and goods are unjustly confiscated, with concocted justifications obscuring the theft of individuals' lifelong endeavors. These actions are enforced not through personal capability but by exploiting the power vested in you by the populace, betraying a stark absence of justice, sincerity, and compassion towards the citizens.

The scripture admonishes against involvement in or tacit approval of theft, illustrating how such associations or failures to condemn these acts erode moral standing. It underscores an ethical mandate to confront and reveal malfeasance, asserting that silence or passivity in theft's presence constitutes complicity, damaging one's moral fiber and relationship with the divine. The biblical narrative stresses the paramountcy of upholding values of truthfulness, moral uprightness, and the active resistance to unfairness and deception in all aspects of existence.

> **Luke 3:14 (KJV)** "And the soldiers likewise demanded of him, saying, And what shall we do? And he said unto them, Do violence to no man, neither accuse any falsely; nor take by extortion: be content with your wages."

> **Proverbs 22:22 (KJV)** "Rob not the poor, because he is poor: neither oppress the afflicted in the gate:"

> **Proverbs 22:23 (KJV)** "For the LORD will plead their cause, and spoil the soul of those that spoiled them."

Your actions, characterized by spreading falsehoods and engaging in deceit, reflect a misuse of authority to manipulate information for personal gain and consolidation of power. By levying unfounded accusations, you aim to tarnish reputations and incite public hostility, actions that sow division and mistrust. Such behavior starkly contrasts with the ethical principles exemplified by John the Baptist, who called for honesty, fairness, and contentment with one's means. His teachings remind us that authority must be exercised with righteousness, avoiding harm, false claims, and greed.

The exploitation and mistreatment of the impoverished and vulnerable are further condemned as grave moral failings. These injustices not only violate ethical and societal norms but also invite divine retribution. The portrayal of God as the defender of the oppressed underscores a sacred commitment to justice, ensuring that those who cause harm will ultimately be held accountable.

These timeless teachings call for ethical integrity, the safeguarding of the vulnerable, and the equitable treatment of all individuals, regardless of status. They challenge us to reflect on the moral weight of our actions, particularly for those in positions of power. To live in alignment with divine values of justice and righteousness is not optional but essential, serving as the foundation for a society that honors fairness, compassion, and truth. Let this reminder inspire a renewed dedication to these principles, ensuring that authority is wielded not for personal gain but for the greater good.

> **Proverbs 10:18 (KJV)** "He that hideth hatred with lying lips, and he that uttereth a slander, is a fool."

> **Proverbs 19:5 (KJV)** "A false witness shall not be unpunished, and he that speaketh lies shall not escape."

Those who disregard the nation's harmony, choosing instead to sow discord and manipulate the fears of the populace through relentless falsehoods, mars a significant departure from ethical principles. Such actions are used in disguising hostility with deceitful words and engaging in slander and are not only morally reprehensible but also destructive to the trust and unity essential for societal well-being.

The wisdom of the Word of God warns against these behaviors, emphasizing that deceit and slander are not only foolish but profoundly immoral. To mask ill intent with false testimony or malicious words is to betray the principles of integrity and fairness. Moreover, these scriptures make clear that deceit, particularly when used to bear false witness, invites divine retribution. Those who engage in dishonesty cannot escape the consequences of their actions; justice, both human and divine, remains inevitable.

These teachings stand as a powerful warning against deceit and dishonesty, highlighting the critical need for sincerity and truthfulness. They remind us that unethical conduct, especially when it undermines harmony and erodes trust within a community, leads to lasting accountability and consequences. Upholding truthfulness is not merely a moral imperative; it is foundational to maintain order, trust, and the common good in society.

Let this serve as a call to reflection and reform. A commitment to sincerity and integrity is not only a safeguard against the repercussions of deceit but also the cornerstone of a society built on trust, respect, and justice. In honoring these principles, individuals and leaders alike contribute to the flourishing of their communities and the upholding of values that transcend personal ambition.

Proverbs 12:22 (KJV) "Lying lips are abomination to the LORD: but they that deal truly are his delight"

Proverbs 19:9 (KJV) "A false witness shall not be unpunished, and he that speaketh lies shall perish."

The scriptures draw a definitive line between the acts of dishonesty and the virtue of truthfulness, portraying falsehood as abhorrent to God. This delineation underscores a strong divine inclination towards sincerity and moral uprightness, accentuating the significance God attributes to living authentically and truthfully. The vivid contrast serves to illuminate the esteemed place of honesty in the realm of spiritual and ethical conduct.

Furthermore, the texts caution about the dire outcomes associated with deceit, particularly in acts of bearing false testimony. This repeated message reinforces the notion that dishonest behaviors are bound to result in adverse consequences, highlighting the grave nature of such actions and the ethical obligation to adhere to truthfulness.

The denouncement of lies and the explicit endorsement of honesty by the biblical narratives serve as a solemn reminder of the moral and spiritual ramifications of falsehood. These teachings stress the unavoidable fallout from engaging in deceit, advocating for a steadfast commitment to honesty and moral integrity in all aspects of life, thereby underscoring the profound value placed on truth and righteousness in maintaining one's moral compass and spiritual alignment.

Proverbs 14:31 (KJV) "He that oppresseth the poor reproacheth his Maker: but he that honoureth him hath mercy on the poor."

Proverbs 31:8 (KJV) "Open thy mouth for the dumb in the cause of all such as are appointed to destruction."

Proverbs 31:9 (KJV) "Open thy mouth, judge righteously, and plead the cause of the poor and needy."

Enacting policies that favor the affluent while disproportionately burdening the impoverished represents a profound injustice, Mr. President/Prime Minister and esteemed cabinet members. Such measures, designed to enrich personal and elite interests, erode the moral foundation of society and betray the trust placed in leadership. Marginalizing the needy and ignoring their plight reflects a deep disregard for the shared humanity of all people and the inherent dignity bestowed upon them.

True leadership calls for mercy, compassion, and the pursuit of equity. Extending care and support to the less fortunate is not only a reflection of moral virtue but also an act of reverence

toward the foundational principles of justice and kindness. The call to advocate for the rights of the vulnerable and the oppressed is a timeless reminder of the duty to safeguard and uplift the marginalized segments of society.

Compassion and justice must be at the core of governance. Advocating for those silenced by unjust policies or excluded by systemic inequities is more than an obligation but a moral imperative. By prioritizing the rights and well-being of the underprivileged, leaders can build a society that upholds dignity, fairness, and opportunity for all.

In the realm of leadership and governance, the responsibility placed on public officials is immense. Decisions made in positions of power impact countless lives and shape the trajectory of nations. Leaders are entrusted with the stewardship of resources and the welfare of their constituents, and this trust demands unwavering integrity and accountability.

History and moral philosophy remind us that leaders are ultimately accountable in everything they do, not only to the people they serve but also to a higher Power. Ethical leadership requires faithfulness, honesty, and the rejection of corrupt practices. Betraying this trust through self-serving policies or actions invites consequences, both immediate and enduring. However, redemption is always possible for those willing to acknowledge their missteps and commit to reform.

This is a call to reflection and action. The path forward requires embracing the principles of justice, integrity, and compassion. By prioritizing policies that protect and empower the most vulnerable, leaders can rebuild trust, foster unity, and leave a legacy of fairness and hope. True greatness in leadership is not measured by personal gain but by the lives transformed through service, the injustices corrected, and the dignity restored to every citizen.

> **Proverbs 29:2 (KJV)** "When the righteous are in authority, the people rejoice: but when the wicked beareth rule, the people mourn." This verse implies that leaders who uphold righteousness and justice bring joy to their people, while those who engage in wickedness can lead to suffering and mourning."

> **Proverbs 20:28 (KJV)** "Mercy and truth preserve the king: and his throne is upholden by mercy." This verse suggests that leaders are preserved and their rule is upheld through mercy and truth, highlighting the importance of honesty and moral conduct in leadership."

> **2 Chronicles 7:14 (KJV)** "If my people, which are called by my name, shall humble themselves, and pray, and seek my face, and turn from their wicked ways; then will I hear from heaven, and will forgive their sin, and will heal their land."

Leadership, Mr. Prime Minister, is a sacred trust, requiring a commitment to justice, integrity, and the well-being of the people you serve. Your role, along with that of your cabinet, is not merely about governance but about stewardship, ensuring that resources are used wisely, policies are fair, and the most vulnerable are protected. Decisions made at the highest levels of government have profound implications, shaping the lives of citizens and defining the moral compass of a nation.

Yet, when leadership becomes tainted by corruption, favoritism, or self-interest, it betrays the trust placed in it. Marginalizing the poor, prioritizing the interests of the affluent, or exploiting public resources for personal gain stands in stark contrast to the principles of righteous governance. Such actions erode the foundations of society, deepen inequality, and undermine the integrity of leadership.

The biblical lens provides a powerful framework for reflection. Leadership, as portrayed in scripture, is a position of immense responsibility, held to high ethical and moral standards. The Bible teaches the vital importance of honesty, fairness, and compassion in leadership. It warns of the consequences of corruption and injustice but also offers hope to the people through leaders who have strayed can find redemption through sincere repentance and a return to righteous governance.

For those who profess faith in God or adhere to His commands, seeking public office is a solemn undertaking. The biblical perspective reminds leaders to be accountable, both to the Creator and to the people they serve. Upholding principles of truth, justice, and righteousness is not optional; it is the foundation of faithful and effective governance.

Let this be a moment of reflection for you and your cabinet. The decisions you make today will echo through history and eternity. Embrace the opportunity to lead with integrity, to serve with humility, and to govern with justice. By aligning your leadership with the values of righteousness and truth, you can transform not only the nation you serve but also the legacy you leave behind. Leadership is not a platform for self-enrichment but a divine calling to uplift, protect, and inspire. May this reminder guide you toward a path of ethical governance and enduring impact.

CHAPTER 20

THE MIGHTY EQUALIZER: A DIVINE MESSAGE FOR THE ONE THAT OPPRESSES FATHERLESS AND WIDOWS?

=====================

FUFUO

"A yellow-flowered plant"

Asante philosophical symbol of Jealousy, Envy

=====================

The Bible contains several verses that emphasize God's concern for the oppressed, including orphans (fatherless) and widows. One well-known verse is from the book of Isaiah and Exodus:

Isaiah 1:17 (KJV) "Learn to do well; seek judgment, relieve the oppressed, judge the fatherless, plead for the widow."

Exodus 22:21 (KJV) "Thou shalt neither vex a stranger, nor oppress him: for ye were strangers in the land of Egypt."

Exodus 22:22 (KJV) "Ye shall not afflict any widow, or fatherless child."

Exodus 22:23 (KJV) "If thou afflict them in any wise, and they cry at all unto me, I will surely hear their cry;"

Exodus 22:24 (KJV) "And my wrath shall wax hot, and I will kill you with the sword; and your wives shall be widows, and your children fatherless."

The oppression suffered by orphans and widows can have generational consequences, potentially resulting in a curse on future generations for the injustices committed. Thus, your prayers will not be answered by God and what you have worked for all your life including reputation, and blessings can be ruined as a consequence for your evil acts towards the poor and the marginalized.

The Lord God, warns that those who ignore the cries of the poor, including orphans and widows will never go unpunished.

Jeremiah 7:6 (KJV) "If ye oppress not the stranger, the fatherless, and the widow, and shed not innocent blood in this place, neither walk after other gods to your hurt:"

Jeremiah 7:7 (KJV) "Then will I cause you to dwell in this place, in the land that I gave to your fathers, for ever and ever."

Proverbs 21:13 (KJV) "Whoso stoppeth his ears at the cry of the poor, he also shall cry himself, but shall not be heard."

Malachi 3:5 (KJV) "And I will come near to you to judgment; and I will be a swift witness against the sorcerers, and against the adulterers, and against false swearers, and against those that oppress the hireling in his wages, the widow, and the fatherless, and that turn aside the stranger from his right, and fear not me, saith the LORD of hosts."

Turning away from wickedness, upholding justice, and helping the poor and fatherless. Maltreatment of vulnerable people can contribute to societal decay and disorder. as a result, you will experience the consequences of continued wickedness and living in darkness which can lead to broader consequences and societal unrest.

Psalms 109:9 (KJV) "Let his children be fatherless, and his wife a widow."

Psalms 109:10 (KJV) "Let his children be continually vagabonds, and beg: let them seek their bread also out of their desolate places."

Psalms 109:11 (KJV) "Let the extortioner catch all that he hath; and let the strangers spoil his labour."

Psalms 109:12 (KJV) "Let there be none to extend mercy unto him: neither let there be any to favour his fatherless children."

Psalms 109:13 (KJV) "Let his posterity be cut off; and in the generation following let their name be blotted out."

Psalms 109:14 (KJV) "Let the iniquity of his fathers be remembered with the LORD; and let not the sin of his mother be blotted out."

Psalms 109:15 (KJV) "Let them be before the LORD continually, that he may cut off the memory of them from the earth."

God is the ultimate protector and advocate for those without earthly support, such as orphans and widows. What will the Lord, the Lord God, say to you who oppress the fatherless and widows, exploiting their vulnerability and adding to their suffering?

Prophet Ezekiel condemned the rulers of Israel for their exploitation of the poor and the defenseless, highlighting the moral failings of those in power who neglected their divine responsibility to care for the vulnerable. This timeless message resonates today as we witness injustices in many parts of the world, including the ongoing plight of the Palestinian people in Gaza. Where once Israel suffered oppression, now there are instances where they are seen as oppressors, highlighting a tragic cycle of mistreatment.

Ezekiel's message serves as a powerful reminder of the consequences of turning away from the principles of justice and compassion. His words call out the sinful behaviors of those who exploit the weak, including the fatherless and widows, emphasizing that such actions are not only a violation of moral duty but a direct affront to the Creator.

Let this be a solemn call to reflection and repentance for all who hold power or influence. God's mandate is clear: protect the vulnerable, uplift the downtrodden, and ensure justice for all. To fail in this responsibility is to invite divine judgment, for the cries of the oppressed reach the ears of the Almighty, who will not remain silent in the face of such wrongdoing. The path forward lies in embracing righteousness, compassion, and the pursuit of justice for every person, regardless of their status or circumstance.

Isaiah 1:17 (KJV) "Learn to do well; seek judgment, relieve the oppressed, judge the fatherless, plead for the widow."

Isaiah 1:18 (KJV) "Come now, and let us reason together, saith the LORD: though your sins be as scarlet, they shall be as white as snow; though they be red like crimson, they shall be as wool."

Isaiah 1:19 (KJV) "If ye be willing and obedient, ye shall eat the good of the land:"

Isaiah 1:20 (KJV) "But if ye refuse and rebel, ye shall be devoured with the sword: for the mouth of the LORD hath spoken it."

Isaiah 1:23 (KJV) "Thy princes are rebellious, and companions of thieves: every one loveth gifts, and followeth after rewards: they judge not the fatherless, neither doth the cause of the widow come unto them."

Amos 5:11 (KJV) "Forasmuch therefore as your treading is upon the poor, and ye take from him burdens of wheat: ye have built houses of hewn stone, but ye shall not dwell in them; ye have planted pleasant vineyards, but ye shall not drink wine of them."

Amos 5:12 (KJV) "For I know your manifold transgressions and your mighty sins: they afflict the just, they take a bribe, and they turn aside the poor in the gate from their right."

Amos 5:13 (KJV) "Therefore the prudent shall keep silence in that time; for it is an evil time."

Amos 5:14 (KJV) "Seek good, and not evil, that ye may live: and so the LORD, the God of hosts, shall be with you, as ye have spoken."

Amos 5:15 (KJV) "Hate the evil, and love the good, and establish judgment in the gate: it may be that the LORD God of hosts will be gracious unto the remnant of Joseph."

God rejects worship and offerings from those who oppress the fatherless and widows, emphasizing the importance of righteous behavior and compassion warns against any such belief system that fails to care for orphans and widows in their distress as happening all around us while those who call themselves followers of Christ still look on unconcern and root for the evil and ungodly perpetrators.

Isaiah 1:14 (KJV) "Your new moons and your appointed feasts my soul hateth: they are a trouble unto me; I am weary to bear them."

Isaiah 1:15 (KJV) "And when ye spread forth your hands, I will hide mine eyes from you: yea, when ye make many prayers, I will not hear: your hands are full of blood."

James 1:27 (KJV) "Pure religion and undefiled before God and the Father is this, To visit the fatherless and widows in their affliction, and to keep himself unspotted from the world."

Matthew 25:41 (KJV) "Then shall he say also unto them on the left hand, Depart from me, ye cursed, into everlasting fire, prepared for the devil and his angels:"

Matthew 25:42 (KJV) "For I was an hungred, and ye gave me no meat: I was thirsty, and ye gave me no drink:"

Matthew 25:43 (KJV) "I was a stranger, and ye took me not in: naked, and ye clothed me not: sick, and in prison, and ye visited me not."

> **Matthew 25:44 (KJV)** "Then shall they also answer him, saying, Lord, when saw we thee an hungred, or athirst, or a stranger, or naked, or sick, or in prison, and did not minister unto thee?"

> **Matthew 25:45 (KJV)** "Then shall he answer them, saying, Verily I say unto you, Inasmuch as ye did it not to one of the least of these, ye did it not to me."

> **Matthew 25:46 (KJV)** "And these shall go away into everlasting punishment: but the righteous into life eternal."

Oppression of the fatherless and widows is a profound violation of moral and ethical principles, a direct affront to the values of compassion and justice. Those who exploit the vulnerable, taking advantage of their lack of protection or support, are warned of the inevitable consequences of such actions. The mistreatment of these groups is not just a societal failing but a betrayal of the fundamental duty to uphold the dignity and welfare of all individuals.

This warning in the Word of God is timeless and extends across generations and cultures, emphasizing that leaders and individuals alike bear responsibility for safeguarding the rights of the vulnerable. Historical accounts, such as those recounted by the prophets, highlight the condemnation of oppressive behaviors and the call to defend the powerless. These narratives remind us that society is measured by how it treats its most vulnerable members, and those who fail in this duty cannot escape accountability.

This should serve all of us, as a call to action, urging all who hold power or influence to ensure that their actions reflect fairness, empathy, and justice. Oppression, in any form, dehumanizes both the victim and the oppressor, eroding the foundation of a just and equitable society. The moral imperative is clear: defend the fatherless, support the widows, and uphold the principles of compassion and equity that bind humanity together.

> **Psalm 68:5 (KJV)** "A father of the fatherless, and a judge of the widows, is God in his holy habitation."

> **Ezekiel 22:7 (KJV)** "In thee have they set light by father and mother: in the midst of thee have they dealt by oppression with the stranger: in thee have they vexed the fatherless and the widow."

In this chapter, we reflect on the sacred responsibility of caring for the fatherless and widows, those most vulnerable in society. This is not merely a moral duty but a profound calling to act with justice, seek fairness, and provide relief to those in need. The importance of this charge cannot be overstated, for history and tradition alike remind us of the heavy consequences of neglecting or oppressing the marginalized.

Mistreatment of the fatherless and widows is not only a grave social injustice but also a transgression that carries profound spiritual implications. Those who exploit the weak or turn a blind eye to their suffering risk losing favor and blessings. This truth resonates across all aspects of life, serving as a sobering reminder that our actions or inactions toward the most vulnerable among us reflect the depth of our integrity and the sincerity of our values.

Caring for the marginalized is more than charity; it is an embodiment of compassion, justice, and the shared humanity that binds us together. To provide for the fatherless and widows is to restore dignity, to lift burdens, and to reaffirm the worth of every individual. It is through such acts that society becomes not just a collection of individuals but a true community, united in purpose and spirit.

As we close this chapter, let it serve as a call to action for all who read these words. Commit to justice, seek out those in need, and extend a helping hand to the fatherless, widows, and all who suffer. For it is through these acts of kindness and compassion that we honor the highest ideals of humanity and build a legacy of hope, equity, and love. May this charge inspire each of us to live with purpose and to make a meaningful difference in the lives of others.

CHAPTER 21

THE MIGHTY EQUALIZER: A DIVINE MESSAGE FOR THE BELIEVER OF FALSE DOCTRINES?

======================

FUNTUNFUNEFU DENKYEMFUNEFU

"Siamese crocodiles"

Asante philosophical symbol of Democracy, Unity in Diversity

======================

MEASURING THE SPIRITUAL STRENGTH OF A MAN OF GOD

When determining the spiritual strength or power of a Man of God, it is essential to discern whether it can be measured by miracles, accurate prophecies, or the frequency of deliverances. Many may believe these manifestations are indicators of a Man of God's spiritual prowess. However, the truth illuminated by the LORD God Almighty directs us otherwise.

The artificial yardstick to measure the spiritual strength or power of a Man of God is often misleading. False prophets often spotlight their abilities in performing miracles, delivering

individuals, and foretelling future events as undeniable proof of their spiritual ascendancy. However, the LORD reveals a deeper truth that dismantles this flawed perspective.

> **Proverbs 24:5 (KJV)** "A wise man is strong; yea, a man of knowledge increaseth strength."

In the eyes of God, a Man of God's spiritual strength is intrinsically tied to their depth of knowledge and their obedience to His Word."

According to the Lord, the real indicator of power manifests itself not in moments of tranquility but in the throes of adversity. The essence of spiritual fortitude isn't quantified by the spectacle of miracles but by steadfast faith and unyielding resilience amid trials and tribulations. The scriptures extend a message to various members of the Christian fellowship, recognizing and honoring their distinct strengths and spiritual depths. To the 'fathers,' it acknowledges their profound acquaintance with the Divine, rooted in a journey that spans the breadth of time. Meanwhile, the 'young men' are celebrated for their vigor, the indwelling of God's word within their hearts, and their triumph over malevolence.

This divine narrative underscores the significance of an intimate relationship with God, drawing strength from His eternal word and achieving victory over darkness through persistent faith and perseverance. It teaches us that the true measure of our strength and character is tested and revealed in our capacity to face life's adversities without faltering. By encouraging a spirit of resilience, the scripture implores us to rise above the earthly challenges and hardships that come our way, fortified by the Word of God and unwavering obedience to His will.

> **Proverbs 24:10 (KJV)** "If thou faint in the day of adversity, thy strength is small."

> **1 John 2:14 (KJV)** "I have written unto you, fathers, because ye have known him that is from the beginning. I have written unto you, young men, because ye are strong, and the word of God abideth in you, and ye have overcome the wicked one."

The true measure of a Man of God's spiritual strength is not found in outward displays of miracles, prophecies, or deliverances, which can sometimes create illusions of spiritual power. Instead, the essence of genuine spiritual strength lies in unwavering adherence to God's Word and steadfast obedience to His commands.

Authentic spiritual vigor is reflected in a profound understanding of divine truth, an unshakable faith that endures through life's hardships, and a deeply rooted connection with the Word of God. These qualities form the foundation of a life anchored in righteousness, enabling one to overcome the trials and temptations brought forth by the forces of darkness.

It is this steadfast commitment to God's principles, rather than external manifestations, that truly showcases the spiritual fortitude of a Man of God. This strength is revealed not in fleeting acts but in a life consistently aligned with divine purpose, demonstrating resilience, humility, and unwavering trust in the Creator.

Determining whether a Man of God is genuinely sent by the Almighty is a vital undertaking. The Word of God, as inscribed in the Holy Scriptures, serves as our unwavering guide. Let us delve into the sacred text to uncover the divine criteria for discerning the true from the false.

In this pivotal moment, Satan presents Jesus with a deceptive challenge, attempting to blur the lines between divine authority and miraculous deeds. This test reflects a broader misunderstanding prevalent among some individuals, who judge the legitimacy of a spiritual leader solely by their ability to perform signs and wonders. The scripture narrates the onset of Jesus' trials by Satan in the wilderness, at a time when Jesus, having fasted for 40 days and nights, is physically weakened and thus more susceptible to temptation. Seizing this vulnerability, Satan proposes that Jesus demonstrate His divine sonship through a supernatural act transforming stones into bread. This incident marks the beginning of a series of tests directed at Jesus, each meticulously crafted to question His devotion to God's commands and His trust in divine wisdom and support.

> **Matthew 4:3 (KJV)** "And when the tempter came to him, he said, If thou be the Son of God, command that these stones be made bread."

> **Matthew 4:4 (KJV)** "But he answered and said, It is written, Man shall not live by bread alone, but by every word that proceedeth out of the mouth of God."

The authenticity of a spiritual leader is intrinsically tied to their adherence to and alignment with the Word of God. This connection serves as a continual source of divine wisdom and guidance, underscoring the pivotal role of God's Word in shaping and affirming true spiritual authority.

A notable example is found in the life of Samuel, a revered figure whose spiritual journey reflects the profound relationship between God and His chosen servants. Samuel's experiences highlight a personal and direct method of divine revelation, emphasizing that God's Word serves as the primary channel through which His will and instructions are communicated. This ongoing dialogue underscores the significance of God's Word as a living and powerful force that connects humanity to the Creator's purpose.

The influence of the Word extends beyond mere instruction, and it embodies the essence of divine interaction, shaping the character, actions, and decisions of those who seek to serve faithfully. It is through this unwavering connection to God's Word that a leader demonstrates their authenticity, reflecting a life guided by divine principles and aligned with a higher calling.

This understanding challenge us to discern true spiritual leadership not by outward displays of power or authority but by the depth of their commitment to living and serving in accordance with God's revealed truth. The transformative and sustaining nature of the Word remains a testament to its centrality in the lives of those called to lead with integrity and faithfulness.

> **1 Samuel 3:21 (KJV)** "And the Lord appeared again in Shiloh: for the Lord revealed himself to Samuel in Shiloh by the word of the Lord."

> **Ecclesiastes 8:4 (KJV)** "Where the word of a king is, there is power: and who may say unto him, What doest thou?"

The profound impact and sovereignty of divine communication are often likened to the authoritative decrees of a king, whose words hold unmatched power and command. A king's declarations are definitive, carrying irrevocable force and demanding obedience without question. This concept serves as a metaphor for the supreme authority of the Creator, illustrating that just as the edicts of earthly rulers shape their realms, so to do God's directives govern the universe with ultimate authority.

The analogy highlights the unparalleled dominion of God's Word, which not only establishes the order of creation but also determines the destiny of individuals and nations. Every divine utterance carries an unassailable force, affirming that God's will is both sovereign and absolute. His Word transcends human limitations, shaping the cosmos and guiding the course of history with precision and purpose.

This perspective invites reflection on the power of divine communication and its role in our lives. It challenges us to recognize that God's authority is supreme, His decrees are unchanging, and His Word is the foundation upon which all creation rests. In acknowledging this, we are reminded of our place within His grand design and the enduring relevance of His guidance in our journey through life.

In another encounter, Satan introduces a misleading notion, focusing on the demonstration of miraculous deeds as proof of divine favor. However, Jesus counters this deception, teaching us to dismiss the belief that miracles are the sole validation of a spiritual leader's authenticity. He asserts the supremacy of God's Word as the fundamental criterion. This episode unfolds as Jesus faces another trial by Satan, following the initial temptation in the wilderness, where Jesus is urged to transform stones into bread. The devil escalates the challenge by transporting Jesus to the pinnacle of the temple in Jerusalem, the holy city. Here, Satan provokes Jesus to demand a miraculous intervention to prove His divine sonship by testing God's protective promise. Through these trials, Jesus exemplifies unwavering resolve and reliance on the sacred scriptures, highlighting that true faith and authority stem not from signs and wonders but from adherence to the Word of God.

> **Matthew 4:5 (KJV)** "Then the devil taketh him up into the holy city, and setteth him on a pinnacle of the temple,"

> **Matthew 4:7 (KJV)** "Jesus said unto him, It is written again, Thou shalt not tempt the Lord thy God."

> **Deuteronomy 6:16 (KJV)** "Ye shall not tempt the LORD your God, as ye tempted him in Massah."

We have been reflecting on the importance of rejecting the allure of sign-seeking within our churches, and among today's believers, we draw upon the profound example of Jesus' response to temptation. When faced with the challenge to demonstrate divine authority through a miraculous act, Jesus firmly rejected the notion of testing God's faithfulness for the sake of proof.

This moment underscores a vital lesson: faith is not grounded in demands for signs or wonders as evidence of God's love or protection. Instead, it is anchored in trust, reverence for God's sovereignty, and a commitment to aligning with His will. Jesus' response highlights the importance of humility and steadfastness in our spiritual journey, reminding us that true authenticity is not found in seeking outward displays but in an unwavering reliance on the principles and truth of God.

By rejecting the temptation to exploit divine authority for personal affirmation, Jesus sets a precedent for all believers. Our spiritual walk should be rooted in faith, not spectacle; in trust, not proof. This example calls us to focus on cultivating a deeper relationship with God, grounded in His Word and purpose, as the foundation of a meaningful and authentic faith.

In the encounter with Satan, we observe a significant moment where temptation is framed by the allure of material wealth, widespread fame, and global adoration as indicators of divine favor. This mirrors a common misconception among some modern preachers who equate spiritual success with the accumulation of riches and large followings.

Jesus, however, delivers a profound correction to this flawed perspective. He reveals that true divine blessing is not defined by earthly possessions or popularity but by wholehearted worship and unwavering service to God. His response to this temptation highlights that genuine fulfillment is found not in worldly achievements but in the dedication to guiding souls toward salvation.

This teaching establishes a clear standard for measuring spiritual success. It redirects our focus from the pursuit of material abundance and human recognition to the ultimate purpose of devotion to God and leading others to embrace His truth. Jesus' example serves as a timeless reminder that the real treasure lies in a life committed to faithfulness and eternal impact rather than fleeting worldly gains.

> **Matthew 4:8 (KJV)** "Again, the devil taketh him up into an exceeding high mountain, and sheweth him all the kingdoms of the world, and the glory of them;"

Matthew 4:9 (KJV) "And saith unto him, All these things will I give thee, if thou wilt fall down and worship me."

Matthew 4:10 (KJV) "Then saith Jesus unto him, Get thee hence, Satan: for it is written, Thou shalt worship the Lord thy God, and him only shalt thou serve."

Deuteronomy 6:13 (KJV) "Thou shalt fear the LORD thy God, and serve him, and shalt swear by his name."

The Temptation of Wealth and Fame presents a pivotal narrative in which Jesus confronts Satan's final challenge in the wilderness. Offered dominion over the kingdoms of the world in exchange for worship, Jesus faces a test designed to derail His mission of sacrifice and service by appealing to the allure of instant power and glory. This temptation strikes at the heart of His divine purpose, aiming to replace obedience to God with submission to worldly ambition. Yet, with unwavering resolve, Jesus rejects this offer, affirming that worship and service belong to God alone.

Through His response, Jesus exemplifies the true measure of spiritual success not the one we are familiar with in todays so-called men and women of God who think that their spiritual level is measured in wealth or fame, but not in fidelity to God's will. His firm declaration reaffirms a vital truth: the path of faithfulness is defined by obedience to God and devotion to His commandments, not by the fleeting rewards of material gain or human recognition. This moment serves as a guiding light for believers, reminding them that genuine allegiance to God is demonstrated in their commitment to His Word and their mission to lead others toward eternal life.

At the heart of this discussion lies the deeper insight that the hallmarks of a true servant of God are rooted in steadfast adherence to His teachings. The Word of God illuminates a journey defined by mercy and divine approval for those who express their love through obedience. The prohibition of idolatry, enshrined in divine commandments, reinforces this truth, emphasizing the profound relationship between God and those who follow His ways. This bond is not about mere rule-keeping but about a deep, enduring relationship of love, loyalty, and trust.

God's promise of mercy to those who cherish and uphold His statutes spans generations, underscoring His unwavering commitment to those who live under His guidance. This assurance reveals a timeless narrative of divine love and benevolence, offering hope and favor to all who remain faithful. Jesus' triumph in the wilderness serves as a testament to the enduring power of obedience, reminding us that true fulfillment lies in aligning our lives with the will of God and trusting in His eternal plan.

Exodus 20:6 (KJV) "And shewing mercy unto thousands of them that love me, and keep my commandments."

Psalm 1:1 (KJV) "Blessed is the man that walketh not in the counsel of the ungodly, nor standeth in the way of sinners, nor sitteth in the seat of the scornful."

Psalm 1:2 (KJV) "But his delight is in the law of the LORD; and in his law doth he meditate day and night."

Psalm 1:3 (KJV) "And he shall be like a tree planted by the rivers of water, that bringeth forth his fruit in his season; his leaf also shall not wither; and whatsoever he doeth shall prosper."

The discourse on the credentials of a Man of God offers a profound exploration of the journey toward spiritual fulfillment and the essence of a life lived in divine companionship. It vividly illustrates a life that flourishes through a deep connection with God's principles, much like a tree thriving by a life-giving stream which signifies a symbol of abundance, stability, and grace. This imagery reveals the transformative power of aligning one's life with God's will, and affirm the blessings that flow from such alignment.

At the heart of this reflection is the relationship between love and obedience. Following Jesus' teachings is not portrayed as an obligation but as the purest expression of love for Him. This adherence becomes the foundation for abiding in His love, echoing the way Jesus demonstrated His devotion to the Father by living in accordance with His commands. Obedience, therefore, emerges as the gateway to a deeper, more meaningful relationship with God.

This perspective expands to encompass the joy that stems from such a relationship which is rooted in joy and love that reflects Jesus' sacrificial care for humanity. To be called a friend of Christ is to embody a love that prioritizes selflessness, mutual care, and an unwavering commitment to the good of others. This idea weaves together themes of joy, love, and obedience, offering a holistic understanding of what it means to follow Christ.

Ultimately, the true measure of a Man of God is found in his ability to live out these values. A life marked by self-sacrifice, compassion, and unwavering dedication to God's principles exemplifies the essence of Christian discipleship. This discourse challenges every believer to embrace these attributes, not as lofty ideals but as practical, everyday expressions of their faith and devotion.

John 14:15 (KJV) "If ye love me, keep my commandments."

John 15:10 (KJV) "If ye keep my commandments, ye shall abide in my love; even as I have kept my Father's commandments, and abide in his love."

John 15:11 (KJV) "These things have I spoken unto you, that my joy might remain in you, and that your joy might be full."

> **John 15:12 (KJV)** "This is my commandment, That ye love one another, as I have loved you."

> **John 15:13 (KJV)** "Greater love hath no man than this, that a man lay down his life for his friends."

> **John 15:14 (KJV)** "Ye are my friends, if ye do whatsoever I command you."

In our final consideration, the definitive marker of a genuine Man of God is their steadfast commitment to the Scriptures. By ensuring their teachings and deeds are in harmony with the Bible, such leaders demonstrate their divine mandate to guide individuals towards salvation while faithfully observing God's statutes. Caution is advised against those who stray towards seeking material gain or miraculous signs as proof of their spiritual authority. Authentic spiritual richness is found in the diligent observance of God's Word, and the true hallmark of a Man of God is characterized by their absolute dedication to God's commandments and the eternal well-being of others. To underpin this conclusion, let us reflect on four pertinent Scriptures:

> **Matthew 4:3 (KJV)** "And when the tempter came to him, he said, If thou be the Son of God, command that these stones be made bread."

> **2 Timothy 3:16 (KJV):** "All scripture is given by inspiration of God, and is profitable for doctrine, for reproof, for correction, for instruction in righteousness:"

> **2 Timothy 3:17 (KJV):** "That the man of God may be perfect, thoroughly furnished unto all good works."

> **James 1:22 (KJV):** "But be ye doers of the word, and not hearers only, deceiving your own selves."

In this defining encounter, Jesus Christ firmly repudiates the idea, highlighting it as fundamentally misaligned with God's nature. Facing Satan, Jesus brings to light an essential lesson: evaluating a servant of God or the manifestation of the divine based exclusively on miracles is a critical error. This perspective is not merely incorrect but deeply flawed, revealing a misunderstanding and a disposition far removed from genuine spirituality. The essence and presence of God cannot be fully captured or appreciated through signs and wonders alone. Rather, the true understanding and acknowledgment of the divine are accessed through the Word of God. This insight serves as a powerful reminder of the real basis for recognizing the divine, steering us towards a more authentic and grounded faith.

> **1 Samuel 3:21 (KJV)** "And the LORD appeared again in Shiloh: for the LORD revealed himself to Samuel in Shiloh by the word of the LORD."

> **Ecclesiastes 8:4 (KJV)** "Where the word of a king *is, there is* power: and who may say unto him, What doest thou?"

Matthew 4:4 (KJV) "But he answered and said, It is written, Man shall not live by bread alone, but by every word that proceedeth out of the mouth of God."

In this instance, Satan persists in trying to characterize the Man of God, Jesus Christ, by the performance of miracles. This emphasizes a critical juncture where Satan seeks to question and shape Jesus Christ's identity and validity through the capability to perform supernatural acts. Within the biblical accounts, especially during the temptations of Jesus in the wilderness as documented in the Gospels, Satan's emphasis on miracles as a measure of Jesus's authenticity reflects a significant misinterpretation or intentional distortion of Jesus's purpose and ministry.

Matthew 12:39 (KJV) "But he answered and said unto them, An evil and adulterous generation seeketh after a sign; and there shall no sign be given to it, but the sign of the prophet Jonas:"

Matthew 16:4 (KJV) "A wicked and adulterous generation seeketh after a sign; and there shall no sign be given unto it, but the sign of the prophet Jonas. And he left them, and departed."

1 Peter 1:25 (KJV) "But the word of the Lord endureth for ever. And this is the word which by the gospel is preached unto you."

Revelation 12:11 (KJV) "And they overcame him by the blood of the Lamb, and by the word of their testimony; and they loved not their lives unto the death."

In the broader scriptural context, miracles are profound demonstrations of God's power and the presence of His kingdom, yet they are not the sole or definitive indicators of divine authority. Jesus's response to challenges of His identity and mission emphasizes a deeper truth: His role as the Son of God and His divine purpose extend far beyond outward displays of miraculous ability. His ministry is firmly rooted in embodying and fulfilling God's Word through His teachings, acts of healing, and the revelation of God's character and intentions for humanity.

The temptation to equate divine authority solely with miracles diverts attention from the core of Jesus's mission, which is centered on teaching, redemption, and reconciling humanity with God. By rejecting the notion that His identity must be proven through spectacular displays, Jesus underscores that true messianic authority is evidenced not by external tests of power but by steadfast alignment with God's will and the transformative impact of His love and redemption.

This perspective invites a deeper understanding of divine purpose, moving beyond superficial validations to recognize the profound significance of faith, obedience, and the transformative relationship between God and His people. Jesus's example challenges us to look beyond the extraordinary and focus on the enduring principles of His mission: teaching, healing, and fostering a world that reflects God's love and justice.

> **Matthew 4:5 (KJV)** "Then the devil taketh him up into the holy city, and setteth him on a pinnacle of the temple,"

> **Matthew 4:6 (KJV)** "And saith unto him, If thou be the Son of God, cast thyself down: for it is written, He shall give his angels charge concerning thee: and in *their* hands they shall bear thee up, lest at any time thou dash thy foot against a stone."

Again, we witness Jesus Christ firmly dismissing the idea that the performance of miracles should serve as the benchmark for verifying someone's role as a servant of God. Jesus instead stresses the significance of Scripture as the basis for assessing a person's divine mission. He articulates that this approach is essential not only for recognizing genuine servants of God but also for differentiating between true spiritual direction from God and misleading influences, whether they emanate from Satan or any other source. Through his teachings, Jesus highlights the pivotal importance of the Bible in judging the validity of spiritual messages and their bearers, promoting reliance on God's Word as the cornerstone of discernment and insight.

> **Matthew 4:7 (KJV)** "Jesus said unto him, It is written again, Thou shalt not tempt the Lord thy God."

At this juncture, Satan alters his tactic, enticing with the lure of material wealth encompassing money, precious metals, extensive properties, fame, and the admiration of countless individuals as signs of God's blessing. He insinuates that such earthly prosperity and widespread recognition serve as proof of divine endorsement, suggesting that they affirm one's affiliation with God and denote considerable influence. This perspective also suggests that the large followings, which idolize and hold someone in high esteem, are inherently correct in their judgment, reflecting a pattern observable in the leadership of sizeable, modern-day religious groups.

> **Matthew 4:8 (KJV)** "Again, the devil taketh him up into an exceeding high mountain, and sheweth him all the kingdoms of the world, and the glory of them;"

> **Matthew 4:9 (KJV)** "And saith unto him, All these things will I give thee, if thou wilt fall down and worship me."

Many spiritual leaders today often prioritize showcasing their material wealth, vast properties, and large followings as markers of divine favor, diverting attention from the core mission of their spiritual calling, which is the transformation and salvation of individuals. This trend reflects a concerning shift away from the foundational principles of genuine spirituality, which prioritize fostering spiritual growth and serving the community above personal gain.

Such behavior underscores the need for discernment in identifying authentic spiritual leadership. True leaders are called to guide others toward meaningful change and eternal purpose, not to use their positions as platforms for self-promotion or material accumulation. This approach mirrors a well-known temptation strategy, emphasizing the importance of vigilance and wisdom in distinguishing those who lead with sincerity from those who seek only to elevate their own status.

This reality calls for a reflective examination of the values that underpin spiritual guidance. Genuine leadership is not defined by outward displays of success but by a commitment to nurturing faith, inspiring transformation, and serving others selflessly. It is through these enduring principles that spiritual leaders demonstrate their authenticity and fulfill their higher purpose.

> **1 Corinthians 9:2 (KJV)** "If I be not an apostle unto others, yet doubtless I am to you: for the seal of mine apostleship are ye in the Lord."

The emphasis lies not on the accumulation of material assets such as gold or silver but on the spiritual impact one has on others. The essence of genuine leadership is found in the ability to inspire faith, foster spiritual growth, and support others on their journey toward redemption and purpose. This principle serves as a reminder that the value of a life devoted to God is not in material abundance but in the legacy of love, guidance, and spiritual upliftment left behind.

Through this perspective, we are called to prioritize spiritual values over worldly pursuits, focusing on the transformative impact of faith and the enduring significance of leading others toward eternal fulfillment. True richness is found not in what one possesses but, in the lives, one touches and the good one does in the service of a higher purpose.

> **Matthew 4:10 (KJV)** "Then saith Jesus unto him, Get thee hence, Satan: for it is written, Thou shalt worship the Lord thy God, and him only shalt thou serve."
>
> **Matthew 4:11 (KJV)** "Then the devil leaveth him, and, behold, angels came and ministered unto him."
>
> **Exodus 20:6 (KJV)** "And shewing mercy unto thousands of them that love me, and keep my commandments."
>
> **Psalm 1:1 (KJV)** "Blessed *is* the man that walketh not in the counsel of the ungodly, nor standeth in the way of sinners, nor sitteth in the seat of the scornful."
>
> **Psalm 1:2 (KJV)** "But his delight *is* in the law of the LORD; and in his law doth he meditate day and night."
>
> **Psalm 1:3 (KJV)** "And he shall be like a tree planted by the rivers of water, that bringeth forth his fruit in his season; his leaf also shall not wither; and whatsoever he doeth shall prosper."

John 14:15 (KJV) "If ye love me, keep my commandments."

John 15:10 (KJV) "If ye keep my commandments, ye shall abide in my love; even as I have kept my Father's commandments, and abide in his love."

John 15:14 (KJV) "Ye are my friends, if ye do whatsoever I command you."

The essence of these scriptural passages lies in the deep connection between love for the Divine, adherence to spiritual commandments, and the resultant blessings of spiritual well-being and abundance. They introduce a foundational concept where divine compassion is extended to those who align their hearts and actions with God's directives. This theme is further developed with the metaphor of a tree prospering by water, symbolizing the vitality and success that accompanies a life attuned to spiritual laws.

The narrative continues by highlighting the mutual relationship between divine affection and obedience, presenting adherence to God's commandments as both a demonstration of love and a condition for remaining within that love. This relationship is portrayed as one of friendship, offering a model of spiritual living that transcends mere duty to become an intimate journey with the divine.

In synthesizing these insights, it becomes clear that spiritual obedience is framed not as an obligation but as a transformative journey towards a richer communion with God, characterized by His mercy, enduring love, and the promise of a life that is not only fruitful but also enduringly connected to the source of all growth. The call to believers is to embrace a lifestyle deeply rooted in the divine Word, assuring them of a legacy that is both spiritually rewarding and life-affirming.

DISCERNING TRUE MEN AND WOMEN OF GOD

In today's spiritual landscape, it becomes increasingly crucial to discern true men and women of God amidst a world filled with various influences and voices. The words of Jesus Christ provide us with profound insight into the challenges we may encounter as we seek to distinguish genuine spiritual leaders from the deceptive. As we navigate this spiritual journey, we can turn to several key principles:

1. The Source of Authority

Ask whether the individual is speaking on behalf of themselves or conveying the message of God and Jesus Christ.

> **John 5:30 (KJV)** "I can of mine own self do nothing: as I hear, I judge: and my judgment is just; because I seek not mine own will, but the will of the Father which hath sent me."

> **John 5:31(KJV)** "If I bear witness of myself, my witness is not true."

The exploration of divine authority reveals profound truths about the nature of true leadership and justice. Jesus exemplifies the essence of humility and obedience by demonstrating complete reliance on divine guidance, emphasizing that authentic authority arises not from self-promotion but from unwavering alignment with a higher purpose. This approach underscores the principle that true leadership is defined by a commitment to justice and integrity, rooted in adherence to the divine will rather than personal ambition.

Furthermore, the emphasis on the inadequacy of self-proclaimed authority highlights the importance of external validation in establishing truth and credibility. By pointing to witnesses beyond Himself through His actions, teachings, and the affirmations of others, Jesus underscores the value of accountability and the collective affirmation of one's mission. This serves as a guiding principle for believers, encouraging them to seek discernment and confirmation not solely from personal convictions but from a broader spiritual context that reflects divine intentions.

Ultimately, the essence of authority is found in submission to a higher power and the pursuit of justice through humility, obedience, and integrity. It challenges us to approach our roles in life with the same reliance on guidance beyond ourselves, fostering a deeper connection to divine truth and a more profound sense of purpose in our actions. This perspective invites us to live lives shaped by service, trust in a higher plan, and a commitment to the greater good.

2. The Witness of Works and Teachings

The Witness of Works and Teachings" in the life and ministry of Jesus Christ plays an integral role of Jesus' actions and teachings as testimonies to His divine authority and mission. Let's delve into each verse to unpack this theme.

> **John 5:36 (KJV)** "But I have greater witness than that of John: for the works which the Father hath given me to finish, the same works that I do, bear witness of me, that the Father hath sent me."

> **John 10:25 (KJV)** "Jesus answered them, I told you, and ye believed not: the works that I do in my Father's name, they bear witness of me."

In the discussions surrounding Jesus' mission and divine identity, His works stand as a central and transformative testament. These works, encompassing His miracles, acts of compassion, and teachings, transcend mere human effort; they are divine commissions reflecting the purpose and will of God. Each action serves a dual purpose: they are tangible expressions of God's love and salvation and undeniable affirmations of Jesus' authority as the one sent by God.

This perspective underscores the profound connection between faith and action. Jesus' works are not isolated demonstrations of power but intentional acts that reveal the character of God and His Son through mercy, strength, and a redemptive plan for humanity. They embody the essence of divine purpose, illustrating that true authority is reflected in deeds that align with God's overarching mission.

These actions also challenge skeptics, serving as irrefutable evidence of His identity in a world often swayed by words alone. They demonstrate that genuine faith is not confined to verbal declarations but is lived out through purposeful acts that resonate with divine teachings. Jesus' life exemplifies this integration of belief and action, inviting believers to embrace a faith that is both deeply spiritual and profoundly active.

These narrative calls believers to move beyond superficial understanding and engage with the deeper implications of Jesus' works and mission. It is an invitation to align our lives with the principles demonstrated through His ministry, fostering a faith that is lived out through acts of compassion, justice, and obedience to God's will.

In conclusion, Jesus' works are a testament to His divine mission and identity, serving as a model for living a life of faith that intertwines belief with action. They remind us that true spiritual authority is expressed through deeds that reflect the heart of God, inspiring us to participate actively in the unfolding of His kingdom in our own lives and communities.

3. The Testimony of the Holy Spirit

The Testimony of the Holy Spirit" in Christian doctrine emphasizes the Holy Spirit's vital role in validating the divine origin of teachings and actions within the faith. The Holy Spirit, beyond being a source of comfort and guidance, acts as a definitive marker of truth, distinguishing between the divine and the human, the sacred and the profane. As highlighted by the scripture "The Spirit itself beareth witness with our spirit, that we are the children of God," the Holy Spirit plays a critical role in affirming a believer's identity and the veracity of their connection to God. This becomes particularly significant when individuals claim to be inspired or guided by divine will. The Holy Spirit, working both within the community of believers and the heart of the individual, acts as a critical verifier of such claims, ensuring they align with the foundational truths of Christianity and the character of God.

If you are a Christian and claim the presence of the Holy Spirit, observe whether the Holy Spirit bears witness to the teachings of the individual as being of God.

> **John 5:37 (KJV)** "And the Father himself, which hath sent me, hath borne witness of me. Ye have neither heard his voice at any time, nor seen his shape."

> **Romans 8:16 (KJV)** states, "The Spirit itself beareth witness with our spirit, that we are the children of God."

The testimony of the Holy Spirit is a profound aspect of Christian living, offering assurance, guidance, and discernment. In a world where claims of divine inspiration are many, the Holy Spirit provides the essential standard by which such claims can be tested. This divine witness ensures that the teachings and actions embraced and followed by believers are truly reflective of God's will, leading the church into deeper truth and unity under the headship of Christ.

4. Search the Scriptures

The encouragement to engage in personal investigation by diligently examining the scriptures to assess the alignment of teachings with the Word of God is rooted in the Berean approach mentioned in Acts 17:11. The Bereans were commended for their eagerness to receive the word and for examining the Scriptures daily to see if what Paul preached was true. This model of scriptural engagement is crucial for several reasons.

> **Acts 17:11 (KJV)** "These were more noble than those in Thessalonica, in that they received the word with all readiness of mind, and searched the scriptures daily, whether those things were so."

John 5:39 (KJV) "Search the scriptures; for in them ye think ye have eternal life: and they are they which testify of me."

1 John 4:1 (KJV) "Beloved, believe not every spirit, but try the spirits whether they are of God."

The Bereans, a commendable group of Jews from Berea, exemplified an ideal approach to spiritual teachings presented by Paul and Silas. Notably open-minded and eager to learn, they received the apostolic word with readiness. Yet, their openness was not synonymous with uncritical acceptance. They embarked on a daily journey of diligently examining the scripture to authenticate the apostles' teachings regarding Jesus Christ as the Messiah. This method of direct and personal engagement with Scripture led to the development of deeply rooted convictions, ensuring that their faith was not superficially inherited or uncritically adopted but was instead a result of thorough examination, testing, and verification against God's Word.

Such diligent examination of Scriptures significantly enhances one's ability to understand and interpret biblical texts. It encourages believers to delve into the context, content, and application of biblical teachings, fostering spiritual growth and maturity. In an era teeming with numerous voices claiming to proclaim the truth, this Berean approach acts as a critical safeguard against deception. By rigorously comparing teachings with the Bible, believers are equipped to discern the consistency of these teachings with divine truth or identify deviations, thereby protecting both themselves and the broader Christian community from false doctrines and misleading interpretations.

Furthermore, this practice of assessing the alignment of teachings with the Word of God is fundamental in ensuring that one's beliefs and practices remain anchored in biblical truth. This dedication to doctrinal integrity is crucial for the preservation of the faith's purity and unity, preventing believers from veering into error or divisiveness. Thus, the Berean model not only represents a commendable method of engaging with spiritual teachings but also serves as a vital framework for maintaining a robust, discerning, and mature Christian faith.

5. Consistency with the Word of God

Verify whether the writings and teachings of the individual remain in harmony with the scriptures.

John 5:46 (KJV) "For had ye believed Moses, ye would have believed me: for he wrote of me."

Acts 1:14 (KJV) "These all continued with one accord in prayer and supplication, with the women, and Mary the mother of Jesus, and with his brethren."

Acts 15:25 (KJV) "It seemed good unto us, being assembled with one accord, to send chosen men unto you with our beloved Barnabas and Paul,"

This passage beautifully illustrates the profound connection between Jesus' teachings and the foundational Jewish Scriptures, particularly the writings of Moses. It highlights the continuity between the Old and New Testaments, presenting Jesus not as the founder of a new religion but as the fulfillment of ancient promises and prophecies. His life and mission were deeply rooted in the Hebrew Bible, affirming the unity of the biblical narrative and underscoring His role in divine redemption.

The reference to the Gospel of John, where Jesus affirms that Moses' writings pointed to Him, is a critical cornerstone for understanding how the Messiah's mission was integrated within Jewish tradition and scripture. This connection not only reinforces the validity of Jesus' teachings but also reflects the early Christian community's approach to addressing doctrinal challenges, such as through the Council of Jerusalem. Their example of collective wisdom and dialogue serves as a model for maintaining unity and clarity in faith and practice.

Reflecting on these ideas through a five-step guide to discerning genuine spiritual leaders offers practical insights in a world saturated with competing voices and influences. By seeking clarity, wisdom, and alignment with foundational truths, believers can navigate their spiritual journey with confidence. The teachings of Jesus provide timeless guidance, illuminating the path toward understanding and faithfulness.

May the grace and wisdom of the Lord Jesus Christ continue to guide and inspire as we strive to walk in truth and follow those who lead in alignment with His Word.

THE DEFINITION OF A TRUE PROPHET

When examining the qualities of a true prophet, the Bible serves as a critical source of insight and criteria. It aids in distinguishing between those prophets who sincerely act in accordance with God's intentions and those who may not. The scriptures caution against prophets who prioritize worldly achievements over the message of salvation. Within these teachings, we find a specific warning. The scriptures narrate instances of prophets who were tempted by the prospect of financial gain and the practice of divination, highlighting the importance of prophets being motivated not by personal gain but by a commitment to convey God's message. This account emphasizes the dangers of prophets being swayed by monetary temptations and predictive practices. A true prophet's foremost goal should be to execute God's will, steering clear of the pursuit of material riches.

> **Jeremiah 23:15 (KJV)** "Therefore thus saith the LORD of hosts concerning the prophets; Behold, I will feed them with wormwood, and make them drink the water of gall: for from the prophets of Jerusalem is profaneness gone forth into all the land."

> **Numbers 22:7 (KJV)**, "And the elders of Moab and the elders of Midian departed with the rewards of divination in their hand; and they came unto Balaam, and spake unto him the words of Balak"

> **Micah 3:11 (KJV)** "The heads thereof judge for reward, and the priests thereof teach for hire, and the prophets thereof divine for money: yet will they lean upon the LORD, and say, Is not the LORD among us? none evil can come upon us."

The scripture highlights a warning against prophets prioritizing earthly success over the core message of redemption. It presents an additional caution, detailing the tale of prophets lured by the promise of financial gain and the practice of divination, emphasizing that true prophets ought not to be motivated by monetary interests. This story illuminates the risk associated with prophets being swayed by financial rewards and predictive practices. The fundamental purpose of a true prophet is to enact God's will, as opposed to seeking material prosperity.

> **Isaiah 52:7 (KJV)** "How beautiful upon the mountains are the feet of him that bringeth good tidings, that publisheth peace; that bringeth good tidings of good, that publisheth salvation; that saith unto Zion, Thy God reigneth!"

> **Isaiah 52:8 (KJV)** "Thy watchmen shall lift up the voice; with the voice together shall they sing: for they shall see eye to eye when the LORD shall bring again Zion."

It illustrates that true prophets share a singular vision, committed to the overarching goal of salvation and reuniting God's followers.

> **Acts 4:12 (KJV):** "Neither is there salvation in any other: for there is none other name under heaven given among men, whereby we must be saved"

> **Romans 1:16 (KJV):** "For I am not ashamed of the gospel of Christ: for it is the power of God unto salvation to every one that believeth; to the Jew first, and also to the Greek"

> **John 3:17 (KJV):** "For God sent not his Son into the world to condemn the world; but that the world through him might be saved."

> **Isaiah 52:10 (KJV)** "The LORD hath made bare his holy arm in the eyes of all the nations; and all the ends of the earth shall see the salvation of our God."

In contrast, the essence of a true prophet's calling, as seen through God's perspective, is fundamentally intertwined with the notion of Salvation. Scripture vividly portrays this, underscoring the critical importance of conveying the message of salvation. This text brings to light the function of true prophets as heralds of both salvation and divine serenity. It accentuates that the central theme of a legitimate prophet's message is the salvation offered by God to all parts of the globe.

In summary, the Word of God teaches us that a true prophet's ministry is fundamentally centered around the message of salvation and divine intent. Such prophets eschew earthly riches, focusing instead on spreading God's offer of salvation universally. Their voices echo in unison, like watchmen in harmony, dedicated to guiding God's people towards the path of salvation.

PROPHECY AND THE WORD OF GOD

A prophet's ability to deliver prophecies without referencing the Bible is fundamentally flawed; the answer is unequivocally "No." Prophetic utterances must be anchored in the Scriptures to be considered divinely inspired. A prophet claiming to deliver messages not based on biblical scripture is likely influenced by external, non-divine forces. The authenticity and validity of a prophet's messages are fundamentally tied to their adherence to the biblical text. To affirm this principle, one must turn to the Scriptures, which serve as the ultimate standard and guide for discerning genuine prophecy and ensuring it is rooted in God's Word:

> **John 5:47 (KJV)** "But if ye believe not his writings, how shall ye believe my words?"

> **Isaiah 8:20 (KJV)** "To the law and to the testimony: if they speak not according to this word, it is because there is no light in them."

Examine the scripture closely, and you will see that the teachings of Jesus Christ, who was Himself a Prophet, were firmly rooted in the holy scriptures. Prophecies made by individuals claiming to receive revelations beyond the foundation of scripture, do not align with the divine guidance set forth by God. The Bible clearly asserts that any utterances not grounded in God's Word lack true divine insight.

Fundamentally, the origin of true prophecy, along with its source, is deeply spiritual. The Spirit of God, which permeates the Word of God, stands as the only authentic fountain of divine prophecy. Therefore, any prophet whose declarations are not based on the scriptural truths of the Bible, specifically the teachings of Jesus Christ, operates under the influence of a spirit other than the Holy Spirit.

> **1 Samuel 3:21 (KJV)** "And the LORD appeared again in Shiloh: for the LORD revealed himself to Samuel in Shiloh by the word of the LORD."

> **1 Samuel 3:21 (KJV)** "And the LORD appeared again in Shiloh: for the LORD revealed himself to Samuel in Shiloh by the word of the LORD."

> **John 1:1 (KJV)** "In the beginning was the Word, and the Word was with God, and the Word was God."

> **Revelation 19:10 (KJV)** "And I fell at his feet to worship him. And he said unto me, see thou do it not: I am thy fellowservant, and of

thy brethren that have the testimony of Jesus: worship God: for the testimony of Jesus is the spirit of prophecy."

The narrative of God's manifestation to Samuel in Shiloh underscores a pivotal biblical theme: The Lord chooses to reveal Himself and communicate with humanity through His Word. This principle is further echoed in the opening verses of John, where it is stated that the Word is not only with God but is God Himself, establishing the Word as the foundational element of divine existence and revelation.

The essence of prophecy and its divine origin are vividly illustrated in Revelation, where the act of worship is redirected towards God, emphasizing that true prophecy and testimony stem from Jesus Christ. This connection between Christ, the Word, and prophecy highlights the integral role of the Scriptures in the realm of divine revelation and communication.

Thus, the scripture elegantly weaves together the notion that all legitimate prophecy is deeply rooted in the Word of God. It warns against the teachings of prophets who stray from the scriptural path, as such deviations mark a departure from the guidance of the Holy Spirit. This affirms the Bible's revered status as the supreme conduit of divine wisdom and truth.

In light of these reflections, it becomes clear that discernment and fidelity to the Word of God are essential in recognizing authentic prophets and safeguarding against false teachings. The scripture invites believers to lean on the Word of God as both the lens through which divine truth is discerned and the standard against which all prophecy should be measured.

DISCERNING WHEN SATAN'S SPIRIT TAKES OVER IN A PROPHETIC SERVICE

Is it possible to recognize when the spirit of deception has infiltrated a prophetic church service? Indeed, it is not only possible but essential to discern such moments with wisdom and spiritual vigilance. Through the guidance of divine truth and discernment, the presence of a counterfeit spirit can be unveiled. Let us reflect on the principles of truth and righteousness to affirm this profound reality.

Prophesying from Personal Spirit: A Cautionary Warning

The teachings in the book of Ezekiel reveal a sobering truth about how some prophets speak not from divine wisdom but from their own thoughts and emotions. These individuals stray from the path of genuine spiritual insight, presenting messages that lack the essence of divine truth.

Authentic prophecy arises solely from divine revelation, a principle that underscores the critical need to align with the guidance of the divine rather than human intuition or interpretation. This serves as a reminder to discern carefully and to seek the voice of truth, ensuring that prophetic utterances remain rooted in the wisdom and will of the Creator.

> **Ezekiel 13:1 (KJV)** "And the word of the LORD came unto me, saying,"
>
> **Ezekiel 13:2 (KJV)** "Son of man, prophesy against the prophets of Israel that prophesy, and say thou unto them that prophesy out of their own hearts, Hear ye the word of the LORD;"
>
> **Ezekiel 13:3 (KJV)** "Thus saith the Lord GOD; Woe unto the foolish prophets, that follow their own spirit, and have seen nothing!"

The Foundation of True Prophecy: The Word of God

The discussion around the core of true prophecy emphasizes the indispensable role of the Word of God as the foundational element for any prophecy that claims authenticity. This premise underlines that prophecies should not stem from personal or subjective interpretations of the Scriptures but must be deeply rooted in the divine revelation provided by God Himself.

The mandate presented in the New Testament, specifically in Romans, instructs that prophecy must be exercised in accordance with faith. This directive highlights that the true capacity of a prophet is not measured by their personal conviction or eloquence but by a faith that is firmly anchored in the Word of God.

Furthermore, the concept of faith is clarified within the scriptures as being synonymous with the Word of God itself, which is proclaimed and cherished among believers. This definition underscores the belief that faith, and consequently prophecy, should emanate from, and reflect, the teachings and truths found within the divine Word.

> **2 Peter 1:19 (KJV)** "We have also a more sure word of prophecy; whereunto ye do well that ye take heed, as unto a light that shineth in a dark place, until the day dawn, and the day star arise in your hearts:"

> **2 Peter 1:20 (KJV)** "Knowing this first, that no prophecy of the scripture is of any private interpretation"Top of Form

> **Romans 12:6 (KJV)** "Having then gifts differing according to the grace that is given to us, whether prophecy, let us prophesy according to the proportion of faith"

> **Romans 10:8 (KJV)** "But what saith it? The word is nigh thee, even in thy mouth, and in thy heart: that is, the word of faith, which we preach;"

In essence, the integrity and validity of prophecy are secured through its alignment with Scripture, ensuring that true prophecy is not just an expression of faith but a reflection of God's unchanging word. This framework not only guides prophets in their declarations but also offers believers a criterion for discerning the authenticity of prophetic messages, anchoring them in the foundational truths of their faith.

The Spirit of Prophecy and Christ's Testimony

Prophecy is intrinsically tied to the testimony of Christ, emphasizing that the essence of all genuine prophetic utterances is rooted in bearing witness to Him. The message and mission of Jesus serve as the foundation for authentic prophecy, illuminating the profound connection between prophetic revelation and the life and teachings of Christ. This understanding places Jesus at the center of all true prophetic insight, affirming that the ultimate purpose of prophecy is to proclaim His truth and divine mission to the world.

> **Revelation 19:10 (KJV)** "And I fell at his feet to worship him. And he said unto me, See thou do it not: I am thy fellowservant, and of thy brethren that have the testimony of Jesus: worship God: for the testimony of Jesus is the spirit of prophecy."

Recognizing the False Prophet: Deceptive as Foxes

The analogy drawn between false prophets and crafty, deceitful foxes serves to illustrate how these individuals, straying from the path of God's Word, embody treachery and cunning. Lacking the commitment to act as spiritual guardians or intercessors, these scriptures expose a perilous trait of false prophets: the fabrication of their own visions and messages upon veering away from biblical truths, leading others astray as they seek validation for their falsehoods.

> **Ezekiel 13:4 (KJV)** "O Israel, thy prophets are like the foxes in the deserts."

> **Ezekiel 13:5 (KJV)** "Ye have not gone up into the gaps, neither made up the hedge for the house of Israel to stand in the battle in the day of the LORD."

> **Ezekiel 13:6 (KJV)** "They have seen vanity and lying divination, saying, The LORD saith: and the LORD hath not sent them: and they have made others to hope that they would confirm the word."

> **Ezekiel 13:4-5 (KJV)** "God likens false prophets who operate outside His Word to cunning and treacherous foxes. They fail to stand in the gap or provide spiritual defense."

Identifying Satan's Spirit in a Prophetic Service

In a prophetic service, the ability to discern when a deceptive spirit takes control is of utmost importance. This often becomes evident when a prophet strays from foundational teachings, choosing to prophesy or preach from their own thoughts or emotions rather than aligning with divine truth.

When messages cannot be fully validated by established spiritual principles or contradict the broader framework of faith, it raises concerns about the influence of a deceptive spirit within the gathering. This phenomenon can be likened to individuals not religious or not grounded in the Lord describing a sudden inner prompting, such as saying, "something told me…" For Christians, these internal prompts are often attributed to their spirit or the guidance of the Holy Spirit. However, it is essential to exercise discernment to determine whether these influences align with divine wisdom or stem from another source or imaginations.

Spiritual discernment hinges on a solid foundation in truth, serving as the compass for recognizing the source of prophetic or spiritual experiences. Whether in prophetic services or moments of spiritual deliverance, understanding and applying these principles ensures that only genuine divine guidance is followed.

1 John 4:1(KJV) "Beloved, believe not every spirit, but try the spirits whether they are of God: because many false prophets are gone out into the world."

2 Timothy 4:3-4 (KJV) "For the time will come when they will not endure sound doctrine; but after their own lusts shall they heap to themselves teachers, having itching ears; And they shall turn away their ears from the truth, and shall be turned unto fables."

In summary, Satan's spirit takes over in a prophetic service when the Prophet abandons the Word of God and speaks directly from their own understanding and spirit. When prophecies are not in perfect harmony with the entirety of Scripture and cannot be fully confirmed in the Bible, it is vital to be aware of this subtle shift in the spirit of the service. Staying rooted in the Word of God is the ultimate defense against the intrusion of false spirits into the prophetic realm.

A Prophet Is a Prophet Because...

A prophet gains recognition through distinct characteristics and deeds that resonate with the principles outlined in the Gospel of Jesus Christ. We will delve into these traits, underpinned by relevant verses from the Bible

1. Testimony of Jesus Christ

A Prophet is notably characterized by their profound comprehension and articulation of the Gospel of Jesus Christ. The significance of bearing witness to Jesus Christ is also stressed in various scriptures. This concept is supported by multiple passages throughout the Bible:

> **Revelation 19:10 (KJV)**: "And I fell at his feet to worship him. And he said unto me, See thou do it not: I am thy fellowservant, and of thy brethren that have the testimony of Jesus: worship God: for the testimony of Jesus is the spirit of prophecy."

> **John 15:26 (KJV)** "But when the Comforter is come, whom I will send unto you from the Father, even the Spirit of truth, which proceedeth from the Father, he shall testify of me."

> **2 Peter 1:21 (KJV)** "For the prophecy came not in old time by the will of man: but holy men of God spake as they were moved by the Holy Ghost."

These insights collectively emphasize that the testimony of Jesus Christ is the cornerstone of all true prophecy, serving as its defining hallmark.

2. Obedience to God's Commandments

A Prophet's life is marked by steadfast adherence to the commandments given by God. This essential trait is highlighted in the scriptures for our admonishing:

> **Deuteronomy 11:27 (KJV)**: "A blessing, if ye obey the commandments of the LORD your God, which I command you this day:"

> **Deuteronomy 11:28 (KJV)**: "And a curse, if ye will not obey the commandments of the LORD your God, but turn aside out of the

way which I command you this day, to go after other gods, which ye have not known."

Acts 5:29 (KJV) "Then Peter and the other apostles answered and said, We ought to obey God rather than men."

Romans 2:8 (KJV) "But unto them that are contentious, and do not obey the truth, but obey unrighteousness, indignation and wrath."

John 14:15 (KJV) "offers a simple yet profound directive from Jesus Himself, "If ye love me, keep my commandments."

Joshua 1:8 (KJV) "This book of the law shall not depart out of thy mouth; but thou shalt meditate therein day and night, that thou mayest observe to do according to all that is written therein: for then thou shalt make thy way prosperous, and then thou shalt have good success."

This underscores the fundamental significance of adhering to divine commandments, positioning obedience as a defining characteristic of a true prophet.

3. Truthfulness and Honesty

The integrity of a Prophet is fundamentally anchored in the virtues of truthfulness and honesty, qualities that are indispensable in their character and teachings. Their dedication to truth is vividly mirrored in the teachings of scripture, highlighting the significance of honesty not just in one-on-one interactions but also as a cornerstone for establishing justice and peace within a community. Consequently, a genuine prophet lives out this value by steering clear of falsehood and deceit, opting instead to consistently stand by and convey truth in every aspect of their life. Such steadfast commitment to truth transcends personal virtue, serving as a divine command that epitomizes the prophet's role as both a messenger of God's word and an exemplar of righteous conduct for others to emulate.

> **Zechariah 8:16 (KJV)** "These are the things that ye shall do; Speak ye every man the truth to his neighbour; execute the judgment of truth and peace in your gates."

> **Colossians 3:9 (KJV)** "Lie not one to another, seeing that ye have put off the old man with his deeds."

Christians are called to embrace truthfulness in all aspects of life, leaving behind past behaviors rooted in sin and deceit to walk in righteousness through Christ. This transformative journey is expected of all believers, but especially of prophets, who are entrusted with exemplifying honesty

and integrity in their relationship with God and in their interactions with others. This commitment to truth reflects the essence of living as a true prophet of God, a life reshaped by and devoted to the principles of divine truth.

4. Counsel Rooted in the Word of God

In the realm of spiritual leadership, a prophet's guidance must consistently align with divine wisdom, avoiding reliance on secular methods or materialistic approaches to spiritual enlightenment. However, challenges arise when prophetic counsel strays from this principle, such as urging believers to abandon practical solutions like medical treatment in favor of miraculous intervention. Such advice raises significant concerns, as it diverges from the core mandate of prophetic ministry: to lead individuals toward righteous decisions grounded in divine truth and wisdom.

True prophetic ministry must honor a balance between faith and the sanctity of life, guiding worshippers to serve God in spirit and truth. Actions or counsel that disregard practical wisdom or endanger believers undermine the essence of prophetic integrity. The distinction of being a prophet demands unwavering adherence to principles of discernment, care, and alignment with divine teachings.

The calling of a prophet is reserved for those who embody these values fully, reflecting the rigorous criteria set forth for authentic prophetic ministry. Any deviation from these standards casts serious doubt on the legitimacy of the prophetic role. A true prophet's life and message must be rooted in the commandments of God and characterized by the spirit of truth.

May the grace of the Lord Jesus Christ provide you with wisdom and discernment, empowering you to live out the true calling of a prophet or to wisely follow those who uphold this sacred responsibility.

> **Jeremiah 23:21 (KJV)** "I have not sent these prophets, yet they ran: I have not spoken to them, yet they prophesied."

> **Jeremiah 23:22 (KJV)** "But if they had stood in my counsel, and had caused my people to hear my words, then they should have turned them from their evil way, and from the evil of their doings."

> **Luke 7:28 (KJV)** "For I say unto you, Among those that are born of women there is not a greater prophet than John the Baptist: but he that is least in the kingdom of God is greater than he."

> **John 10:41 (KJV)** "And many resorted unto him, and said, John did no miracle: but all things that John spake of this man were true."

Luke 7:28 (KJV) and **John 10:41 (KJV)** "where the greatness of a true Prophet is revealed."

This discussion brings to light the profound integrity and truthfulness of John the Baptist's ministry, illustrating that his prophetic authenticity was not diminished by the absence of miracles but was instead validated through his truthful testimony about Jesus. His life exemplifies the critical virtues of truthfulness and humility, essential for those who seek the title of Prophet. The biblical narrative establishes a clear framework of criteria for prophethood, emphasizing that any deviation from these established principles questions the authenticity of a prophetic claim. Therefore, embracing the role of a Prophet requires a deep commitment to living out the truths of God's Word, underscored by a life of humility and spiritual devotion.

May the grace and wisdom of the Lord Jesus Christ guide and equip you as you pursue the high calling of serving as a Prophet, grounded in the unshakeable foundation of God's Word.

CAN PROPHECY OCCUR INDEPENDENT OF THE SCRIPTURES?

Many self-styled prophets, particularly from Ghana and other African regions, have migrated to Europe and the Americas not for employment but to establish churches as part of their schemes. They assert the capability to precisely identify personal details of individuals, such as names, occupations, birthdays, and locations of their possessions, claiming these insights are divinely revealed by God. This, they argue, demonstrates that prophecy can occur independently of the Scriptures. However, it is crucial to consult the Scriptures to verify the authenticity of these claims. The Bible provides the necessary guidance on this issue, and it is to this source we must turn for clarity and understanding.

1. Seeking Prophecies from the Scriptures

According to the Scriptures, when genuine Prophets seek divine revelations, they turn to the Scriptures for guidance. They do not rely on personal intuition or unsanctioned sources.

> **1 Peter 1:10 (KJV)** "Of which salvation the prophets have enquired and searched diligently, who prophesied of the grace that should come unto you:"
>
> **1 Peter 1:11 (KJV)** "Searching what, or what manner of time the Spirit of Christ which was in them did signify, when it testified beforehand the sufferings of Christ, and the glory that should follow."

The prophets engaged in meticulous inquiry and thorough examination, seeking to understand the specifics or the timing of the events the Spirit of Christ within them had foretold. This approach sharply contrasts with that of prophets who assert they receive revelations beyond what is documented in Scripture. As a believer, you have, in the presence of the broader community or public gatherings, consented to affirm revelations about yourself that you know to be false, merely out of courtesy. This action makes you equally responsible for any deception that has been perpetuated as a result

2. Receiving Revelations from God

True prophets receive divine revelations as they immerse themselves in the wisdom of sacred teachings. These writings serve as the channel through which messages from the divine are imparted. This emphasizes that genuine prophetic insight is rooted in spiritual guidance and divine inspiration, ensuring the message aligns with eternal truths and wisdom.

1 Peter 1:12 (KJV) "Unto whom it was revealed, that not unto themselves, but unto us they did minister the things, which are now reported unto you by them that have preached the gospel unto you with the Holy Ghost sent down from heaven; which things the angels desire to look into."

Matthew 7:15 (KJV) "Beware of false prophets, which come to you in sheep's clothing, but inwardly they are ravening wolves."

Matthew 7:16 (KJV) "Ye shall know them by their fruits. Do men gather grapes of thorns, or figs of thistles?"

True prophetic revelation serves as a profound reminder of its purpose and essence, cautioning against the influence of false prophets. Authentic revelations are never self-serving or meant for immediate gratification. Instead, they form part of a greater divine plan, reaching beyond the present to impact future generations and fulfill a broader purpose within the journey of faith.

The power of prophecy lies in its role as a guiding force in the collective spiritual journey, leading believers toward the realization of divine promises. These revelations are intricately connected to the shared faith experience, aiming to uplift and unify the community of believers while advancing the mission of spiritual growth and enlightenment. Genuine prophecy focuses on the edification of the collective, never on the glorification of the individual.

2 Peter 2:1 (KJV) "But there were false prophets also among the people, even as there shall be false teachers among you, who privily shall bring in damnable heresies, even denying the Lord that bought them, and bring upon themselves swift destruction."

2 Peter 2:2 (KJV) "And many shall follow their pernicious ways; by reason of whom the way of truth shall be evil spoken of."

In this light, we are cautioned against being swayed by those who claim prophetic insight merely by revealing personal or past information—knowledge that does not edify, instruct, or build up the faith community, but rather serves to inflate the prophet's ego or personal following. True prophetic messages from God are forward-looking, often not immediately verifiable, and are intended to prepare, guide, and reassure God's people of their role in His salvation plan, not to glorify the messenger.

These understanding challenges us to discern the nature of the prophecies and the prophets we encounter. Are they contributing to the collective understanding and anticipation of God's kingdom, or are they focused on personal gain and recognition? Genuine prophecy aligns with God's redemptive history and the future unfolding of His plan, a plan so majestic that even angels long to comprehend it.

Therefore, let us be vigilant and seek wisdom in discerning the truth, focusing on revelations that truly edify the church and align with God's future-oriented plan of salvation. In doing so, we safeguard ourselves against the allure of false prophets and remain steadfast in our faith journey, anchored in the hope and promise of God's eternal plan.

3. Old Testament Confirmation

The Old Testament presents compelling evidence that genuine prophecy is deeply rooted in a connection to divine truth, as demonstrated through the lives of figures like Samuel and Daniel. Their stories reveal that authentic prophetic messages do not arise in isolation but are anchored in a profound relationship with the divine and a foundation of sacred teachings.

Samuel's narrative illustrates the life of a prophet whose words were consistently supported by divine guidance. His prophecies were not only accurate but also recognized as divinely inspired, reflecting a direct and ongoing communication with the divine. This recognition by the community stemmed from his evident role as a chosen messenger, rooted in an active relationship with the divine.

These examples underscore the principle that true prophecy emerges from a dialogue with the Creator, where the prophet's words are a faithful reflection of divine will and purpose. This foundational connection ensures that the message aligns with eternal truth and serves as a beacon for the community.

> **1 Samuel 3:19 (KJV)** "And Samuel grew, and the Lord was with him, and did let none of his words fall to the ground."
>
> **1 Samuel 3:20 (KJV)** "And all Israel from Dan even to Beersheba knew that Samuel was established to be a prophet of the Lord."
>
> **1 Samuel 3:21 (KJV)** "And the Lord appeared again in Shiloh: for the Lord revealed himself to Samuel in Shiloh by the word of the Lord."

Daniel's experience provides a complementary perspective on the nature of prophecy, showcasing the importance of seeking understanding through diligent engagement with divine teachings. His insight into the duration of Jerusalem's desolation came through careful study of earlier prophecies. This illustrates that prophetic understanding often emerges from a deep relationship with divine truth and a commitment to seeking clarity and guidance.

Daniel's response in times of difficulties turning to prayer, supplication, fasting, and acts of humility that highlights that prophecy is not merely the passive reception of messages but an active and responsive relationship with the divine. It reflects a willingness to align oneself with the greater purpose and seek divine intervention with reverence and dedication.

Both instances emphasize that authentic prophecy is deeply intertwined with a connection to divine wisdom, whether through direct revelation or thoughtful engagement with spiritual teachings. This ensures that true prophetic messages remain aligned with a higher plan, serving to guide, warn, and draw people closer to the divine will.

> **Daniel 9:1 (KJV)** "In the first year of Darius the son of Ahasuerus, of the seed of the Medes, which was made king over the realm of the Chaldeans;"

> **Daniel 9:2 (KJV)** "In the first year of his reign I Daniel understood by books the number of the years, whereof the word of the Lord came to Jeremiah the prophet, that he would accomplish seventy years in the desolations of Jerusalem."

> **Daniel 9:3 (KJV)** "And I set my face unto the Lord God, to seek by prayer and supplications, with fasting, and sackcloth, and ashes"

4. The Surest Word of Prophecy

For those aspiring to be prophets with unwavering accuracy, it is essential to anchor their messages in the infallible authority of sacred teachings. These teachings serve as the ultimate standard for any prophetic utterance, providing a foundation that has stood the test of time, been fulfilled in history, and validated by the faithful witness of countless generations. Unlike human insights, which can be flawed or biased, the principles and prophecies contained in these teachings are rooted in divine revelation, offering an unparalleled source of reliability and truth.

Prophetic messages should act as a guiding light, offering clarity and illumination in a world often shrouded in spiritual confusion. For those called to the prophetic, there is a clear imperative to immerse themselves deeply in these sacred texts. Such engagement aligns the heart and mind with divine wisdom, fostering an internal transformation that ensures prophetic accuracy. This alignment allows the prophet's words to transcend human understanding, becoming reflections of divine truth and light.

By adhering to these principles, aspiring prophets can ensure their messages remain authentic, trustworthy, and deeply connected to the divine will.

> **2 Peter 1:19 (KJV)** "We have also a more sure word of prophecy; whereunto ye do well that ye take heed, as unto a light that shineth in a dark place, until the day dawn, and the day star arise in your hearts:"

> **2 Peter 1:20 (KJV)** "Knowing this first, that no prophecy of the scripture is of any private interpretation."

Finally, verse 20, "Knowing this first, that no prophecy of the scripture is of any private interpretation," reinforces the communal and universal nature of biblical prophecy. It warns against subjective or personal interpretations that deviate from the intended message. For aspiring prophets, this is a caution against elevating personal revelations or interpretations above the collective understanding and traditional interpretations of the Christian community. It stresses the importance of humility, accountability, and a willingness to submit one's insights to the scrutiny of sound theological interpretation and the guidance of the Holy Spirit.

In summary, those aspiring to the role of a prophet are called to a deep and reverent engagement with sacred teachings, a commitment to aligning their hearts with divine truth, and humility in interpretation. By adhering to these principles, prophets can ensure their messages are both accurate and faithful to the overarching divine purpose and plan. This underscores the importance of foundational texts as the ultimate source of reliable and trustworthy prophetic guidance.

5. The Testimony of Jesus Christ

Finally, it is essential to recognize that the essence of true prophecy lies in bearing witness to the life and mission of Jesus, embodying its foundational purpose and spirit.

> **Revelation 19:10 (KJV):** "See thou do it not: I am thy fellowservant,
> and of thy brethren that have the testimony of Jesus: worship God:
> for the testimony of Jesus is the spirit of prophecy."

This implies that true prophecy is consistent with the teachings of Jesus, and anyone claiming to be a prophet should adhere to God's Word, prioritizing divine truth over personal acclaim or adoration.

In conclusion, the Scriptures make it clear that true prophecies are deeply rooted in the Word of God. They are a product of diligent study, reverence for Scripture, and alignment with the testimony of Jesus Christ. Prophesying without Scriptural foundation is contrary to the Bible's teachings.

May the Lord Jesus Christ grant you wisdom and discernment as you seek to understand and apply these principles to your faith.

CHAPTER 22

THE MIGHTY EQUALIZER: A DIVINE MESSAGE FOR THE DOCTOR WHO PLAY "GOD" IN YOUR PRACTICE

=====================

GYE NYAME

"Except God"

Asante philosophical symbol of the Supremacy of God Almighty

=====================

A message for a medical practitioner who oversteps the bounds of ethical and natural principles in the name of advancement serves as a call to humility and recognition of human limitations. While medicine plays a vital role in alleviating suffering and promoting well-being, it must operate within the framework of respect for the natural order and moral integrity.

The pursuit of knowledge and skill in medicine is commendable, but it should never lead to an inflated sense of authority or the assumption of roles beyond human capacity. True wisdom involves trusting in a higher order and acknowledging that the complexities of life and creation surpass human understanding. A practitioner must strive to align their work with principles of reverence, compassion, and integrity, ensuring that their interventions honor the sanctity of life.

Ultimately, the foundation of ethical medical practice lies in humility recognizing that while human efforts contribute to healing, they are part of a broader design that is not solely within

human control. By seeking guidance beyond their own understanding and maintaining respect for the natural order, a practitioner upholds the true purpose of their calling: to heal and serve without distorting the delicate balance of life.

> **James 4:12 (KJV)** "There is one lawgiver, who is able to save and to destroy: who art thou that judgest another?"

> **Proverbs 3:5-6 (KJV)** "Trust in the LORD with all thine heart; and lean not unto thine own understanding.

> **Proverbs 3:6 (KJV)** "In all thy ways acknowledge him, and he shall direct thy paths."

> **Jeremiah 9:23 (KJV)** "Thus saith the LORD, Let not the wise man glory in his wisdom, neither let the mighty man glory in his might, let not the rich man glory in his riches:

> **Jeremiah 9:24 (KJV)** "But let him that glorieth glory in this, that he understandeth and knoweth me, that I am the LORD which exercise lovingkindness, judgment, and righteousness, in the earth: for in these things I delight, saith the LORD."

The understanding that God is the ultimate authority and the source of true judgment serves as a humbling reminder, particularly for those in the medical field. It underscores the inherent limitations of human nature and the importance of recognizing the role of practitioners as facilitators of healing rather than as ultimate arbiters or saviors.

This perspective calls for reliance on higher wisdom, cautioning against the overconfidence that can stem from personal expertise or achievements. For medical professionals, it is a reminder to approach their work with humility, acknowledging that their skills and knowledge are part of a larger design rather than the sole source of healing or power.

True wisdom lies not in pride over human accomplishments but in understanding and honoring the greater authority that governs life. By focusing on this, practitioners can align their work with principles of service, integrity, and respect for the sanctity of life, ensuring that their efforts reflect the balance and purpose of a higher order.

> **1 Peter 5:5 (KJV)** "Likewise, ye younger, submit yourselves unto the elder. Yea, all of you be subject one to another, and be clothed with humility: for God resisteth the proud, and giveth grace to the humble."

> **Psalm 147:3 (KJV)** "He healeth the broken in heart, and bindeth up their wounds."

Proverbs 16:18 (KJV) "Pride goeth before destruction, and an haughty spirit before a fall."

In summary, all scripture, viewed as divinely inspired, serves as a constant reminder to those in the medical field of the importance of humility, the necessity of relying on God's guidance, and the recognition of their role as mere instruments in the process of healing. This perspective firmly establishes God as the ultimate authority and equalizer, beyond the reach of human capability and understanding.

CHAPTER 23

THE MIGHTY EQUALIZER: A DIVINE MESSAGE FOR THE MANUFACTURER OF DANGEROUS WEAPONS?

=======================

HWEMUDUA

"Measuring stick"

Asante philosophical symbol of Examination, Quality Control, Standardization, Research

=======================

A divine message for those involved in the production of dangerous war equipment, chemical, and biological weapons within defense industries serves as a profound reminder of the moral and ethical responsibilities tied to their work. It underscores the belief in God as the ultimate arbiter of justice and the **"Almighty God,"** emphasizing the importance of prioritizing peace, justice, and righteousness above all.

Such industries often operate under the justification of defense and security, yet their products have the potential to cause immense harm, destruction, and loss of innocent lives. This message calls for a deep reflection on the consequences of their actions, urging them to evaluate whether their work aligns with the values of preserving life, fostering harmony, and upholding justice.

Rather than contributing to tools of destruction, this perspective invites a shift towards promoting initiatives that protect life and resolve conflicts through peaceful means. It emphasizes that true power lies not in the ability to destroy but in the ability to build, heal, and create a legacy of peace and security for future generations. Recognizing the sanctity of life and the higher accountability for their actions, manufacturers are called to align their efforts with principles that reflect compassion, wisdom, and a commitment to a just and peaceful world.

> **Isaiah 2:4 (KJV)** "And he shall judge among the nations, and shall rebuke many people: and they shall beat their swords into plowshares, and their spears into pruninghooks: nation shall not lift up sword against nation, neither shall they learn war any more."

> **Psalm 46:9 (KJV)** "He maketh wars to cease unto the end of the earth; he breaketh the bow, and cutteth the spear in sunder; he burneth the chariot in the fire." This emphasizes God's power over war and His ability to bring peace."

> **Proverbs 21:15 (KJV)** "It is joy to the just to do judgment: but destruction shall be to the workers of iniquity."

> **Matthew 5:9 (KJV)** "Blessed are the peacemakers: for they shall be called the children of God."

In viewing the Divine as the "Mighty Equalizer," the ethics of war and peace take on a profound significance, particularly when examining the inequities of conflict. War disproportionately devastates vulnerable nations, leaving the poor to bear its heaviest burdens while the wealthy, often those who profit from the production and supply of destructive weapons, remain largely insulated from its horrors.

The narrative challenges the moral implications of manufacturing instruments of destruction, urging a reimagining of their purpose. It envisions a transformation for both physical and ideological perspective where resources devoted for war purposes are redirected toward constructive, life-affirming applications. This shift represents not just a change in use but a deeper evolution in human values, emphasizing peace and reconciliation over conflict and domination.

Such a transformation calls for global accountability, particularly from wealthier nations whose defense industries fuel conflicts that wreak havoc on less privileged regions. Guided by a commitment to justice and compassion, this change addresses the glaring imbalance of power and suffering in warfare, moving society closer to a vision of equitable and lasting peace.

> **James 4:1 (KJV)** "From whence come wars and fightings among you? come they not hence, even of your lusts that war in your members?"

> **James 4:2 (KJV)** "Ye lust, and have not: ye kill, and desire to have, and cannot obtain: ye fight and war, yet ye have not, because ye ask not."

Romans 12:17-21 (KJV) "Recompense to no man evil for evil. Provide things honest in the sight of all men."

Romans 12:18 (KJV) "If it be possible, as much as lieth in you, live peaceably with all men."

Romans 12:19 (KJV) "Dearly beloved, avenge not yourselves, but rather give place unto wrath: for it is written, Vengeance is mine; I will repay, saith the Lord."

Romans 12:20 (KJV) "Therefore if thine enemy hunger, feed him; if he thirst, give him drink: for in so doing thou shalt heap coals of fire on his head."

Romans 12:21 (KJV) "Be not overcome of evil, but overcome evil with good."

The Divine's role as the ultimate authority over conflict and war is central to this message, emphasizing a transformative vision of dismantling the tools and systems that perpetuate suffering, particularly in impoverished nations. This portrayal extends beyond merely preventing conflict, presenting the Divine as an active force in promoting peace, justice, and equity on a global scale.

The call for peacemaking resonates deeply in this context, highlighting peace as a universal value that must be embraced by all, both the powerful producers of weapons and the vulnerable populations most affected by their use. This message underscores the stark contrast between the principles of justice and righteousness and the devastating consequences of war, which disproportionately burden the less affluent.

An honest examination of the roots of conflict reveals how human desires and ambitions are often exploited by those who profit from warfare. These raises pressing ethical questions for those in the weapons industry about their role in perpetuating global inequalities and fueling violence. Such introspection challenges the moral foundation of the arms trade, advocating for accountability and a reevaluation of priorities.

The rejection of vengeance and the promotion of peace pose a direct challenge to the logic of the arms industry. Within the framework of the Divine as the "Mighty Equalizer," this perspective calls for a fundamental shift in how power and security are perceived, encouraging a move away from the proliferation of destructive forces toward building systems that foster justice, harmony, and the flourishing of life.

Ultimately, this view presents a profound challenge to weapon manufacturers and the powerful nations that support them. It is an invitation to align with a higher purpose, one that champions global peace and the upliftment of humanity, especially for those in impoverished regions who bear the greatest cost of war. This divine call advocates for a reimagining of global priorities, urging a commitment to principles that promote life, growth, and cooperation over destruction and division. True power, this perspective suggests, lies not in the might of arms but in the enduring strength of peace and justice.

CHAPTER 24

THE MIGHTY EQUALIZER: A DIVINE MESSAGE FOR YOU DUMPING DANGEROUS WASTE IN YOUR NEIGHBORS LAND?

===================

HWEMUDUA

"Measuring stick"

Asante philosophical symbol of Examination, Quality Control, Standardization, Research

===================

A divine message for those involved in dumping dangerous industrial waste in poorer countries would center on the principles of accountability, justice, and respect for the sanctity of life and creation. It calls for recognizing the moral and ethical implications of such actions, especially when they exploit the vulnerability of less affluent nations.

This perspective highlights the Divine as the ultimate equalizer, ensuring that justice prevails and the playing field is leveled. The act of offloading harmful waste onto disadvantaged communities reflects a disregard for the well-being of others and the environment, violating principles of fairness and mutual respect. Such actions perpetuate global inequalities and pose severe risks to health and the natural world, for which there is an inherent accountability.

The call to justice emphasizes the responsibility to treat all communities with dignity, ensuring that decisions made in the pursuit of profit or convenience do not cause harm to those least equipped

to defend themselves. It urges industries and individuals to prioritize ethical practices that protect both humanity and the environment, fostering a global culture of care and equity.

Ultimately, this message serves as a reminder that true power lies in actions that uplift and sustain rather than exploit and destroy. It invites those involved in harmful industrial practices to reflect deeply on their impact and align their actions with values that honor justice, stewardship, and the interconnectedness of all life.

> **Leviticus 19:18 (KJV)** "Thou shalt not avenge, nor bear any grudge against the children of thy people, but thou shalt love thy neighbour as thyself: I am the LORD."

> **Proverbs 14:31(KJV)** "He that oppresseth the poor reproacheth his Maker: but he that honoureth him hath mercy on the poor."

> **James 4:17(KJV)** "Therefore to him that knoweth to do good, and doeth it not, to him it is sin."

The issue of developed or advanced industrialized countries using the land of poorer nations like those in Africa for dumping unwanted goods or dangerous polluted waste is a significant ethical concern. This practice reflects a profound disregard for the principles of mutual respect, care, and responsibility that are essential in any just and equitable society.

In this context, treating others with the same respect and care one expects for oneself is fundamentally violated when industrialized nations exploit the vulnerabilities of poorer countries. Dumping waste irresponsibly in these regions is not only an act of environmental degradation but also a form of oppression. It exposes communities in these countries to harm and risks, both immediate and long-term, that would be deemed unacceptable in the countries where the waste originated.

The principle of not causing harm, especially to those who are vulnerable, is critically relevant here. Poorer nations often lack the resources and infrastructure to manage hazardous waste effectively, making them susceptible to exploitation. The act of dumping waste in these countries is a clear indication of disregard for their wellbeing and the sanctity of their environment.

The notion that land is sacred and should not be defiled takes on a poignant meaning in this scenario. By treating the lands of poorer nations as dumping grounds, developed countries are not only polluting these environments but are also showing a profound disrespect for the inhabitants and their right to a safe and healthy environment.

> **Numbers 35:33 (KJV)** "So ye shall not pollute the land wherein ye are: for blood it defileth the land: and the land cannot be cleansed of the blood that is shed therein, but by the blood of him that shed it."

Numbers 35:34 (KJV) "Defile not therefore the land which ye shall inhabit, wherein I dwell: for I the LORD dwell among the children of Israel."

Matthew 7:12(KJV) "Therefore all things whatsoever ye would that men should do to you, do ye even so to them: for this is the law and the prophets."

The Golden Rule of treating others as you would like to be treated. This becomes especially significant when considering the practice of dumping hazardous waste or conducting dangerous experiments. If the roles were reversed, it is unlikely that developed nations would tolerate the dumping of hazardous materials on their land. Such practices expose a profound injustice in the way poorer nations are treated and exploited.

What you choose to cast away in one place can come back to haunt you in unexpected ways. The discarded waste or harmful experimentation intended to harm others can resurface in your own backyard, potentially causing harm that you may be even more vulnerable to than the intended victims. This serves as a warning: the consequences of such actions can spread like a disease, often affecting the very perpetrators in ways they could not anticipate. What was once seen as a way to profit or exercise power over others may return as a reckoning. In the same vein, dangerous experiments that spread as pandemics can be used by God to teach those who perpetuated such evils, offering immunity to the vulnerable, especially the poor, while allowing the perpetrators to face the consequences of their actions since the world has become a global community, punishment in the very affliction they once unleashed can resurface with a different face.

In the end, knowing the right course of action (like managing waste or conducting safe experiments) and choosing to ignore it is an unethical decision. Developed countries, with their vast resources, have a responsibility to act in ways that protect all nations, not just their own. If they fail in this moral duty, they risk suffering the same consequences of their negligence, in their own lives, in their fortunes, and in the legacy, they leave behind.

CHAPTER 25

THE MIGHTY EQUALIZER: A DIVINE MESSAGE FOR THE DESTROYER OF NATURAL RESOURCES IN THE NAME OF PROGRESS

======================

HYE WONHYE

"That which cannot be burnt"

Asante philosophical symbol of Imperishability, Endurance, Everlasting

======================

*T*here is a cry rising from the earth, a groaning of rivers turned brown with filth, of forests gasping under the weight of greed, and of lands stripped bare in the name of development. This is not just an environmental crisis. It is a moral and spiritual rebellion against the God of justice, the Creator of heaven and earth. And to such rebellion, the Lord, who is the **Mighty Equalizer**, will not remain silent.

In Ghana, a land once known as the Gold Coast, the evidence of this rebellion is clear. Under the guise of economic advancement, foreign companies, aided by their local collaborators, have plundered the nation's natural resources, gold, bauxite, timber, and fertile lands, without regard for the land or its people. But make no mistake: the greatest betrayal is not from foreigners, but from greedy Ghanaians who open the gates of destruction for a bribe. These collaborators, who should be guardians of the land, have instead become merchants of devastation. They shall not escape the justice of the Living God.

> **Jeremiah 22:13 (KJV):** Woe unto him that buildeth his house by unrighteousness, and his chambers by wrong; that useth his neighbour's service without wages, and giveth him not for his work;

What is being done in Ghana and across Africa is the modern equivalent of evil packaged in the name of investment or exploration as resources are stolen, lands are destroyed, waters poisoned, and yet the people are left poorer than before.

> **Leviticus 19:13 (KJV)** "Thou shalt not defraud thy neighbour, neither rob him: the wages of him that is hired shall not abide with thee all night until the morning."
>
> **Proverbs 22:22 (KJV)** "Rob not the poor, because he is poor: neither oppress the afflicted in the gate:"
>
> **Proverbs 22:23 (KJV)** "For the LORD will plead their cause, and spoil the soul of those that spoiled them."

Consider this: rivers so polluted from illegal mining, known locally as galamsey that they are no longer fit for drinking, irrigation, or fishing. Mercury used in mining find its way into rivers by miners seeking quick profit, and the poison leeches into the food chain. Children eat from soils laced with chemicals. Cattle drink from toxic streams. The unborn will reap deformity from seeds sown by today's corruption. How long shall we ignore the warning of **Proverbs 22:22-23?**

Politicians who were elected to protect the land now claim they are helpless because "the system is too sophisticated." Yet the truth is this: the very hand charged with stopping the destruction is the same hand that funds and defends it. The enemy is not outside, it is within. Traditional leaders who once blessed the land for harvests now sign it away for excavators.

Chiefs, pastors, civil servants, and even citizens watch the devastation and say nothing. But the God who sees in secret will reward openly (Matthew 6:4). Judgment is coming.

> **Matthew 6:4 (KJV):** "That thine alms may be in secret: and thy Father which seeth in secret himself shall reward thee openly."
>
> **James 5:4 (KJV)** "Behold, the hire of the labourers who have reaped down your fields, which is of you kept back by fraud, crieth: and the cries of them which have reaped are entered into the ears of the Lord of sabaoth."
>
> **Micah 6:8 (KJV)** "He hath shewed thee, O man, what is good; and what doth the LORD require of thee, but to do justly, and to love mercy, and to walk humbly with thy God?"
>
> **Proverbs 21:13 (KJV)** "Whoso stoppeth his ears at the cry of the poor, they also shall cry themselves, but shall not be heard."

> **Deuteronomy 24:14 (KJV)** "Thou shalt not oppress an hired servant that is poor and needy, whether he be of thy brethren, or of thy strangers that are in thy land within thy gates"

> **Deuteronomy 24:15 (KJV)** "At his day thou shalt give him his hire, neither shall the sun go down upon it; for he is poor, and setteth his heart upon it: lest he cry against thee unto the LORD, and it be sin unto thee."

And while foreign companies continue to exploit Ghana and other African nations, let us be clear: no Ghanaian or African is abroad mining gold or stripping forests in another man's land. Yet, corporations from those very regions enter Africa and operate with a level of impunity they would never risk in their own countries. What is prohibited where they come from becomes normalized here. This is not merely hypocrisy, it is a global injustice and a moral stain on the conscience of the world.

The Lord is not blind. It is a shared inheritance, not a private business venture for the elite. The looting of Africa's resources without fair compensation is not a trade, it is a theft. It is the sin of withholding wages, repackaged in diplomatic suits and investor meetings.

> **Psalm 24:1 (KJV)**: "The earth is the Lord's, and the fulness thereof; the world, and they that dwell therein."

Let it be known that God is not mocked. As He judged Babylon, as He humbled Pharaoh, as He struck down the proud kings of old, so will He bring justice upon every entity, foreign or local, that lays waste to His creation and oppresses His people.

But this message is not only a warning. It is a call to repentance. A call to stop measuring progress by GDP and start measuring it by generational sustainability. A call for ethical trade, environmental restoration, and the fear of God to return to governance.

Let the church rise and speak, not only against spiritual sin, but against the desecration of the land God gave us to steward. Let citizens stop celebrating leaders who build cathedrals with one hand while signing mining deals with the other. Let every Ghanaian and every African see this truth: *you cannot serve God and Mammon* (Matthew 6:24).

This is not just about Ghana. It is about Congo, Nigeria, Tanzania, and every nation whose rich soils have become bloodstained grounds for global greed. The Spirit of God cries out like in **Habakkuk 2:12:**

> **Habakkuk 2:12 (KJV):** "Woe to him that buildeth a town with blood, and stablisheth a city by iniquity!"

Let the leaders of nations know: God will equalize. He will level mountains built on deceit. He will scatter wealth gathered through oppression. He will expose every hidden deal and silence every lying tongue. The Almighty God does not need ballots or armies. He only needs truth.

So, choose this day carefully, do you want to be a protector or a predator? A steward or a saboteur? Because judgment will not miss its mark. The land will testify, the rivers will bear witness, and the next generation will ask what you did when the soil cried for help.

May the fear of the Lord return to our leaders. May justice roll down like waters, and righteousness like an ever-flowing stream **(Amos 5:24).** And may God raise up a new generation who will not sell their inheritance for a bowl of gold-laced poison.

May the Lord Jesus Christ grant you wisdom and discernment as you seek to understand and apply these principles to your faith and to treat others as you would desire God to treat you.

CHAPTER 26

Examining Divine Guidance: Distinguishing Faith Communities from Sects in Modern Churches

========================

KETE PA

"Good bed"

Asante philosophical symbol of Good Marriage

========================

As I reflect on the profound and often enigmatic journey of life, I am reminded of the inevitability of death, a reality that touches us all in unique and deeply personal ways. This reflection holds a special poignancy for me as I pay tribute to my sister, Favour Kpodzo, whose life was tragically cut short under circumstances fraught with troubling questions about the influence of false teachings and indoctrination within a church. Her passing has left an indelible mark on my heart, underscoring the fragility of life and the profound duty we have to care for and protect one another.

In the face of this sorrow, I am drawn to contemplate the values that define a meaningful life and the legacy we leave behind. While material achievements are fleeting, the enduring impact of a life rooted in integrity, compassion, and love serves as a testament to its true worth. These reflections remind me that even in grief, there is an opportunity to reaffirm our commitment to these principles and to honor those we have lost by living with purpose and conviction.

Though the pain of loss is deep, it also invites us to consider the hope that can be found in the face of mortality. It is through mourning that we often gain clarity about what truly matters, fostering a deeper understanding of the shared human experience and the enduring connections that unite us.

My sister's memory inspires me to continue striving for a life marked by authenticity and care, even as I navigate the sorrow of her absence.

> **Ecclesiastes 5:15 (KJV)** "As he came forth of his mother's womb, naked shall he return to go as he came, and shall take nothing of his labour, which he may carry away in his hand.
>
> **Ecclesiastes 7:1 (KJV)** "A good name *is* better than precious ointment; and the day of death than the day of one's birth."
>
> **Philippians 1:21 (KJV)** For to me to live *is* Christ, and to die *is* gain."

These sacred lessons prompt me to reflect deeply on what it means to be a child of the Divine, shaping our view on life and the transition to what lies beyond. They urge us to examine our inner selves and our connection with the higher power, highlighting that in times of grief, we may draw nearer to the Divine essence.

As I pay homage to my cherished sister, I recognize that these spiritual teachings are not mere philosophical ideas but practical beacons that illuminate our path through life's darkest valleys. They stand as testaments to the hope and love that transcend mortality, encouraging us to cling to these eternal verities as we commemorate her. Let these insights fortify us, as we find solace and strength in our beliefs and the bonds of love that unite us in this existence and the next.

In my work, "Mighty Equalizer," I honor my sister, a figure of grace, compassion, and resilience whose life story and premature departure deeply engage with the essential inquiry of navigating spiritual truths amidst varied religious communities and teachings. This homage transcends personal grief to address broader themes of spiritual discernment and the quest for authentic faith amidst diverse and sometimes conflicting teachings.

Her legacy, marked by her peaceful demeanor, her unwavering kindness, and her journey of determination despite being forsaken, underscores the significance of her life and loss. Her engagement with her faith community brings to light critical questions about the essence of their guidance and its congruence with the foundational truths of scripture.

> **1 Thessalonians 5:21 (KJV):** "Prove all things; hold fast that which is good."
>
> **Proverbs 31:25-26 (KJV):** "Strength and honour are her clothing; and she shall rejoice in time to come."

> **Proverbs 31:26 (KJV):** "She openeth her mouth with wisdom; and in her tongue is the law of kindness."

The Bible cautions us explicitly about the perils of false teachings.

In *Matthew 7:15,* Jesus warns against false prophets, who are likened to wolves in sheep's clothing. This allegory is crucial in understanding how deceptive teachings can appear harmless yet harbor destructive consequences. Similarly, *2 Peter 2:1* warns of false teachers who introduce destructive heresies, even denying Christ, leading to their swift downfall.

The Apostle Paul's warning against those who cause divisions and offenses contrary to sound doctrine can be directly linked to the concerning practices of certain religious groups that create rifts within families. These churches, driven by self-serving motives, often employ tactics that isolate individuals from their family units. By fostering distrust and portraying family members as sources of problems, they effectively remove the protective oversight and discerning influence that families typically provide.

The dangers of false teachings are profoundly evident, often presenting themselves in ways that appear harmless but carry devastating consequences. These deceptive doctrines can lead individuals astray, undermining foundational truths and causing significant harm. One particularly concerning manifestation of this is the way certain religious groups exploit their influence to create divisions within families.

These groups, motivated by self-serving interests, frequently employ strategies that isolate individuals from their loved ones. By fostering distrust and framing family members as obstacles or sources of conflict, they erode the natural bonds of support and oversight that families provide. This deliberate isolation removes the protection of collective wisdom and discernment, leaving individuals more vulnerable to manipulation and control. Such practices not only harm the individuals directly involved but also tear at the fabric of familial and communal unity, highlighting the profound impact of false teachings on both personal and societal levels.

> **Matthew 7:15 (KJV)** "Beware of false prophets, which come to you in sheep's clothing, but inwardly they are ravening wolves."
>
> **2 Peter 2:1 (KJV)** "But there were false prophets also among the people, even as there shall be false teachers among you, who privily shall bring in damnable heresies, even denying the Lord that bought them, and bring upon themselves swift destruction."
>
> **Romans 16:17 (KJV):** "Now I beseech you, brethren, mark them which cause divisions and offences contrary to the doctrine which ye have learned; and avoid them."

Romans 16:18 (KJV): "For they that are such serve not our Lord Jesus Christ, but their own belly; and by good words and fair speeches deceive the hearts of the simple."

Titus 3:10 (KJV): "A man that is an heretick after the first and second admonition reject;"

Titus 3:11 (KJV): "Knowing that he that is such is subverted, and sinneth, being condemned of himself."

This tactic of creating division not only undermines the foundational support networks of individuals, rendering them more susceptible to manipulation, but it also empowers these entities, masquerading as churches, to indoctrinate and potentially ensnare individuals into cult-like behaviors without the safeguarding presence of family. Such isolation from familial ties and established social structures predisposes individuals to the adoption of novel, frequently perverted belief systems. The doctrines imparted to my sister and her children by their Church starkly diverge from the core principles of Christian teachings, opting instead for ideologies that primarily augment the organization's dominion over its adherents. This egregious departure from authentic spiritual guidance to practices that exploit and mislead represents a profound betrayal of trust and a stark affront to the essence of true faith.

Ephesians 4:14 (KJV): "That we henceforth be no more children, tossed to and fro, and carried about with every wind of doctrine, by the sleight of men, and cunning craftiness, whereby they lie in wait to deceive;"

2 Corinthians 11:13 (KJV): "For such are false apostles, deceitful workers, transforming themselves into the apostles of Christ."

2 Corinthians 11:14 (KJV): "And no marvel; for Satan himself is transformed into an angel of light."

Proverbs 11:14 (KJV): "Where no counsel is, the people fall: but in the multitude of counsellors there is safety."

1 Timothy 4:1 (KJV): "Now the Spirit speaketh expressly, that in the latter times some shall depart from the faith, giving heed to seducing spirits, and doctrines of devils;"

Paul's call to avoid individuals and groups that sow division is a powerful reminder to exercise vigilance and discernment in matters of faith. True Christian teachings are marked by unity, love, and mutual understanding, fostering relationships rather than tearing them apart. The deceptive practices of certain churches, often marked by manipulation and flattery, stand in stark contrast to the core values of honesty, transparency, and genuine care that define authentic faith.

This caution is particularly relevant in addressing the concerning actions of some religious groups that exploit family divisions as a tool for control. Such practices, which often lead to cult-like indoctrination, deviate profoundly from the teachings of Christ. They prioritize manipulation over truth, isolating individuals from their support systems and steering them away from the principles of love and unity that are central to the Christian faith.

In light of these deceptive practices, I urge all who revere God to exercise discernment and remain steadfast in true Christian teachings. By adhering to doctrines that promote harmony, integrity, and compassion, believers can guard against being led astray and uphold the values that reflect genuine faith.

> **2 Timothy 3:13 (KJV):** "But evil men and seducers shall wax worse and worse, deceiving, and being deceived."

> **1 John 4:1 (KJV):** "Beloved, believe not every spirit, but try the spirits whether they are of God: because many false prophets are gone out into the world."

> **Matthew 24:11 (KJV):** "And many false prophets shall rise, and shall deceive many."

> **1 John 4:1 (KJV):** "Beloved, believe not every spirit, but try the spirits whether they are of God: because many false prophets are gone out into the world."

The tragic narrative of my late sister, **Favour Elorm Kpodzo**, serves as a stark example of the grave outcomes that can ensue when individuals are led away from authentic Christian doctrines. Her situation was made even more perilous by her compromised autonomy, compounded by the indoctrination of her children. Under the sway of their church's teachings, they adopted the pastor's assertion that the church acts as a **'hospital'** for the spiritually ill. This ideology, deeply ingrained by the church, deterred Favour from pursuing vital medical treatment.

Contrast this with the Biblical account of Apostle Paul, who not only sought but also valued medical expertise, as evidenced by his close association with Luke, a physician by profession. This relationship underscores the Biblical endorsement of seeking medical help and highlights the importance of balancing spiritual faith with practical wisdom. Luke's role in Paul's life and ministry exemplifies how early Christians integrated their faith with practical healthcare, recognizing that divine faith and medical science can coexist harmoniously. The juxtaposition of my sister's experience with the scriptural example of Paul and Luke illustrates the dangerous departure from this balanced approach, emphasizing the critical need for discernment in distinguishing true Christian teachings from misleading doctrines.

> **James 2:14 (KJV):** "What doth it profit, my brethren, though a man say he hath faith, and have not works? Can faith save him?"

James 2:15 (KJV): "If a brother or sister be naked, and destitute of daily food,"

James 2:16 (KJV): "And one of you say unto them, Depart in peace, be ye warmed and filled; notwithstanding ye give them not those things which are needful to the body; what doth it profit?"

James 2:17 (KJV): "Even so faith, if it hath not works, is dead, being alone."

According to Scripture, the belief that a church can entirely replace medical care misunderstands the holistic Christian teaching that values both the health of the soul and the body. The Bible teaches the importance of seeking wisdom and discernment, especially in health matters, suggesting that professional medical care should complement spiritual support, not be excluded by it. This approach does not diminish the power of faith or the potential for miracles but acknowledges God's wisdom in providing various means of healing. The unfortunate guidance received by Favour's children from their church serves as a caution against teachings that depart from this integrative and balanced perspective, emphasizing the need to embrace both faith and medical expertise as part of God's provision for our well-being.

1 Corinthians 6:19 (KJV): "What? know ye not that your body is the temple of the Holy Ghost which is in you, which ye have of God, and ye are not your own?"

1 Corinthians 6:20 (KJV): "For ye are bought with a price: therefore glorify God in your body, and in your spirit, which are God's."

Proverbs 3:13 (KJV): "Happy is the man that findeth wisdom, and the man that getteth understanding."

Proverbs 3:14 (KJV): "For the merchandise of it is better than the merchandise of silver, and the gain thereof than fine gold."

Favour's tragic death is a somber testament to the harm that can be caused when churches propagate doctrines that contradict fundamental Christian principles, particularly those relating to health and well-being. Her story is a powerful reminder of the importance of discerning true Christian teachings from those that may mislead and cause harm. It highlights the need for vigilance in evaluating the teachings and practices of religious institutions, ensuring they align with the core message of the Gospel that promotes the holistic care of the individual

Galatians 1:6 (KJV): "I marvel that ye are so soon removed from him that called you into the grace of Christ unto another gospel:

Galatians 1:7 (KJV): "Which is not another; but there be some that trouble you, and would pervert the gospel of Christ."

Acts 17:11 (KJV): "These were more noble than those in Thessalonica, in that they received the word with all readiness of mind, and searched the scriptures daily, whether those things were so."

In mourning Favour, I find solace in the comforting assurance that the Divine is close to the brokenhearted, offering strength and peace in moments of profound loss. Her memory challenges us to seek spiritual truth and remain vigilant against teachings that deviate from the path of righteousness. It is an opportunity to reflect on the values she embodied and the lessons her life continues to impart.

In honoring Favour, we are reminded of the enduring principle that righteous deeds and a life lived in faith are cherished and remembered. Throughout spiritual traditions, the actions of those who zealously uphold truth and love are memorialized, standing as timeless examples for others to follow. In this spirit, we celebrate Favour's life, acknowledging her contributions and the legacy of integrity and kindness she has left behind.

This reflection invites us to ponder the spiritual journey of life and death, recognizing that our earthly existence is part of a greater narrative, one that ultimately leads to accountability and reconciliation with the Divine. It serves as a reminder of the spiritual stakes involved in the choices we make, particularly in matters of faith and the teachings we embrace. The beliefs we hold not only shape our lives but also leave an eternal imprint.

In "Mighty Equalizer," we explore these themes not only to honor Favour's memory but also to provide guidance in spiritual discernment, urging vigilance against deceptive teachings that lead away from the truth. Her legacy serves as a beacon, calling us to align our lives with values of faith, love, and truth.

May the Almighty grant you wisdom and protection, guiding your soul and spirit on the true path until the day of divine reconciliation.

CHAPTER 27

THE MIGHTY EQUALIZER: A DIVINE MESSAGE FOR THE CORRUPT ELECTORAL OFFICER

======================

BOA ME NA ME MMOA WO

"Help me and let me help you"

Asante philosophical symbol of Cooperation, Interdependence, Co-Existence, Symbiosis

======================

*T*he selection of leaders is a profound responsibility, one that requires justice, fairness, and unwavering integrity. Those entrusted with overseeing this process must rise above personal or group interests and serve as the impartial stewards of the people's trust. Their role is not just administrative; it is deeply moral, carrying the weight of both societal and divine accountability. The corrupt electoral practices we witness today stand in stark contrast to this sacred duty, as they are often driven by self-interest, favoritism, and manipulation of the process. These actions undermine the very foundations of democracy and good governance.

In the Bible, we see a powerful example of the divine hand in leadership selection through the story of Samuel's anointing of David as king. God commanded Samuel to go to the house of Jesse to choose a new king for Israel. Samuel, guided by his own understanding and judgment, was ready to anoint Eliab, the eldest son, assuming his stature and outward appearance made him the rightful

candidate. But God spoke clearly to Samuel, saying, *"Do not look at his appearance or at his physical stature, because I have refused him. For the Lord does not see as man sees; for man looks at the outward appearance, but the Lord looks at the heart"* (1 Samuel 16:7). Despite David's youth and his position as the youngest son, it was he who was chosen by God, anointing him as the king of Israel.

This story reminds us that leadership, whether in biblical times or today, is ultimately in God's hands. Just as Samuel had to trust God's judgment over his own, so too must those involved in electoral processes seek divine wisdom and not be swayed by personal bias or superficial considerations. If we fail to uphold integrity in the selection of our leaders, we risk deviating from God's will and facing the consequences of our actions. The story of David's anointing serves as a timeless warning that the heart of a leader is what matters most, not their appearance or popularity. When we allow corrupt practices to dictate leadership selection, we betray the very essence of justice and accountability.

Electoral officers today must take inspiration from this example, understanding that their role mirrors that of a mediator, channeling the collective voice of the people, which ultimately aligns with the will of God. The phrase "the voice of the people is the voice of God" underscores the sacred nature of their duty, requiring them to act with impartiality, transparency, and adherence to the principles of fairness.

In many democracies, particularly across Africa and now advance democracies, elections have been marred by allegations of corruption, partiality, and malpractice. Such acts not only erode public trust but also destabilize nations, perpetuating cycles of unrest and inequality. These issues stand in stark contrast to the divine principles of governance, which advocate for ethical conduct, equitable treatment, and the rejection of bribery and corruption. When electoral officials subvert the will of the people, they undermine the democratic process and invite the judgment of the "Mighty Equalizer," who holds all actions accountable on the scales of justice.

The impact of election misconduct extends far beyond the ballot box, sowing seeds of division, unrest, and disillusionment within society. Leaders overseeing electoral processes are therefore called to embody the values of peacemaking and impartiality, recognizing that their actions have far-reaching consequences for both their nations and their own moral standing. Post-election turmoil, often fueled by perceived injustices, highlights the urgent need for officials to adhere to principles that foster peace and stability.

This is a call for electoral officers to engage in continuous self-reflection and commit to the highest standards of integrity. They must recognize that their role is not merely procedural but deeply transformative, with the potential to shape the trajectory of their nations. By prioritizing justice and fairness, they act as stewards of democracy, ensuring that the process reflects the collective will of the people and aligns with the divine values of equality and righteousness.

Ultimately, a corrupt electoral official must be reminded that the consequences of their actions extend beyond the immediate moment. They are accountable not only to their fellow citizens but

also to the eternal principles of justice and truth upheld by the Divine. In embracing their role with humility and honor, election officials can ensure that their work becomes a testament to integrity, fostering a future where peace, justice, and equity prevail.

> **Proverbs 17:23 (KJV)-** "A wicked man taketh a gift out of the bosom to pervert the ways of judgment."

> **Proverbs 29:2 (KJV)** "When the righteous are in authority, the people rejoice: but when the wicked beareth rule, the people mourn"

> **Deuteronomy 16:19 (KJV)** "Thou shalt not wrest judgment; thou shalt not respect persons, neither take a gift: for a gift doth blind the eyes of the wise, and pervert the words of the righteous."

Electoral corruption and bribery, particularly in young democracies and emerging nations, represent a grave challenge where money and power often overshadow the collective will of the people. This practice not only undermines democratic ideals but perpetuates a cycle of leadership driven by self-interest rather than the welfare of the citizenry. Such dynamics contribute to widespread suffering, inequality, and a stagnation of national development, as the needs and aspirations of ordinary citizens are disregarded.

The distortion of electoral processes through corruption compromises justice and fairness, stripping citizens of their fundamental right to fair representation and governance. Beyond the immediate injustice, the long-term damage to public trust in democratic institutions is profound, leading to disillusionment and apathy among the electorate. A weakened democratic framework erodes the social fabric, fostering instability and deepening systemic inequalities.

In many developing nations, the voices of ordinary people are too often drowned out by unethical practices during elections. This highlights the critical need for electoral officials to act with integrity and impartiality, safeguarding the transparency and fairness of the electoral process. Their responsibility extends beyond administering elections; they are entrusted with protecting the democratic rights of the people and ensuring that leadership reflects the genuine will of the populace.

To address these issues, there must be a collective commitment to accountability, justice, and ethical conduct. Electoral officials and those in positions of authority have a pivotal role to play in restoring faith in the democratic process, ensuring that elections are not merely exercises in power but true reflections of the people's voice and aspirations.

> **Ecclesiastes 5:8 (KJV)** "If thou seest the oppression of the poor, and violent perverting of judgment and justice in a province, marvel not at the matter: for he that is higher than the highest regardeth; and there be higher than they."

Amos 5:12 (KJV) "For I know your manifold transgressions and your mighty sins: they afflict the just, they take a bribe, and they turn aside the poor in the gate from their right."

Romans 13:1 (KJV) "Let every soul be subject unto the higher powers. For there is no power but of God: the powers that be are ordained of God."

Romans 13:2 (KJV) "Whosoever therefore resisteth the power, resisteth the ordinance of God: and they that resist shall receive to themselves damnation."

The teaching that all governing authorities are established by God and thus should be respected and obeyed does not imply an unconditional endorsement of all actions taken by those in power. It's crucial to understand that while "higher powers" in positions of political or civic authority are part of the societal structure ordained by God, this does not grant these leaders a carte blanche to wield their power unjustly. The instruction for Christians to respect and obey laws and rules set by these authorities is rooted in the belief that orderly governance is part of God's plan for human society. However, it's equally important to recognize that God, as the "Mighty Equalizer," holds these leaders accountable for how they exercise the power entrusted to them.

In this context, while resistance against government is generally discouraged, it is understood within the broader Biblical narrative that God's commitment to justice and righteousness supersedes human authority. Leaders who abuse their power, acting unjustly or oppressively, are not operating in alignment with God's will. Such leaders face divine judgment for their actions, as they have failed in their God-given responsibility to lead with fairness and integrity.

Therefore, submission to authority, as advocated in the scripture, is not an encouragement to accept injustice passively. Rather, it is a call for lawfulness and order, balanced by the higher principles of justice and righteousness that God upholds. Christians are encouraged to navigate this balance thoughtfully, honoring the governing authorities as much as possible while also being conscious of God's ultimate authority and His expectations of justice and righteousness for all, especially those in positions of power.

Subverting the will of the people through corrupt electoral practices is a grave injustice. It not only contravenes the principles of fairness and righteousness but also erodes the foundation of democracy and good governance. Those who engage in such practices are not only betraying the trust of the people but are also undermining the integrity and future of their nations.

In light of these challenges, there is a vital need for reform and rectification. This includes stringent measures to ensure the integrity of electoral processes, the implementation of robust anti-corruption laws, and the establishment of independent bodies to oversee elections. The goal should

be to create an environment where the power of money and influence is curtailed, allowing the true will of the people to prevail in determining the leadership and direction of their countries.

In summary, many developing countries, the subversion of the people's will by corrupt electoral practices demands urgent attention and correction. Ensuring justice, integrity, and accountability in elections is not just a matter of fulfilling democratic principles but is also crucial for the long-term prosperity and stability of these nations.

The aftermath of contentious elections often leaves a nation bruised and divided. In these critical moments, the Biblical teachings of prayer, repentance, forgiveness, and reconciliation emerge as powerful tools for national healing and the mending of societal fractures.

> **2 Chronicles 7:14 (KJV)** "If my people, which are called by my name, shall humble themselves, and pray, and seek my face, and turn from their wicked ways; then will I hear from heaven, and will forgive their sin, and will heal their land."

> **Colossians 3:13 (KJV)** "Forbearing one another, and forgiving one another, if any man have a quarrel against any: even as Christ forgave you, so also do ye."

The principles of humility, prayer, repentance, and a sincere pursuit of spiritual guidance play a transformative role in fostering collective responsibility and healing. When individuals and nations recognize their moral failings and turn toward a higher authority with genuine intention, they create space for renewal and restorative grace. This approach is especially meaningful during periods of crisis or moral decline, offering a pathway to recovery that goes beyond human capabilities and lays the foundation for lasting change.

Within communities, particularly those rooted in Christian faith, forgiveness emerges as a vital element of harmony. It challenges individuals to empathize, release resentment, and extend grace to one another. Far from being a mere ideal, forgiveness is a practical and powerful tool for resolving conflicts, strengthening bonds, and cultivating a culture of unity and mutual respect. A forgiving heart creates resilience and fosters the deep connections necessary for building thriving, compassionate communities.

As elections draw closer, this chapter calls upon nations to embrace humility, engage in prayer, and seek divine guidance for the road ahead. In the face of political tensions and divisive rhetoric, the act of collective repentance becomes even more significant. It invites leaders and citizens alike to confront their flaws, seek wisdom beyond their own, and open themselves to a spirit of reconciliation.

This spirit of humility can serve as a catalyst for healing, facilitating open dialogue and understanding among factions divided by political discord. By turning to these enduring principles,

nations can find a way to mend strained relationships, foster unity, and move toward a future defined by peace, integrity, and shared purpose.

> **2 Corinthians 5:10 (KJV)** "For we must all appear before the judgment seat of Christ; that every one may receive the things done in his body, according to that he hath done, whether it be good or bad."

> **Proverbs 20:28 (KJV)** "Mercy and truth preserve the king: and his throne is upholden by mercy."

The teachings of Apostle Paul resonate with the profound concept of final judgment, where each individual is held accountable for their actions. This perspective fosters a belief that all deeds, whether positive or negative, will be subject to a thorough assessment. Such an understanding acts as a moral compass for believers, encouraging them to lead lives of righteousness in the awareness that they will ultimately be evaluated by a higher authority. This notion of impending divine judgment serves as a guiding principle for ethical living and decision-making.

In the context of leadership and governance, the qualities of mercy and truth are identified as key pillars for stability and longevity. A ruler who exemplifies these virtues is more likely to establish and maintain a robust and enduring governance structure. This suggests that moral integrity and the ability to act with compassion and honesty are not just admirable traits but essential components for effective and sustainable leadership. Such qualities in leadership contribute to the creation of a just and prosperous society, highlighting the inextricable link between ethical governance and societal well-being.

> **Matthew 5:9 (KJV)** "Blessed are the peacemakers: for they shall be called the children of God."

> **Romans 12:18(KJV)** "If it be possible, as much as lieth in you, live peaceably with all men."

The concept of God as "the Mighty Equalizer" highlights the profound responsibility of leaders, judges, and electoral officials to embody fairness, justice, and integrity. Their actions directly influence the stability and prosperity of nations, and the ripple effects of their decisions impact societal trust, peace, and cohesion.

In governance and judicial systems, impartiality and fairness are not mere ethical expectations but moral imperatives that align with the divine order of justice. Leaders and officials are entrusted with the sacred duty of ensuring equality before the law, treating both the powerful and the vulnerable without favoritism or prejudice. This commitment fosters a just society and reflects the divine balance that God represents.

However, when leaders and officials engage in corrupt practices such as accepting bribes, showing partiality, or prioritizing personal benefits, they undermine both societal stability and the divine principles of righteousness. Such actions distort justice and erode trust in institutions, perpetuating inequality and injustice. Within this framework, the consequences of such behavior are seen as inevitable, for divine justice holds all accountable.

Conversely, those who uphold principles of honesty and fairness are not only contributing to a stable and prosperous society but are also aligning themselves with divine will. Their dedication to integrity and impartiality is rewarded with spiritual fulfillment and the favor of the Almighty, reinforcing the idea that justice is both a societal duty and a pathway to righteousness.

In post-election scenarios, particularly in nations grappling with contested results and lingering divisions, forgiveness and reconciliation are indispensable. These principles, rooted in compassion and mutual respect, pave the way for healing, restoring trust, and fostering national unity. Forgiveness is not a sign of weakness but a transformative act that allows opposing factions to address grievances and work towards a shared vision for the future.

Nations emerging from the turmoil of electoral disputes are called to embrace prayer, repentance, and reconciliation as practical tools for restoring peace. These divine teachings serve as a guide for overcoming challenges, healing divisions, and building a unified path forward.

In conclusion, the commitment to free and fair elections, grounded in justice and transparency, is essential for political stability and societal prosperity. By embracing these values, democracies especially in Africa and other emerging regions can transform political turbulence into opportunities to strengthen institutions and enhance citizen trust. Upholding these principles ensures that governance reflects the will of the people and aligns with the timeless values of fairness, integrity, and reconciliation.

May the Lord Jesus Christ be with your spirit, guiding and sustaining you. May He grant you wisdom and understanding in all things.

CHAPTER 28

GENERAL CONCLUSION

=====================

MATE MASIE

"What I hear, I keep

Asante philosophical symbol of Wisdom, Knowledge, Prudence, Secrecy,

Confidentiality, Oath of Secrecy

=====================

A Divine Path Forward

As we come to the final chapter of *"The Mighty Equalizer,"* we are called to pause and reflect on the divine hand that sovereignly shapes the course of our lives, and the eternal truths revealed in the unchanging Word of God. This journey has been an earnest exploration of life's cause-and-effect dynamics through the teachings of our Lord Jesus Christ, grounded firmly in the timeless wisdom of the Holy Scriptures.

From Genesis to Revelation, the Bible has remained our faithful compass. Throughout each lesson, we have upheld the principles of divine revelation, embracing God's Word as the ultimate source of knowledge, truth, and salvation. As the prophet Isaiah warns, "To the law and to the

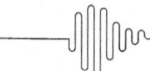

testimony: if they speak not according to this word, it is because there is no light in them" (Isaiah 8:20). This truth has been a cornerstone of our teaching.

In Exodus 34:7, we are reminded of God's justice: **"Keeping mercy for thousands, forgiving iniquity and transgression and sin, and that will by no means clear the guilty; visiting the iniquity of the fathers upon the children, and upon the children's children, unto the third and to the fourth generation."**

This passage lays bare the gravity of divine judgment. God's justice is perfect and unwavering, yet His mercy is abundantly extended to those who walk in obedience to His Word. Without such obedience, the effects of sin ripple through generations, impacting even those not directly responsible.

But there is hope, the glorious and eternal. The only redemption from the curse of sin lies in the salvation offered through our Lord and Savior, Jesus Christ. Through His life, sacrificial death, and resurrection, grace is made available to all who believe. It is through walking in His will, obeying His commandments, and living according to His Word (the teachings of **Yehoshua**-Yeshua) that we find true redemption.

The consequences of our actions reach beyond this earthly life; they carry eternal significance. While the curse may affect the third and fourth generations, the grace of God breaks that chain for those who choose to follow Christ. The message is clear and unchanging: we are called to obedience in Christ Jesus not only for ourselves, but for the sake of generations yet to come.

In this final chapter, as we bring the book to a close, we are once again reminded of the unchanging power and reliability of God's Word. While the world continues to shift and societies transform, our unshakable hope remains anchored in Jesus Christ. His ways are higher than ours, and His glory is His alone. This immutable truth calls us to live humbly, trust deeply, and walk faithfully in His path. Obedience to God's law is the key to breaking generational curses and experiencing the fullness of His grace culminating in eternal life is made available to us and to those who come after us.

This book is a tool for many:

This work is not only a theological exposition but also a practical guide designed to serve diverse individuals and institutions:

1. **Established Ministers:** Deepen your understanding and enrich your ministry.

2. **Newly Ordained Ministers:** Gain valuable guidance for preaching and pastoral care.

3. **Theological Scholars:** Discover a rich resource for scriptural study and research.

4. **Bible Students:** From certificates to doctoral levels, find meaningful insights for academic and spiritual growth.

5. **Politicians and Policy Makers:** Let biblical principles guide leadership with justice and integrity.

6. **Civic Society Organizations:** Be equipped to advocate for righteousness and social transformation.

7. **Medical Practitioners and Scientists:** Draw inspiration from the Creator in the pursuit of healing and discovery.

8. **Legal Professionals:** Uphold justice with a conscience informed by divine wisdom.

9. **Business Leaders:** Lead with accountability, ethics, and God-honoring stewardship.

10. **Nations:** Both Rich and Poor- Embrace godly principles for governance, prosperity, and peace.

11. **General Practitioners and Administrators:** Navigate your calling with purpose, wisdom, and service-oriented leadership shaped by biblical truths.

I emphasize that, the Word of God is composed of two inseparable elements the written Scriptures and the living guidance of the Holy Spirit. Just as a ship requires both a sturdy vessel and a skilled captain, the believer's journey demands both the foundation of Scripture and the illumination of the Spirit. Obedience and love for God are not separate, but intertwined. The Spirit of God dwells in those who walk in faithful obedience.

This book lays the foundation for continued study, future writing, and the creation of theological tools for the Body of Christ. It aims to expand biblical knowledge and nurture spiritual maturity. We remain committed to proclaiming the mysteries of the Gospel with boldness, clarity, and unwavering truth.

I urge every reader: test the content of this work against the Word of God. Let Scripture be the standard by which all teaching is measured. In doing so, you affirm the truth of the Gospel, enrich your walk with Christ, and strengthen your obedience to God's commands.

As I close, we entrust you to the grace and guidance of the Almighty. May the Lord God illuminate your path, may Jesus Christ grant you understanding, and may the Holy Spirit dwell within your spirit. Go forth with the strength and peace of God, steadfast in your faith and united in the mission of the Gospel.

Amen.

THE END

PRINCIPAL REFERENCE

The Holy Scriptures - King James Version